The Films of
Robin Williams

The Films of Robin Williams

Critical Essays

EDITED BY JOHNSON CHEU

Foreword by David Misch

McFarland & Company, Inc., Publishers

Jefferson, North Carolina

LIBRARY OF CONGRESS CATALOGUING-IN-PUBLICATION DATA

Names: Cheu, Johnson, 1969– editor.. | Misch, David, author of foreword.
Title: The films of Robin Williams : critical essays / edited by Johnson Cheu ; foreword by David Misch.
Description: Jefferson, North Carolina : McFarland & Company, Inc., Publishers, 2019. | Includes bibliographical references and index. | Includes filmography.
Identifiers: LCCN 2018053972 | ISBN 9781476667331 (softcover : acid free paper) ∞
Subjects: LCSH: Williams, Robin, 1951–2014—Criticism and interpretation.
Classification: LCC PN2287.W473 F55 2019 | DDC 791.4302/8092—dc23
LC record available at https://lccn.loc.gov/2018053972

BRITISH LIBRARY CATALOGUING DATA ARE AVAILABLE

ISBN (print) 978-1-4766-6733-1
ISBN (ebook) 978-1-4766-3563-7

The front cover image is of Robin Williams in *Good Morning, Vietnam!*, 1987 (Buena Vista/Photofest)

Printed in the United States of America

McFarland & Company, Inc., Publishers
Box 611, Jefferson, North Carolina 28640
www.mcfarlandpub.com

In loving memory of
my friend and colleague
Deb Carmichael

Table of Contents

Acknowledgments

First, I must thank McFarland and all the good people there for their continued faith and all the wonderful work they put in to ensure stellar books and the enduring relevance of Popular Culture Studies. Their continued faith in me and my ideas (and their patience), particularly during my own rather turbulent 2017 is particularly appreciated. Thanks to all my contributors for their steadfastness and wanting to get it right.

Every project comes with its own set of challenges and this one happened during a time of unexpected personal and professional upheaval. Though she's in the book, I owe a great debt of gratitude to Cindy Miller for help in securing some of these essays. The book itself took a rather windy road to its final form and shape, and Cindy's help was invaluable at crucial times.

My respect and gratitude to my colleagues at Michigan State: Roger Bresnahan, Deborah Carmichael (we miss you), Cheryl Ceaser, Mary Cook (happy retirement), Kate Fedewa, Richard Manderfield, David Medei, and Elizabeth Spence for the willingness to stop and listen whenever I needed it. My department chair Malea Powell, as well as former chair Jeffrey Grabil, for enduring support with this project. Douglas Noverr and Gary Hoppenstand, who started me down this road and who always make time. Marsha Edington, Diana Shank, Melissa Artherton, Regina Boone, Rhonda Hibbitt, and Angela Hunt who make sure everything keeps spinning. John Dowell, who, once again, came through with both friendship and his technical expertise. The library staff at MSU is beyond reproach. I am grateful for the continued conversations with Linda Mizjewski and Debra Moddelmog who, likewise, always make the time. Matt Wanat and John McCombe still answer every email. Edna Poore, who makes sure I'm up on all the movies and that I'm well-fed. Brian and Ed for coffee and talk. Robert, Pat, and Carolyn who, likewise, always talk things through. And, of course, my family for all manner of love and support in all things.

"You're only given a little spark of madness. If you lose that, you're nothing."

—Robin Williams, *The Roxy*, 1977

"The most we can do is to write—intelligently, creatively, critically, evocatively—about what it is like to live in the world at this time."

—Oliver Sacks, 4-22-15, Journal entry in Bill Hayes's *Insomniac City: New York, Oliver, and Me*, p. 254.

Foreword

Robin Williams—It's Complicated

DAVID MISCH

In medieval Italy, a man consulted a "doctor of the mind."
"I'm always unhappy," said the man. "There is no joy for me
and it's been like this since I can remember. I feel I have no
choice but to take my own life."

"Do not despair," replies the doctor. "There is a jester in
the city named Calveri and they say he is the merriest man
alive; no one can view his performance and remain melancholy. Take my advice and go see him immediately."

"You don't understand," says the man. "I am Calveri."

The "sad clown" is as much a stereotype as the comic who's "always on"
and it's wrong ... but not entirely. David Steinberg had a piece on prejudice,
noting stereotypes have an element of truth. "Some Jews are good with money,
some Blacks have rhythm, and some Orientals all look alike."[1]

Does misery love comedy? Scientific literature on the mental state of
comedians is shockingly sparse. Of course, all comics whine miserably that
all comics are whiny and miserable. (Also sexually indomitable, though that
may be confirmation bias.[2]) But there's no reason to believe sad clowns are
the norm: the offstage comic temperament ranges from Richard Lewis's
numerous neuroses to Steve Martin's mannerly maturity.

And then there's Robin Williams, who—offstage and on—seemed to arc
through every persona imaginable: manic speedball; hyper-intelligent analyst
of science, politics, and culture; intermittent addict of multiple substances
and fluids. Asking where his truth lies beggars the question; Robin contained
multitudes. (That's Walt Whitman,[3] read a book.) The vast and variegated
characters he brought to life clearly came from somewhere. Though I'm not
paid (or remotely qualified) to psychoanalyze, my GPS says "Within."

1

It's terrible that Robin's life and legacy will be defined at least partially by his suicide. "Why?" people asked, including many who knew him. Some had clues, but only partial, because there were so many factors: the cancellation of his TV series, the fadeout of his film career, cardiac surgery, a history of depression, a relapse of alcoholism, diagnoses of dementia and Parkinson's.

That last seems especially potent because Robin craved speed—literally for many years and figuratively his whole life. In any room he was the fastest, physically and mentally. To lose that, to stumble, to fumble for a quip; the prospect must have seemed like death in itself.

No celebrity, no one, is entirely what they present to the world but the concept of a suicidal Mork is cognitive dissonance made flesh. My brief working and personal relationship with Robin gives me no special insight into who he really was, but there is one thing that I think contains clues. Robin was far more than comedy, but I believe his love—need?—to make people laugh was central to his identity.

At 28, I was hired to write for a new TV series about an alien. I grew up with *My Favorite Martian*, so I knew this would be a stupid show. (Which hardly mattered—it was my entry into show biz.) But I got a counter-cautionary word from my manager: "The guy who's starring, I manage him too, and he's pretty good."

How good was clear from the moment production began, but its full measure exploded in our first show. I remember standing onstage (I hosted the tapings) as Robin came out. He hadn't been introduced, he was just walking, and no one knew who he was. But the minute he hit the stage, there was an electric jolt and all eyes turned to him. People started chortling … and he hadn't done anything. Just his presence brought a promise of laughter so intense that it seemed to appear before it was generated. That whole first season was a process of constant incredulous discovery by audiences in the studio and people around the world. Even when we got to know him, Robin's protean inventions of voice and body (I'll get to "words" in a moment) astonished and enticed; we couldn't wait to see what he'd do next.

As for words, therein lies a tale.

Yes, Robin was a great improviser. But everyone who watched him through the years can attest that he, like many improvisers, was as much recycler as originator of quips. Even the finest improv produces huge amounts of unfunny material. (Larry David's semi-improvised *Curb Your Enthusiasm* shoots hours of footage to get a half-hour episode.) Clubs like Chicago's Second City have two shows; late-night's ad-libs form the genesis of the next main show, which is written—improv improved from its rough origins.

And so with Robin.

After seeing him a few times, you became aware that most of his ad-libs were recycled and reconfigured old lines and bits. Once Robin was presenting at the Oscars when Whoopi Goldberg came out. "Whoa," he said. "That dress is so tight you can see what religion you are." The audience roared. It was classic Robin recycling; he already had the line, probably from his Juilliard days doing Shakespeare in leotards: "Those pants are so tight you can see what religion you are" (i.e., you must be Jewish, i.e., you're circumcised). But at the Oscars it made no sense because (a) Whoopi's dress wasn't tight and, perhaps more relevant, (b) Whoopi has no penis. It got a laugh, I think, because it seemed dirty and a great comedian said it.

However, Robin didn't confine his line-borrowing to his own lines. He was a vacuum cleaner; anything interesting said or done in his presence got sucked into his brain and spit out in altered form. And sometimes unaltered—his reputation for joke-stealing was such that many comics refused to perform if he was in the room. But as far as I know, Robin both couldn't stop and was mortified that he did it, making numerous payments to stand-ups whose acts migrated to his.

Robin absorbed everything—jokes and phrases and words—juggled them, turned them inside out, then flung them hither and yon. (Actually, I don't know about hither but definitely yon.) One critic called it "harvested madness." To my mind, this detracts not a whit from his genius, of which his recycling ability and agility, is another example.

The idea that Robin could improvise endlessly led to the myth that he ad-libbed *Mork and Mindy*, and I can trace the canard to its source. Soon after we premiered, the *New York Times* wanted a story. A reporter got access to the set and offices and watched an episode go from script to stage to screen. Then he wrote a story so false it made me wonder if—based on the *Times*' reporting—there was ever a war in Vietnam. The most scandalous of his calumnies was something like "sometimes the writers throw up their hands and write 'Mork does his thing here.'" Not only did that never happen when I was there (during the last two years there were gaps in the script for improvs, which frankly didn't work), but everyone—very much including Robin—would have been outraged if it had. Robin didn't want the pressure of improvising on national TV for 24 minutes each week and the other actors, untrained in improv, weren't equipped to ad-lib beyond a few words or lines. The director, camera-people, script supervisor, and editor all needed a script to follow. Robin may have used the script as a launching pad, but he needed the pad for the launch.

As the myth took hold, we writers would say (quietly, to our loved ones—no need to undermine the legend), "There were ten people up 'til four in the morning writing those ad-libs." The truth, as so often, is more complicated. Robin did improvise, but generally not lines—it was words here and there and, more important, faces and voices and physical business. The show's fabled live tapings burnished the legend with a phenomenon that totally fooled the studio audience.

To wit...

Robin's need for laughter was such that its absence was anathema, but that absence is an inevitable part of the rehearsal process; lines he spoke for the crew to huge hilarity on Monday got chuckles Tuesday and nothing Wednesday. That's when we writers saw the episode for the first time and Robin—horrified at the prospect of ear-shattering silence from people who'd heard the lines repeatedly—improvised like crazy. We'd note the good bits, try to come up with better versions of the others, and so it went until the Friday night taping; we'd even write new lines on the set in the middle of shooting. During the show, if Robin improvised something that didn't work, on the next take he'd sometimes go back to a previous line (often one we'd written) and it'd get a huge laugh: first, because it was funny; second, because the crowd thought—like the legend said—Robin was ad-libbing.

But, and this can't be overstated, we owed everything to our star. Our scripts weren't so brilliant; Robin's the reason we soared to the stratosphere. His talent and charisma, his incarnation of comedy gods going back to the mythological trickster, were what got me residual checks that still arrive (though in increasingly decreasing amounts) today. Robin was unquestionably one of comedy's greatest improvisers/actors/stand-ups, but with so many personas, it's hard to see the tree for the forest. To quote a writer even older than I, to "pluck out the heart of his mystery" means looking more closely at what I believe was his addiction to laughter. (Again: read a book.[4])

I spent a little time with Robin and found him personable, intelligent, thoughtful. What he wasn't, with me, was funny. I'm a comedy writer but no quip-machine; Robin recognized that and adapted to my temperament. But if a comedian happened by, they'd instantly launch into what Robin called "playing" and he came alive, glowing—that's where he lived.

As the years passed, that life seemed to disappear from his movies; to challenge himself, he took projects that were out of his comfort zone, but often not very good. Like many actors, he'd balance risky projects with the more conventional, which often ended up damaging his reputation. (I'm looking at you, RV.)

The genie in *Aladdin* was, I feel, one of the few roles which showcased Robin's unique brilliance, encompassing not a single personality but a collection of astonishing voices and attitudes, morphing like quicksilver one into the other. Word-play intended, no one on earth was more animated than Robin Williams. Maybe beneath that barely fictionalized genie was a clue to the sadness of one clown: a manic, ceaseless, never-satisfied search for laughter. In retrospect, it was right there on the *Mork* stage all along.

Most "live" sitcoms shoot a couple hours to get a half-hour show; not

Mork and Mindy. Once Robin caught on, audiences thronged the studio, dizzy with excitement at the prospect of an evening with a comic genius. (I had a literal front-row seat and can attest to the air practically humming at the start of each show.) But as the evening wore on, and on, the energy level (though not Robin's) plunged. It wasn't just due to our plentiful retakes; people literally got exhausted from laughing. They'd stumble out after three or four hours, almost *unhappy* from so much happiness.

Maybe humans are born with an upper limit to our intake (and output) of joy. After all, isn't laughter, like life, supposed to be ephemeral? If it's intense and continuous, spurred on relentlessly, remorselessly by a fantastical genie/trickster's orgasmic geysering of words, might it become almost a burden? And if it's like that for the audience, what's it like for the genie? Especially one compelled by psychology/biology to extract every last laugh from every last lung.

Dime-store psychoanalysis: I think the facts are enough. Robin Williams was extraordinarily talented, childlike, complex, buoyant, haunted, filled with insatiable appetites for pleasure and experiences. He got a huge amount from life; he gave—arguably—even more. He didn't deserve to die but he wanted to. Is that tragic ... or funny?

Well, it's complicated.

Perhaps, like Robin's life, and like our own, it's a little of both.

David Misch has been a comic folksinger, stand-up comedian and screenwriter; his credits include Mork and Mindy, Saturday Night Live *and* The Muppets Take Manhattan. *He's also an author (*A Beginner's Guide to Corruption, Funny: The Book), *teacher (his own courses on comedy at USC and musical satire at UCLA) and lecturer (Yale, the Smithsonian, Oxford University, University of Sydney, American Film Institute, Austin Film Festival, Actors Studio, Midwest Popular Culture Association, VIEW Cinema Festival, Torino, Italy). His play* Occupied *is in development at the Skylight Theatre in Los Angeles and he blogs for the* Huffington Post.

NOTES

1. Personal electronic correspondence between David Misch and David Steinberg, 12 June 2018. See also Ronald Beck, "David Steinberg Succeeds Despite Wasserman's Words," *The Stanford Daily*, vol. 164, no. 65, 17 January 1974, page 5.

2. Actually, it's not: there *is* scientific literature supporting the hypothesis that comedians give their lovers more and better orgasms. See http://journals.sagepub.com/doi/full/10.1177/147470491401200507 for more ... and *more* ... and *deeper* understanding.

3. Walt Whitman, "Song of Myself," *Leaves of Grass*. Brooklyn, NY, 1855.

4. William Shakespeare, *The Tragedy of Hamlet, Prince of Denmark*. Act III, Scene II. Circa 1599.

BIBLIOGRAPHY

Beck, Ronald. "David Steinberg Succeeds Despite Wasserman's Words," *The Stanford Daily*, vol. 164, no. 65, 17 January 1974, page 5.

Shakespeare, William. *The Tragedy of Hamlet, Prince of Denmark*. Act III, Scene II. Circa 1599.

Whitman, Walt. "Song of Myself," *Leaves of Grass*. Brooklyn, NY, 1855.

FILMOGRAPHY

Clements, Ron, and John Musker, dir. *Aladdin*. Buena Vista Pictures, 1992.

Sonnenfeld, Barry, dir. *RV*. Columbia Pictures, 2006.

Introduction

Robin Williams and the
Weight of Representation

JOHNSON CHEU

At a childhood birthday party, I received a sparkly *NANU-NANU* t-shirt. Robin Williams's *Mork and Mindy* was all the rage in the late 1970s, and though I was more into the coolness of the Fonz on *Happy Days*, I remember that t-shirt fondly. Though I couldn't articulate it as a child, both of Mork's signatures—the end-of-the-show observational codas regarding the curious ways of human beings to his boss, Orson, and his standing on his head to "sit" in the Cunningham's living room—articulated simultaneously what it meant to be an "Other" or alien, and what it meant to try to learn belongingness. He, thus, served a dual purpose in my Asian household: acculturating us into American customs and into idiomatic English language. For me, mainstreamed fully into public education from segregated special education, being gifted that t-shirt meant that I was like any other elementary school child—that I was beginning to belong.

Over the years, I developed an interest in Robin Williams's television and film career. He was one of my generation's stars (and one of the few in the pre–cable TV era to successfully transition from television to the movies), a contemporary, and though we have lost several of my generation's icons in recent years—Michael Jackson, George Michael, David Cassidy, David Bowie, Roger Moore, Margot Kidder, Prince, Carrie Fisher, and others—I have to admit none shocked and angered me more than Robin's suicide. When, by all reports, he had taken his own life because of the onset of disabilities, I wanted to scream. Though I try not to be judgmental of others' pain, I thought to myself: "but you played 'Dr. Sayer' (Dr. Oliver Sacks) in *Awakenings* (1990), you *know* that people can have fulfilling lives living with their disabilities. How could you *do* this?!" Not only because I grew up with him, but also because he became disabled, he was one of *ours*. My visceral response was that he was *mine*. Though the impetus for this book was largely shock that there was no scholarly collection devoted to his vast body of work, part of me wanted to spend some time with Robin, to remember him not for his passing, but for the art he left us, for the joy he left us.

In thinking about him and embarking on this project, I was struck by his work and skill, not just as a zany comic presence with a mind that left "a mile a minute" in the dust, but as a dramatist, a portrayer of darknesses within us, a portrayer of future hopes, and as an Everyman. Building this collection to cover not only the films for which he was more well-known—as well as his darker fare—has been a challenge, but also a goal: to peer keenly at the man and his artistry. Robin's oeuvre may not match some other actors' and may be peppered with "duds" (or money-grab films, depending on the opinion of the critic you're reading), but in this age of repetitive sequels and blockbusters, Robin, it seems to me, tried to be an *artist*. We've had others who waffle between the blockbuster and the smaller film—and television, of course—but Robin, like his oft-characterized comic mind, seemed with his career to be in his own orbit. Looking at his films, I was struck by how much he actually had to say about family, men, culture, and the world that was sometimes lost on audiences who were bedazzled by "merely" his wit. What started out as shock and anger for me blossomed into a world of contemplation and reflection over the course of this book. As arts in our hyper-politicized America are indeed under siege, the willingness of Robin Williams to gift us with art that was joyful, but also art that forced us to be contemplative—to represent darkness, light, and everything in-between—is a good testament to what art and artists can do, be, and represent.

*   *   *

Mork and Mindy writer David Misch's foreword opens the collection, providing us insight into working with Williams early in his career. From there, we move into Part 1 which has the title "Laughing Heroics: Essays on Comedies and Heroes." Tom Prasch offers us a look at the comedy styling of *Aladdin* and his voice and contributions to that film. Sue Matheson offers us a look into the work of *Jumanji*, more current then ever with the 2017 remake. Prajna Parasher's essay takes us into the world of museum space in Williams's *Night at the Museum* series. Elizabeth Leigh Sherman's essay examines Williams's iconic Mrs. Doubtfire as a threshold figure and leads us toward a present-day understanding of gender and identity. Andrew Slade gives us new thoughts on men, masculinity, and education and Williams's celebrated portrayal in *Dead Poets Society*. Michelle Catherine Iden zeros in on men and Cold War issues in *Moscow on the Hudson* and *Good Morning, Vietnam* Gael Sweeney's essay on

Williams's queer portrayals in *Mrs. Doubtfire, The Birdcage, The Night Listener,* and *Boulevard* leads us from his more comedic and heroic portrayals into his darker, more serious, often more politicized work.

These themes of politics and Everyman portrayals constitute much of the work in Part 2 titled "Dark Spirits—Essays on Politics, Everyman and the Universe." Philip L. Simpson opens this section with a fresh look at *The World According to Garp.* Kenya Wolff and Ludovic A. Sourdot take a decidedly darker examination of *Toys* and consider politics and militarization. Rebecca A. Umland and Samuel J. Umland, too, take us down a darker path with their look at decidedly non-heroic men in *Death to Smoochy, Insomnia,* and *One Hour Photo* (all 2002). Cynthia J. Miller and A. Bowdoin Van Riper consider the city in *The Fisher King* and upend genre conventions in re-imagining it as a horror film. Stacy C. Parenteau and Eric J. Sterling search for psychological redemption in *The Fisher King, Good Will Hunting,* and *What Dreams May Come.* Lori L. Parks examines death and memory in his film *The Final Cut.* Lisa K. Perdigao and Alan M. Rosiene examine several of his films including *Being Human,* offering filmgoers—older generations and younger ones—ways to think about his films in the aftermath of his passing.

Like the codas in *Mork and Mindy,* Kathy Merlock Jackson's essay also serves as a sort of observational coda. Jackson considers and connects Williams's films to the formative years of the Millennial generation, giving us a better sense of his enduring legacy.

*   *   *

In an interview in *Catapult,* the writer Maxine Hong Kingston is asked about writing and representation. On the question of representation, she tells interviewer Alexis Cheung that she's writing a novel now to be published 100 years after her death so that she can be free to write what she wants without the burden of representation, without the burden of worrying about criticism of racial or gender representation.[1] It seems odd, and yet natural, to think about representation when it comes to actors who craft whole professions out of representation. However, we live in more divisive times; at least, it appears as such, where everyone's identity, actions, and voices are (or can be)—as the young say—*on blast.* We live in the era of the 24-hour news and entertainment cycle. We live in the era where identity and representation can be anonymous, but also when the very idea of a public self extends to everyone with a smart phone and the internet and social media, not just the actor or entertainer. We live in the era when the lines between what is public and what is private, and the lines between public and private lives are more blurred than ever before. Representation, more than an old-style photograph stuck in a family album, has become a daily task via social media platforms and has indeed become big business.

It is early June 2018 as I make final revisions to this introduction, and Roseanne Barr has just had her sitcom reboot canceled because of her racist tweet. Anthony Bourdain and fashion designer Kate Spade have both just committed suicide. I pause to wonder what Robin Williams would have said about comedians, about Kanye and slavery, about the Trump presidency, about the rise in school shootings, and also about our current openness towards mental health and illness. I think about what fodder all this would have been for him—both as a comedian and as a dramatist—how sad he likely would have been as a father to see some of this, and yet how much he would have had to say. I think about how much the absence of his singular voice aches. But then, in David Itzkoff's new biography, *Robin* (2018), these words are offered to a young reporter profiling Robin early in his career, "Go, young man, and write your story. In a thousand years, roaches will crawl over your words, their little feelers waving, and say: 'Come on, let's keep crawling.'"[2] I think of Williams's words as an indictment of paparazzi-future, rather than one on writing.

In the end, Robin Williams took control of his own time, and ultimately his own narrative, though as Itzkoff points out, Williams "seemed to understand that others would want to piece together his story and try to make sense of it."[3] But for me, it is only because we appreciate his importance as an artist and performer that we would want to do so. Whether we meant to bestow upon him certain stereotypes or not, Robin lived with that burden of representation, the zany-crazy one or the deep thinker, in his roles. But he was also a performer who tried to avoid the *typecasting* of the zany-crazy one in his vast filmic and television output. If we are to remember him, even now in this age of reality TV and social influencers whose fame burns brightly for a hot minute, we will hopefully recall an artist who did more than announce a presence, but one who made us laugh, made us think, who embodied the most powerful of gifts an artist has: through his art he gave of himself, but allowed us to see a little of ourselves too. Perhaps it will matter not in a thousand years *how* we see Robin Williams and his artistry, but we may hope his work will be around to *be* seen—as we all keep crawling, waving with our feelers.

NOTES

1. Alexis Cheung, "What I Learned from Maxine Hong Kingston." *Catapult*. 4 December 2017. https://catapult.co/stories/the-woman-warrior-what-i-learned-from-maxine-hong-kingston.
2. David Itzkoff, *Robin*, p. 440.
3. *Ibid.*, p. 440.

BIBLIOGRAPHY

Cheung, Alexis. "What I Learned from Maxine Hong Kingston." *Catapult*. 4 December 2017. https://catapult.co/stories/the-woman-warrior-what-i-learned-from-maxine-hong-kingston.
Itzkoff, David. *Robin*. New York: Henry Holt and Company, 2018.

PART 1

Laughing Heroics

Essays on Comedies and Heroes

"Can I call you Al?"

Robin Williams's Genie as Subversive Countertext in Disney's Aladdin

Tom Prasch

When, thirty-five minutes into *Aladdin*'s (1992) hour-and-a-half running time, the Genie, voiced by Robin Williams, is finally released from his lamp, he complains about the pains of his cramped living space for just a moment ("Oy, 10,000 years will give you such a crick in the neck") before shape-shifting into the first of his personae, some sort of television host, sticking his tail-turned-microphone into Aladdin's baffled face to ask: "Where you from? What's your name?" Given the name, he riffs off that: "Can I call you Al? Or just Din? Or how about Laddie" (which pivots him into Scottish form, bearded and kilted, and then terriered). And then we're off: a moment of Arnold Schwarzenegger, Julius Caesar et tuing, Groucho Marx in his *You Bet Your Life* phase (complete with hovering duck), French chef, some Cab Callowayesque crooner, Ed Sullivan, William Buckley, Lon Chaney, and Robert De Niro for an "Are you looking at me" moment, among others. That lamp in which the Genie had been confined for the previous few millennia may have been, as he puts it, an "itty bitty living space," but the television reception must have been very good.

Disney's *Aladdin*—following a familiar plotline roughly lifted from the classic Arabian *1,001 Nights,* although borrowing more directly from the 1940 Alexander Korda production of *Thief of Baghdad*[1]; set in an abstracted Baghdad (renamed Agrabah); featuring, aside from Williams's star turn as Genie, a wide range of stereotypes of Middle Easterners and their culture, but with a far more American-featured (and American-valued) hero and heroine— was released in 1992, just a year after the Gulf War. The timing was noticed

12

by critics both then (for example, the *New York Times,* editorializing: "Thanks to current international politics, however, one form of ethnic bigotry retains an aura of respectability in the United States: prejudice against Arabs"[2]) and later (Leslie Felperin, for instance, juxtaposes the two: "In 1991, the West was bombarded with infrared images of the Gulf War and a wrecked Baghdad. A year later, Walt Disney's *Aladdin* was released, set in a mythical city called Agrabah, a near acronym of Baghdad.... Both texts are informed by the discourse of Orientalism, which can broadly be defined as a set of readings and misunderstandings Western institutions impose on what used to be called the Orient, especially ... the Middle East"[3]). The convergence created a range of problems in the film's reception.

While *Aladdin,* with its Middle Eastern (if not exactly Baghdadi) setting and characters, clearly fits the pattern identified by Johnson Cheu in recent Disney animations of the last few decades, whereby "Disney is, in fact, becoming more multicultural in its filmic fare and its image,"[4] the film's reception suggests that the road to diversity is not always smooth. While widely embraced by movie critics (Rita Kempley, for example, wrote in the *Washington Post* that "Disney quite simply has outdone itself with this marvelous adaptation of the ancient fairy tale"[5]) and audiences (*Aladdin* was not only the highest grossing animation to that date, but the highest grossing film of 1992[6]), the film was also lambasted by offended interest groups for its racially and culturally offensive stereotypes (most notably the Arab-American Anti-Discrimination Committee, whose advocacy was largely responsible for the studio's decision to elide two lines of the opening song when the film was released on video[7]) and by a range of academic commentators (cue Edward Said references).

Said's *Orientalism* remains such a touchstone for commentators focused on (mis)representations of the Middle East as *Aladdin* because it lays out so clearly the mechanics of representation and their relationship to structures of power in the systematic process by which Western commentators from the eighteenth century forward have imaged the "Orient" as non–Western Other. The construction of the Orient is at once a projection of the Western imaginary (largely disconnected from actual Middle Eastern realities) and an exercise of power, operating through the process of Othering that insists on that Other's essential inferiority (and thus justifying political forms of subjugation from imperialism forward to contemporary neocolonialism). Thus Said argues: "One ought never to assume that the structure of Orientalism is nothing more than a structure of lies or of myths.... [W]hat we must respect and try to grasp is the sheer knitted-together strength of Orientalist discourse, its very close ties to enabling socio-economic and political institutions, and its redoubtable durability."[8] The tropes of Orientalism rigorously create the Orient as both Other and inferior. Of "the figures of speech associated with the Orient—its strangeness, its difference, its exotic sensuousness, and so forth," Said writes: "They are always declarative and self-evident; the tense they employ is the timeless eternal; they convey an impression of repetition and strength; they are always symmetrical to, and yet diametrically inferior to, a European equivalent."[9] That timelessness operates "as if the Arab had not been subject to the ordinary processes of history," and Said sees this as necessarily an argument for Arab "primitiveness."[10] And these discursive inventions of the era of European imperial power continue to hold sway, Said insists: "contemporary Orientalist attitudes flood the press and the popular mind. Arabs, for example, are thought of as camel-riding, terroristic, hook-nosed venal lechers whose undeserved wealth is an affront to real civilization."[11] We can easily see such tropes at work in Disney's *Aladdin* as early as its opening song, with its references to camels and barbarity. The stereotyped fantasy vision of Agrabah, the racially charged portrayal of the villains, even the princess's harem pants all fit perfectly into Said's construction.

Notable in the positive reviews of the film was the singling out for praise of Robin Williams's voiced performance, and the match between his style and that of the animators. Roger Ebert, for example, wrote: "Robin Williams and animation were born for one another, and in 'Aladdin' they finally meet. Williams's speed of comic invention has always been too fast for flesh and blood; the way he flashes in and out of characters can be dizzying. In Disney's new animated film 'Aladdin,' he's liberated at last, playing a genie who has complete freedom over his form."[12] Janet Maslin also writes: "It is nothing new to find Mr. Williams ... working in a wildly changeable vein. But here are animators who can actually keep up with him."[13] Such reviews not only address the box-office appeal of Williams's Genie, but suggest as well why Williams's comic stylings could not carry the same weight in other, family-focused but live-action projects like *Jack* (1996), *World's Greatest Dad* (2009), *Father's Day* (1997), or *Hook* (1991). David Denby similarly notes: "In a regular movie, Williams is always a bit uncomfortable—you sense that he's artificially slowing himself down. But if Robin Williams's delivery goes faster than the mind of mere mortals, it doesn't go faster than animated movies." Denby concludes: "Robin Williams, of course, *is* a genie, a granter of wishes who has an endless desire to please and can do anything. But because each of his inventions is now embodied, his mind—for all its speed—seems more substantial than before."[14] But what makes Williams magic in the film, I would argue, is not just the form of his work, but its content.

The barrage of impersonations and embodiments provides a countertext that subverts the dominant tropes of the film, fundamentally relocating the universe of the movie to a somewhat attention-deficit-disordered popular-cultural fantasy realm. (It is perhaps noteworthy, in this respect, that Williams's role plays little part in the critical attacks on the film.) Williams's

Genie is less in the medieval Middle East and more in mediated modernity; by being there, he undermines the landscape of the film, which, given the problematic character of its terrain, redeems the movie. To put it another way, it is not so much that Williams steals the show, although he does, becoming the focus of most of the praise lavished on the film by reviewers, and doubtless most of what viewers remember of the film as well.[15] Janet Maslin captures the transformative process with her contrast to previous genies: "'Master, I hear and obey,' said the Genie in the storybook version of 'Aladdin,' and his comments seldom went further than that. For an exercise in contrast, consider the dizzying, elastic miracle wrought by Robin Williams [and] Walt Disney Pictures' bravura animators."[16] The key here is that, in stealing the show, Williams steals it away, relocating it to someplace that is no longer a deeply problematic, and problematically rendered, Middle East.

But to understand the significance of Williams's transformative magic, we need first to understand the critiques of the film, the range of attacks on its representation of the Middle East. Broadly speaking, the film has been challenged for its sources (the distinctly non–Middle Eastern roots of its vision of the Middle East), its negative stereotypes (racial/ethnic, religious, and cultural), and its Americanizing (or Disneyfying, which comes to essentially the same thing[17]) of its main characters (both in terms of their representation and their values systems). The same film can be criticized both for its negative stereotypes and its Americanizing because the heroes are treated differently than its villains and backdrop.

The source problem begins with the Aladdin tale itself. As has long been recognized, the Aladdin story (along with the equally popular Ali Baba tale), while appearing in Antoine Galland's eighteenth-century "translation" of the *1,0001 Nights*, do not occur in the Arabic original manuscripts. When Richard Burton discussed the problem of the stories that Galland "interpolated, or is said to have interpolated" in his (less expurgated than Galland's) translation of the work, it had clearly already become a point of contention among scholars.[18] Even in the eighteenth century, some scholars presumed the stories were penned by Galland himself, and that, since existing Arab versions of the stories postdated his work, they were in fact re-"translations" back into Arabic from French.[19] Leslie Felperin, emphasizing the possibility that Galland wrote the stories himself, drawing on European rather than Middle Eastern sources, concludes: "Thus, the intermingling of Oriental fancy dress and European fantasy ... marks the story of *Aladdin* throughout its history."[20] But however unoriginal the original, that is only part of the problem, because that story is only indirectly Disney's source.

Felperin notes: "The filmmakers have described how the film was visually inspired by a mixture of 'original Middle Eastern material and Western depictions of the East. The studio sponsored book on the making of the film asserts the production designers developed the style of *Aladdin* from the study of the following: (1) Persian miniature paintings from approximately AD 1000 to 1500; (2) various Victorian paintings of Eastern cultures; (3) numerous photo-essay and coffee-table books on the Middle East; (4) Disney animated films from the mid–1940s to the mid–1950s; (5) Alexander Korda's 1940 film, *The Thief of Baghdad*. Apart from the mention of the Persian miniatures, all the sources just cited are Western in provenance."[21] We can complicate Felperin's account a bit: those coffee-table books may have been designed for and produced by Westerners, but the images would have been of actual Middle Eastern sites; and unmentioned in the list are the set of some 2,000 images layout supervisor Rasoul Azadani collected on a trip to his home of Ispahan in 1991.[22] But those images and the Persian miniatures, as a ground for imagining a medieval (even if renamed) Baghdad, also suggest a problematically undifferentiated Disney view of "the Orient," failing to distinguish Arabic and Persian. And the Korda film is an even more problematic source, since it is not just Western in provenance, but an extra level removed from the origins: rooted itself in Raoul Walsh's earlier *Thief of Baghdad* (1924), starring and based on a story by Douglas Fairbanks. Indeed, Michael Cooperson suggests that "Fairbanks's *Thief* most profoundly influenced Disney's *Aladdin,* as indeed it influenced every Arabian fantasy film since 1924, in its visual representation of medieval Arab-Islamic culture," above all in its "efforts to make medieval Baghdad as unreal as possible"[23] (as well as contributing a story line emphasizing the same constellation of characters).

More significant perhaps than the problematic sourcing of the story is the ethnic and cultural stereotyping evident in the film. Indeed, on its release, *Aladdin* faced concerted protests, spearheaded by the American-Arab Antidiscrimination League, over its racial stereotyping of villainous characters and its insensitive handling of the Islamic religion and Arabic cultures (especially in regard to their legal systems).[24] Jack Shaheen put the case perhaps most forcefully at the time of the film's release:

> *Aladdin* … provides a painful reminder that unconscious racism is still alive and well in Hollywood…. Consider the film's opening song, "Arabian Night." It is belted out by a shady-looking *al-rawi* (storyteller) sitting atop a camel crossing the desert.
> The viewer can't say, "Hey, that's just Hollywood," for this song effectively slanders the heritage of 3,000,000,000 Arabs.[25]

Shaheen goes on to detail how the film's Agrabah is "a stereotypical Arabland. Complete with foreboding desert castle featuring Arabesque cupolas and surrounded by poverty and intrigue, Arabland is inhabited mainly by thieves, harem girls, and unscrupulous vendors." He offers a series of questions to consider: "Why are Arabic names mispronounced? Why are storefront signs written in nonsensical scribble-scratch and not a real language?

Why do the palace guards and merchants have large, bulbous noses, sinister eyes, and idiotic accents? Why do the hero and heroine … look and speech so differently than other Arabs? … what impression of Islam is conveyed when a street vendor insists that the standard penalty for stealing is chopping off one's hand?"[26] The problems with the film's representations are clear, indeed so clear that reviewers in the mainstream press noticed it.

Related to the problem of negative stereotyping of Arab villains, the representation of the princess Jasmine follows another familiar Disney pattern of overtly sexualizing exoticized Others. As Celeste Lacroix notes, the Arabic character of the heroine is problematized from the start: "Jasmine of *Aladdin* posed problems for the Disney animators. Her skin tone is appropriately darker for the Middle Eastern setting of the story. Yet, she retains many White features, such as a delicate nose and small mouth. Jasmine differs from Ariel Belle in the size and shape of her eyes…. Other than skin tone, this feature appears to be the only signifier of racial difference."[27] But Jasmine's costuming falls back on Orientalist stereotyping and the sexualizing that accompanies that framing: "Jasmine's costuming emphasizes the Middle Eastern influence of the setting of *Aladdin* and depicts Jasmine in a more sexualized light. The harem-esque look of her off-the-shoulder, cut-at-the-midriff blouse calls to mind some of the iconography associated with orientalization of Middle Eastern women that Said (1978) and Alloula (1986) noted … and plays into Western cultural notions of the Orient through the referencing of the imagery of the harem and the associated exotic, sexual stereotypes."[28] This sexualization, Lacroix notes, even figures in the plotting, when, near the film's conclusion, Jasmine distracts Jafar by flirting with him, something "inconceivable in a character such as Belle."[29] So, even if Westernized in some respects (nose, lips, accent), Jasmine is orientalized in others.

At the same time that the film stereotypes Arabs, it also Americanizes its presentation, a move made possible by the clear separation between good and bad characters; Arabness is associated with the villains. As noted, Aladdin and Jasmine (and even Jasmine's father the sultan to some extent) are representationally differentiated from the more Arabic-featured villains, in facial features and accent.[30] But they are also Americanized at the level of ideals and aspirations, as Jystyna Fruzińska has pointed out: Aladdin's dreams of becoming more than a "street rat" are a "version of the American dream of bypassing the rules of the hierarchical society. Disney's Aladdin behaves as if he faced the possibilities offered by a Western democracy and could easily go 'from rags to riches,'" a notice "tightly connect to individualism" and to American value systems.[31] The same goes for Jasmine, as Greg Metcalf has argued: "In conforming to the pattern of the Disney Princesses, Jasmine plays a role that is cut free of history and cultural context of a young woman in the Arabian past to provide a young woman from contemporary times who ignores history and her responsibilities to family and community in order to satisfy her individual desires."[32] Indeed, even the Genie fits the pattern, as Fruzińska notes: "in the world of the film even a genie … dreams of leaving the hierarchy he was created into.… The American promise of freedom seems to be the dream of all the characters."[33] The villains constitute the sole exception here, left behind in their stereotyped, un–American, Orientalized space.

Critics thus targeted *Aladdin* for a range of distortions and misrepresentations of Middle Eastern realities. But then, enter Genie. David Denby, writing at the time of the film's release, catches the shift, noting in one paragraph that "Cultural historians will note that Disney has brazenly violated recent barriers of taste and cultural respect and has filled the movie with the ripest of Hollywood's Arab clichés" and then opening his next: "And then Robin Williams comes along and saves the movie from possible embarrassment."[34] He does so by shifting the film's basic grounds.

The Genie role, it is clear from accounts of the film's making, was crafted with Williams in mind. Disney in fact pitched the idea to Williams by using his own stand-up material, as animator Eric Goldberg recalls: "John [Musker] and Ron [Clements, the co-directors] said, 'Pick a couple of sections from his comedy albums and animate a genie to them.' That's essentially what I did."[35] The Genie's character thus, from the outset, was crafted around Williams's stand-up routines, known for their hyperkinetic role-shifting mechanics.

And the Genie was then developed through close collaborative work between Williams and the animators, with an occasional glance at the script. As Goldberg recalls: "We had a script, and if you want to call a script a roadmap, then Robin took a lot of detours. And we loved the detours. Robin had so much freedom, and [ad-libbing] was always encouraged."[36] The celebrity impersonations, in particular, were entirely Williams's work, not part of the original script. And the opening narration as well—in which Williams plays the merchant—worked similarly. As Joshua Shaffer notes: "The opening scene with the street merchant was completely unscripted. Robin Williams … was asked to stand behind a table that had several objects on it and a bed sheet covering them all. The animators asked him to remove the sheet, and without looking, take an object from the table and describe it in character."[37] The process then worked from that raw material to edit it down (since they had some sixteen hours of Williams's improvisations[38] to work from) and animating to match his changes.

Williams's work in *Aladdin*, it must be noted, is not a purely anarchic principle inserted into an otherwise routine Disney animated feature. The Genie character has clear diegetic purposes. First of all, he fits that key role—familiar from classic Loony Toons cartoons forward to Jay Ward's comic stylings—of providing something for the parents to do while their children watch a children's film. As director John Musker explains: "'We've mixed adult and kid sensibilities here,' Mr. Musker said. 'Clearly we see that adults and kids come away from the film with different impressions. The kids go for the simpler dialogue and animation"[39] and the Williams impressions to a range of cultural icons children will not know is pitched to adults. The adult audience focus of Williams's Genie was widely noted by reviewers at the time. Desson Howe, for example, notes: "There's a good chance you're going to enjoy 'Aladdin' more than the children. Keep it to yourself, though."[40] Enough broad comedy figures into the character and his animation that the children can buy in as well. That the film thus entices both adult and child viewers (rather than, as more typical of such leavenings of adult in-jokes in child films, simply making children's fare endurable for the adults that have to accompany the children) may well contribute to the enormous box-office success of *Aladdin*: it is a film adults actually want to see, and perhaps re-see, and still, with its hyperkinetics, appeals to children as well.

The Genie also operates within the film as the conscience of Aladdin, essentially playing the Jiminy Cricket role. Indeed, the film makes direct use of that earlier Disney tale: when the Genie urges Aladdin, against the boy's urges to make something more of himself than he is, to "TELL HER THE TRUTH," we see a quick shape-shift into a nose-growing Pinocchio to underline the point. Beyond the playful citing to the classic fairy tale, of course, that shift also marks, as Scott Schaffer notes, one of the several moments of Disney self-referencing in *Aladdin*.[41]

And Aladdin's shape-shifts and also play a more subtle role, underlining the interesting untethered play of identity in the film. This figures partly in the Americanized aspirational ideals, noted above, but partly as well in a sort of postmodern rethinking of the constantly constructed character of identity that, if the Genie most fully embodies it, also provides possibilities to the film's heroes. As Joseph Boone writes of the Genie: "Indeed, this chameleon (whose transformations include several in drag) embodies the polymorphous perverse gone wild once free from the prison of repression symbolized by the lamp."[42] Sean Griffin makes a similar point in relation to the performance of gender in the film. Of the Genie's shiftings, he notes that they "draw on a lot of the heritage of comic transformation in animated cartoons," but take it all to new levels of excess, such that "the manic overabundance of transformation flaunts performance in the viewers face, making it clear that the excess of identity associated with the Genie is precisely what gives the character his appeal." But for Griffin, the effect carries over to Aladdin and Jasmine, who are "constantly performing their gender identities."[43] The fluidity of the Genie thus sanctions the aspiration to changed roles that so centrally underscores both Aladdin and Jasmine's plot arc.

But more critical to the countertext Williams constructs through the

Genie's multiple embodiments is the alternate filmic reality constructed, almost entirely out of the realm of media culture. From his opening words—that utterly un–Arabic "Oy," and soon after that deracinating pitch to his new master, "Can I call you Al?"—the Genie takes us out of the Middle East. But crucial as well is where, in the subsequent pyrotechnic shapechanges, he brings us instead. David Denby captures some of this sense of the film in his review at the time of its release: "I think even children may know that the real subject of *Aladdin*, the new Disney animated feature film, is not the boy who rubbed the magic lamp and got three wishes but the wish-granting pleasures of show business itself. The movie is so filled with grinning references to television, movies and old Disney films that it's practically a celebration of the magic-carpet ride of modern entertainment."[44] Greg Metcalf catches this same principle, although he gives it a more negative spin: "What is most significant about the film is Robin Williams's Genie … a narratively unexplained spectacle of decontextualized media … stripped of historical and social context to become a source of entertainment that promises to satisfy the viewer's wishes. Disney's Genie is the physical manifestation of the contemporary American mediated culture, the McWorld promise of instant gratification and constant stimulation that ultimately refers back to itself—that is mediated spectacle—with no loyalty to any reality beyond that realm."[45] Well, yes, but why be so glum about it? If the filmic reality that such representational play takes us out of is characterized by problematic negative stereotyping of others' cultures, perhaps moving instead to a ludic postmodern terrain provides some relief and release.

For some cultural critics, that will doubtless not be enough. Ian Wojcik-Andrews, for example, not only does not take Williams as countertext, but insists on the Genie's place as key to the ideological work of the film: "The Genie's strategic importance in the manufacturing of consent around US military policy in the Middle East cannot be underestimated…. Indeed, we [he means he] argue that it is precisely this animated form and the Genie's innocent and harmless play that draws our attention to how the Genie works to obfuscate the centralization and accumulative character of empire building. From a bureaucratic point of view, the Genie organizes, administers, caters, and makes possible Aladdin's every wish…. From a military point of view, the Genie represents a weapon of almost unlimited power available for Aladdin to control at will. But, precisely like capital, the Genie's power is unlimited because it is finally shown to bear no particular allegiance except to whomever is the most powerful master."[46] But that reading seems like something of a stretch. Aladdin only gets three wishes, after all.

We can say, finally, that Robin Williams cannot quite redeem *Aladdin* from the full range of its ethnocentric baggage: from its stereotyping, its Orientalizing impulses, its Americanization of the heroes (against the still Arabized villains). But he does open up a postmodern countertext, an alternative space within the film and for is audience. The Genie's presence, Robin Williams's frantic shtick given trickstery embodiment through animation, plays out finally not in any sort of Middle East at all, but in the spaces of mediated culture, in that oh-so-Disney realm of the "imagineer." Sure, that space exists surrounded by the stereotypical faux-medieval faux-Baghdad of the rest of the film, and takes up finally but a third or so of the running time for itself. That it is what most of us most remember of the film says something, at least, about the power of a countertext to shift our understanding of the film it exists in, and perhaps of the world that we live in as well.

NOTES

1. See Leslie Felperin, "The Thief of Buena Vista: Disney's *Aladdin* and Orientalism," in Jayne Pilling, ed., *A Reader in Animation Studies* (London: John Libbey, 1997), 139.

2. "It's Racist, But Hey, It's Disney," *New York Times*, 14 July 1993, at nytimes.com. The timing of the editorial is curious—well after the film's release, indeed after the video version's release, with a few offending lines censored out—and the view was not shared by the more timely movie reviewer. Janet Maslin, although expressing some reservations (about a "shallow" and dated-feeling script and weak lead characters), concludes: "When it comes to Disney animators and children's films, this remains certain: nobody does it better." Janet Maslin, "Disney Puts Its Magic Touch on 'Aladdin,'" *New York Times*, 11 November 1992, at nytimes. com. A similar concern to the editorial's point about the continued respectability of anti-Arabic representations in American media is made by Mayida Zaal: "These demonized and dehumanizing images (often depicted in seemingly harmless ways, as in the Disney film *Aladdin*) have served to desensitize the U.S. populace and to legitimize fear and hatred against Muslims and Islam." Mayida Zaal, "Islamophobia in Classrooms, Media, and Politics," *Journal of Adolescent and Adult Literacy* 55:6 (March 2012), 556.

3. Felperin, "The Thief of Buena Vista," 137.

4. Johnson Cheu, "Introduction: Casting and Diversifying Disney in the Age of Globalization," in Johnson Cheu, ed., *Diversity in Disney Films: Critical Essays on Race, Ethnicity, Gender, Sexuality and Disability* (Jefferson, NC: McFarland & Company, 2013), 1. The other examples Cheu mentions—*Pocahontas* (1995), *Mulan* (1998), *The Princess and the Frog* (2005), and *Toy Story 3* (2010)—were all released after *Aladdin*, and there is some evidence that Disney has learned its lesson from the difficulties surrounding the latter's release.

5. Rita Kempley, "'Aladdin,'" *Washington Post*, 25 November 1992, and washingtonpost.com.

6. Box-office figures at http://www.the-numbers.com/movie/records/domestic/1992. The film also did well at the awards shows: garnering two Oscars (best song, best score) with four nominations, as well as three Golden Globes (song and score again, plus a special award for Williams for his vocal work) with six nominations. See imdb.com.

7. Douglas Little, *American Orientalism: The United States and the Middle East Since 1945* (Chapel Hill: University of North Carolina Press, 2002), 41.

8. Edward Said, *Orientalism* (New York: Vintage Books, 1979), 6.

9. *Ibid.*, 72.

10. *Ibid.*, 230.

11. *Ibid.*, 108.

12. Roger Ebert, "'Aladdin' (1992)," at rogerebert.com.

13. Maslin, "Disney Puts Its Magic Touch."

14. David Denby, "Boy Wonders," *New York Magazine*, 30 November 1992, 110.

15. And, in classic film-stealing form, he accomplishes the theft without dominating the screentime. He does not enter, as noted, until over half an hour into the film. Richard Corliss and Patrick E. Cole credit him with "half an hour onscreen," before going on to detail

his "metamorphoses: a Scotsman, a Scots dog, Arnold Schwarzenegger, Senor Wences, Ed Sullivan, Groucho Marx, a French waiter, a turkey, the crows from Dumbo, Eddie (Rochester) Anderson, a rabbit, a dinosaur, William F. Buckley Jr., Robert De Niro, a stewardess, a bashful sheep, Pinocchio, a magician, a Jean Gabin–style Frenchman, Sebastian the crab from *The Little Mermaid*, Arsenio Hall, a finicky tailor, Walter Brennan, a TV parade host and hostess, Ethel Merman, Rodney Dangerfield, Jack Nicholson, a talking lampshade, a bee, a U-boat, a one-man band and a quartet of cheerleaders." Richard Corliss and Patrick E. Cole, "Aladdin's Magic," *Time* 140: 19 (9 November 1992), accessed through Academic Search Complete.

16. Maslin, "Disney Puts Its Magic Touch."

17. It can be seen as an ironic twist that the form of Americanizing Disney applies to the characters amounts to another form of fantasy projection with heavy ideological baggage, in other words, as the mirror inversion of the Orientalizing impulse. This is part of a broader process that characterizes Disney productions of all kinds; Disneyland's Main Street is no more realistic in its representation of America than Agrabah is as a representation of the Middle East, although the mythic projection of America valorizes and elevates while that of Agrabah critiques and denigrates. At the level of the characters in the film, discussed in more detail below, the imbedded American value system (individualism and the dream of social advancement) is not only anachronistic and out of place, but unrealistic as well.

18. Richard Burton, "Terminal Essay," vol. 6 of *The Book of the Thousand Nights and One Night* (1885; rpt. New York: Heritage Press, 1962), 3680–81; quotation on 3680.

19. See Robert Irwin, *The Arabian Nights: A Companion* (London: Tauris Parke, 2004), 16–18; Irwin also notes Muhsin Mahdi's carefully documented argument that existing Arabic manuscripts of these stories are actually translations from Galland's French edition, 57–58. Michael Cooperson makes a slightly different argument, drawing on the late nineteenth-century researches of M. H. Zotenberg: that Aladdin and other "orphan tales" in the Galland version had Arabic sources that predated Galland's translation, but were not in the original *1001 Nights*. Michael Cooperson, "The Monstrous Births of 'Aladdin,'" in Ulrich Marzolph, ed., *The Arabian Nights Reader* (Detroit: Wayne State University Press, 2006), 266–267.

20. Felperin, "Thief of Buena Vista," 139.

21. *Ibid.*, 139.

22. Joshua C. Shaffer, *Discovering the Magic Kingdom: An Unofficial Disneyland Vacation Guide* (Bloomington, IN: Amber House, 2010), 46.

23. Cooperson, "Monstrous Births," 272, 273.

24. For a detailed contemporaneous account of the protests, see Richard Sheinin, "Angry over 'Aladdin,'" *Washington Post*, 10 January 1993 (at washingtonpost.com). For later accounts of the protests, see Marvin Wingfield and Bushra Karaman, "Arab Stereotypes and American Educators," at the American Arab Anti-Discrimination Committee's website (http://www.adc.org/2009/11/arab-stereotypes-and-american-educators/); Henry A. Giroux, *The Mouse That Roared: Disney and the End of Innocence* (Lanham, MD: Rowman & Littlefield, 1999), 104–105.

25. Jack Shaheen, "Aladdin: Animated Racism," *Cineaste* 20: 1 (1993), 49; Shaheen would reiterate and expand upon the remarks in *Reel Bad Arabs: How Hollywood Vilifies a People* (Northampton, MA: Olive Branch Press, 2001), 50–53, also noting there that, by the second sequel (*Aladdin and the King of Thieves,* 1996), the representations had somewhat improved, and that the response to *Aladdin* did lead Disney to institute focus-group sessions with ethnic groups in later films (thus avoiding such stereotype problems in, for example, *Pocahontas* [1995]). Wingfield and Karaman, in "Arab Stereotypes," note that protests "persuaded the studio to change a phrase in the lyrics for the video version of the film. A reference to chopping off ears was chopped, but the closing line, which refers to the region as 'barbaric,' was left intact."

26. Shaheen, "Aladdin: Animated Racism," 49. For similar charges of stereotyping, see Felperin, "The Thief of Buena Vista," 137–128; Greg Metcalf, "Them Like Us, Then Like Now: The Translation of the Historical and the Non-U.S. in Disney's Animated Films," in Kathleen McDonald, ed., *Americanization of History: Conflation of Time and Culture in Film and Television* (Cambridge, UK: Cambridge Scholars, 2011), 36–37; and, for a treatment that begins

with the stereotypes before making a parallel argument about the music, Nasser Al-Taee, *Representations of the Orient in Western Music: Violence and Sensuality* (Farnham, UK: Ashgate, 2010), ch. 9.

27. Celeste Lacroix, "Images of Animated Others: The Orientalization of Disney's Cartoon Heroines from *The Little Mermaid* to *The Hunchback of Notre Dame*," *Popular Communication* 2: 4 (2004), 220. See also Sarah E. Turner, "Blackness, Bayous and Gumbo: Encoding and Decoding Race in a Colorblind World," in Cheu, ed., *Diversity in Disney Films*, 92, and Dorothy L. Hurley, "Seeing White: Children of Color and the Disney Fairy Tale Princess," *Journal of Negro Education* 74:3 (2005), 225–226; Justyna Fruzińska, *Emerson Goes to the Movies: Individualism in Walt Disney Company's Post-1989 Animated Films* (Cambridge, UK: Cambridge Scholars, 2014), 93.

28. La Croix, "Images of Animated Others," 221.

29. *Ibid.*, 224.

30. Shaffer notes that Jasmine's representation is based in part on Jennifer Connelly, and Aladdin crosses Michael J. Fox with Tom Cruise, none of the models especially noted for their Arabic looks. Shaffer, *Discovering the Magic Kingdom*, 46.

31. Fruzińska, *Emerson Goes to the Movies*, 93.

32. Metcalf, "Them Like Us, Them Like Now," 36. See also Fruzińska, 94.

33. Fruzińska, 95. Scott Schaffer makes a similar argument about all the characters, with a stronger orientation toward the inscription of capitalist ideals, in "Disney and the Imagineering of Histories," *Postmodern Culture* 6:3 (1996), online at http://xroads.virginia. edu/~DRBR2/schaffer.txt, para. 17.

34. Denby, "Boy Wonders," 110.

35. Jeff Labrecque, "Robin Williams in 'Aladdin': Animator Eric Goldberg Remembers Drawing Genie," EW Online, 12 August 2014, at ew.com.

36. *Ibid.* Brackets in original.

37. Shaffer, *Discovering the Magic Kingdom*, 45.

38. *Ibid.*, 36; Labrecque, "Robin Williams in 'Aladdin.'"

39. "Robin Williams Summons Up His Quick Wit as the Genie in 'Aladdin,'" *Baltimore Sun*, 20 November 1992, at bartimoresun.com.

40. Desson Howe, "'Aladdin,'" *Washington Post*, 27 November 1992, at washingtonpost. com.

41. Schaffer, "Disney and the Imagineering of Histories," para. 18.

42. Joseph A. Boone, *The Homoerotics of Orientalism* (Columbia University Press, 2015), 415. Boone links this "polymorphous" shape-shifting as well to the character's appeal to a gay subculture.

43. Sean Griffin, "The Illusion of 'Identity': Gender and Racial Representation in *Aladdin*" in Maureen Furniss, ed., *Animation: Art and Industry* (New Barnet, UK: John Libbey, 2012), 209.

44. Denby, "Boy Wonders," 110.

45. Metcalf, "Them Like Us," 37.

46. Ian Wojcik-Andrews, *Children's Films: History, Ideology, Pedagogy, Theory* (New York: Garland, 2000), 214.

BIBLIOGRAPHY

Al-Taee, Nasser. *Representations of the Orient in Western Music: Violence and Sensuality.* Farnham, UK: Ashgate, 2010.

Boone, Joseph A. *The Homoerotics of Orientalism.* Columbia University Press, 2015.

Burton, Richard. "Terminal Essay." *The Book of the Thousand Nights and One Night*, 6: 3653–3876. 6 vols., 1885; rpt. New York: Heritage Press, 1962.

Cheu, Johnson. "Introduction: Casting and Diversifying Disney in the Age of Globalization." In Johnson Cheu, ed., *Diversity in Disney Films: Critical Essays on Race, Ethnicity, Gender, Sexuality and Disability*, 1–7. Jefferson, NC: McFarland & Company, 2013.

Cooperson, Michael. "The Monstrous Births of 'Aladdin.'" In Ulrich Marzolph, ed., *The Arabian Nights Reader*, 265–282. Detroit: Wayne State University Press, 2006.

Corliss, Richard and Patrick E. Cole. "Aladdin's Magic." *Time* 140, no. 19, 9 November 1992, 74. Accessed through Academic Search Complete.

Denby, David. "Boy Wonders." *New York Magazine*, 30 November 1992, 110–111.

Ebert, Roger. "'Aladdin.'" *Chicago Sun-Times*, 25 November 1992. At http://www.rogerebert.com/reviews/aladdin-1992.

Felperin, Leslie. "The Thief of Buena Vista: Disney's *Aladdin* and Orientalism." In Jayne Pilling, ed., *A Reader in Animation Studies*, 137–42. London: John Libbey, 1997.

Fruzińska, Justyna. *Emerson Goes to the Movies: Individualism in Walt Disney Company's Post-1989 Animated Films*. Cambridge, UK: Cambridge Scholars, 2014.

Giroux, Henry A. *The Mouse That Roared: Disney and the End of Innocence*. Lanham, MD: Rowman & Littlefield, 1999.

Griffin, Sean. "The Illusion of 'Identity': Gender and Racial Representation in *Aladdin*." In Maureen Furniss, ed., *Animation: Art and Industry*, 207–214. New Barnet, UK: John Libbey, 2012.

Howe, Desson. "'Aladdin,'" *Washington Post*, 27 November 1992. At http://www.washingtonpost.com/wp-srv/style/longterm/movies/videos/aladdinhowe_a0af3c.htm,

Hurley, Dorothy L. "Seeing White: Children of Color and the Disney Fairy Tale Princess." *Journal of Negro Education* 74, no. 3, 2005. 221–232.

Irwin, Robert. *The Arabian Nights: A Companion*. London: Tauris Parke, 2004.

"It's Racist, But Hey, It's Disney." *New York Times*, 14 July 1993. At http://www.nytimes.com/1993/07/14/opinion/it-s-racist-but-hey-it-s-disney.html.

Kempley, Rita. "'Aladdin,'" *Washington Post*, 25 November 1992. At http://www.washingtonpost.com/wp-srv/style/longterm/movies/videos/aladdingkempley_a0a32e.htm.

Labrecque, Jeff. "Robin Williams in 'Aladdin': Animator Eric Goldberg Remembers Drawing Genie." *EW Online*, 12 August 2014. At http://ew.com/article/2014/08/12/robin-williams-aladdin-eric-goldberg/.

Lacroix, Celeste. "Images of Animated Others: The Orientalization of Disney's Cartoon Heroines from *The Little Mermaid* to *The Hunchback of Notre Dame*." *Popular Communication* 2, no. 4, 2004. 213–229.

Little, Douglas. *American Orientalism: The United States and the Middle East since 1945*. Chapel Hill: University of North Carolina Press, 2002.

Maslin, Janet. "Disney Puts Its Magic Touch on 'Aladdin.'" *New York Times*, 11 November 1992. At http://www.nytimes.com/1992/11/11/movies/review-film-disney-puts-its-magic-touch-on-aladdin.html.

Metcalf, Greg. "Them Like Us, Then Like Now: The Translation of the Historical and the Non-U.S. in Disney's Animated Films." In Kathleen McDonald, ed., *Americanization of History: Conflation of Time and Culture in Film and Television*, 22–39. Cambridge, UK: Cambridge Scholars, 2011.

"Robin Williams Summons Up His Quick Wit as the Genie in 'Aladdin.'" *Baltimore Sun*, 20 November 1992. At http://articles.baltimoresun.com/1992-11-20/entertainment/1992325013_1_robin-williams-genie-nicholson

Said, Edward. *Orientalism*. New York: Vintage Books, 1979.

Schaffer, Scott. "Disney and the Imagineering of Histories." *Postmodern Culture* 6, no. 3, 1996. Online at http://xroads.virginia.edu/~DRBR2/schaffer.txt.

Shaffer, Joshua C. *Discovering the Magic Kingdom: An Unofficial Disneyland Vacation Guide*. Bloomington, IN: Amber House, 2010.

Shaheen, Jack. "Aladdin: Animated Racism." *Cineaste* 20, no. 1, July 1993. 49.

Shaheen, Jack. *Reel Bad Arabs: How Hollywood Vilifies a People*. Northampton, MA: Olive Branch Press, 2001.

Sheinin, Richard. "Angry over 'Aladdin.'" *Washington Post*, 10 January 1993. At https://www.washingtonpost.com/archive/lifestyle/style/1993/01/10/angry-over-aladdin/46f2aacd-444b-4a81-9aa7-7c43cc84d65b/?utm_term=.1cd06f40eb50.

Turner, Sarah E. "Blackness, Bayous and Gumbo: Encoding and Decoding Race in a Color-blind World." In Johnson Cheu, ed., *Diversity in Disney Films: Critical Essays on Race, Ethnicity, Gender, Sexuality and Disability*, 83–98. Jefferson, NC: McFarland & Company, 2013.

Wingfield, Marvin and Bushra Karaman. "Arab Stereotypes and American Educators." At the American Arab Anti-Discrimination Committee's website, http://www.adc.org/2009/11/arab-stereotypes-and-american-educators/.

Wojcik-Andrews, Ian. *Children's Films: History, Ideology, Pedagogy, Theory.* New York: Garland, 2000.

Zaal, Mayida. "Islamophobia in Classrooms, Media, and Politics." *Journal of Adolescent and Adult Literacy* 55, no. 6, March 2012. 555–558.

Carnival, Free Play and American Horror

Mashup in Joe Johnston's Jumanji

SUE MATHESON

In 1995, the *New York Times* reviewer Janet Maslin found Joe Johnston's *Jumanji* "[a] mixture of random gimmicks and easy sentimentality"[1]; Roger Ebert of the *Chicago Sun-Times* noted that the film, promoted as "a jolly holiday season entertainment, with ads that show Robin Williams with a twinkle in his eye," was "likely to send younger children fleeing form the theatre, or hiding in their parents' arms"[2]; the *Los Angeles Times* reviewer Jack Matthews remarked, "Something bad happened on the way from the book to the movie," noting that "[t]he animals don't exactly look real—the monkeys' faces are too humanly expressive, the lion's mouth a bit too large and hungry—but they're close enough to fool anyone peering through their fingers, and they just keep coming, one after another, with little relief from the film's clumsy efforts at humor."[3] *Jumanji*, however, was an unqualified box office success— earning $100,475,249 in the United States and Canada and $162,322,000 overseas—despite being a critical failure, and has remained surprisingly popular: an animated television series based on the movie ran from 1996 to 1999 and a videogame based on the movie was released in Europe for PlayStation2 in 2006. A brand new *Jumanji* adventure, *Jumanji: Welcome to the Jungle* (2017), released on December 20th, 2018, overtook Rian Johnson's *Star Wars: The Last Jedi* (2017) at the domestic box office on New Year's Day. Also an unqualified box office success, Jake Kasdan's standalone sequel at the time of this writing has grossed $ 531,206,923 at the worldwide box office, nearly doubling the $262 million the first *Jumanji* film earned when it opened in 1995.[4]

Reassessing *Jumanji*, critics have concluded the film was misunderstood on its release. Dragan Antulov, for example, points out that the presence of

darker tones in this movie are "refreshing when compared with the high
levels of saccharine that plague Hollywood family-oriented films in recent
memory," Jonathan Hensleigh's script is "very good" and in many ways resembles Frank Capra's classic *It's a Wonderful Life*, and the acting is "more than
satisfying with Robin Williams's surprisingly constrained and realistic portrayal of a character who is in many ways a boy in a man's body"—the result,
Antulov concludes, is that *Jumanji* "is one of those rare films that could be
recommended to children and adults alike."[5] Mark Harrison, on the other
hand, finds *Jumanji* a "wacky fantasy adventure" that is notable for its "wild"
tone, its "impeccable" production, and its board game's highly exaggerated
characters Peter Hyde's performance in a dual role as Alan's father and Van
Pelt, for example, gives that actor the chance to "camp it up."[6] On the whole,
children, unaware of the film's campiness, have also been enthusiastic: for
example, on *common sense media*, "Kid, 12 years old" posted on January 30,
2010—"Jumanji is really good!!!!!!!! It is funny and it is quite entertaining. It
is a good family movie, and I would watch it again. It is GREAT!!!!!!!!"; Kid,
11 years old" posted on August 29, 2010, posted—"The movie, in my opinion,
is fine. Adventurous but will be scary for the really young kids. There was a
spider and huge bugs in there, so if your child is scared of seeing spiders or
big bugs like me, skip that part of the movie or don't watch it."[7]

To date, only two scholars have considered this film. Joel D. Chaston
who identifies parallels between *Jumanji* and *The Wizard of Oz* (1939) in "The
'Ozification' of American Children's Fantasy Films: The Blue Bird, Alice in
Wonderland and Jumanji." He concludes that "[o]nce again, a popular children's story is rewritten, inevitably, in the Hollywood idiom, to satisfy the
classical film's need for goal-oriented plots."[8] The search for home in *Jumanji*,
Chaston says, "is a goal that has next to nothing to do with [Chris] Van Allsburg's original book."[9] In *Coining for Capital: Movies, Marketing, and the
Transformation of Childhood*, Jyotsna Kapru finds Johnston's film goes much
farther in depicting fantasies unleashed by bourgeois boredom than Allsburg's
book. *Jumanji* erases boredom as the starting point of the children's adventure,
she asserts, but the wild events experienced in the privacy of the home burst
into the town of Brantford: in short order, world runs "amok," while fantastic
reversals of the ordinary drive the film's narrative: "people die before they
are born; people do not play games but games play people; and children's
fantasies and imaginations threaten not only to subvert the home but also to
spill out into the streets."[10] This paper is another step in the consideration of
Jumanji as a site in which the real and the fantastic meet and overlap. In
Jumanji, it is no coincidence that *ludus*, the Latin word for play, also means
board game. Robin Williams, playing Alan Parrish, presides as *magister ludi*
in a carnival mashup of free play, American horror, and the jungle adventure
movie.

Jumanji begins in 1869 as two brothers, Caleb (Cyrus Thiedeke) and Benjamin (Brandon Obray) bury a chest outside Brantford, New Hampshire. One hundred years later, young Alan Parrish discovers the chest and becomes trapped in the board game it contains (and after which the film is named) while playing with his best friend Sarah Whittle. Twenty-six years later, in 1995, Judy and Peter Shepherd find the game, begin playing and unwittingly release Alan who has become an adult. Alan, Judy, and Peter resolve to finish the game in order to reverse the destruction it has caused, they locate Sarah, and persuade her to join them. With each roll of the die, the players come closer to ending the game as pieces on the board move by themselves and a message outlining the rolls' outcomes appear in a globe located at the board's center. Every roll releases obstacles which must be surmounted, ranging from gigantic mosquitoes and bats, to lions, to aggressive and poisonous carnivorous plants, to a board-stealing pelican, to monsoon downpours and giant crocodiles, to a big game hunter named Van Pelt. Each calamity escapes the house in which the game is being played and upends the ordered, peaceful town of Brantford. When Alan is finally able to make the winning roll, the disaster that has been unleashed is sucked back into the board game, and order is restored: in 1969, Alan and Sarah are children once again, but with full memories of the game's events. Accordingly, Alan reconciles with his father and does not have to attend boarding school. Alan and Sarah, like Caleb and Benjamin a century earlier, dispose of *Jumanji* by throwing it into the river. By 1995, Alan and Sarah are married and expecting their first child. They meet Judy, Peter, and their parents Jim and Martha. Alan offers Jim a job, and convinces them to cancel their upcoming ski trip, averting what had been their untimely deaths. But on a beach in France, two young girls hear drumbeats while walking, as *Jumanji* lies partially buried in the sand. The board game has returned to be played again.

Upending the ordinary and the everyday, *Jumanji* is concerned with "an alternative cosmovision characterized by the ludic undermining of all norms."[11] In carnival, the world is "turned upside down."[12] As Kapru notes, in *Jumanji* "adults act like children; children act like adults; people remember not just the past but also the future; people die before they are born; people do not play games but games play people."[13] The young and the old change places: Judy and Peter, for example, become their guardian's caretaker. Rescuing her when she returns home from work to find a jungle in her house and a lion in her bedroom, Peter has no time for the niceties of etiquette, politeness, and good manners.[14] He shoves Nora Shepherd into a linen closet and locks her in.

Elements of the carnivalesque driving a film's narrative is not an unusual or startling in American film. As Stam points out in *Subversive Pleasures: Bakhtin, Cultural Criticism, and Film*, in the dominant Hollywood tradition, carnival is at times evoked in its local sense of "fairground, side show, amusement park," historically latter-day (often commercialized) echoes of old–time carnival. The link between carnival and American cinema, in this sense, Stam notes, is both metonymic and metaphoric: metonymic in the sense that the entertainment is quite literally situated near the fairground and the penny arcade; and metaphoric in the sense that countless films cite the regressive pleasures of commercial carnivals—roller coasters, carousels, Ferris wheels— to analogize those of the cinema itself."[15] Among such films, one finds *Freaks* (1932), *Carnival of Souls* (1962), *Vampire Circus* (1972), *Carnival of Blood* (1970), *The Funhouse* (1981), *Something Wicked This Way Comes* (1983), *Killer Clowns From Outer Space* (1988), *Waxwork* (1988), *Final Destination 3* (2006), *The Last Circus* (2010), *The Devil's Carnival* (2012), and *31* (2016).

Konrad Eisenbichler and Wim Hüsken remark in *Carnival and the Carnivalesque: The Fool, the Reformer, the Wildman and Others in Early Modern Theatre* that carnival and gaming have been linked in literature since the fifteenth century. In *Ein Schönes Spil*, board games and dice feature among the social activities of Carnival. Attempting to escape reality, and particularly, his "spying" and controlling wife, a character who is a "wild man" attempts "to insinuate" himself securely into the Carnival revellers' interactions, calling "Bring us games and cards and dice!"[16] Aptly, Alan Parrish (Robin Williams), *Jumanji's* magister ludi, first appears as a "wild man" dressed in skins and leaves. Metaphorically linked to carnival, *Jumanji's* unabashed action acts as a narrative rollercoaster ride for viewers already intimately acquainted with the principles and pleasures of the filmic fairground. Paradoxically, the unpredictability of *Jumanji's* action, produced by the players' (and the viewer's) inability to guess what will happen next, is a familiar and comforting trope for any American who has been brought up playing board games.

Because participation in board games involves the player inhabiting "a twilight zone where he/she is both outside the game *and* undertakes a role inside the game,"[17] *Jumanji* itself becomes a participatory spectacle which, as a board game, erases "the boundaries between spectator and performer."[18] On the one hand, the narrative of the film rests on action that has been preset. That is the game contains a narrative, available to be discovered or realized, in whole or in part, or, in some cases, in one version or another, depending on the paths taken by the player. On the other hand, while play takes place, a particular realization of the potential offered by the game is created, because the precise shape or outcome (depending on the roll of the die) is indeterminate. The carefully predetermined board game's narrative provides changes in pacing and changing tensions of the film narrative, while the extent to which *Jumanji's* narrative dimensions are experienced as being separate from, or part of, the gameplay is determined by the storytelling devices of the board game itself. In particular, dramatic tension is generated by the board game's predetermined narrative that is structured into the game and the variable "player's story" generated in each individual experience of the game. Since the overarching narrative trajectory of the film is focused on Alan Parrish's experience, the player's story in *Jumanji* is the most important story produced by the game. It is the story with which the players (and hence the audience) are most involved, and it is the story in which the players' decisions have the most impact.

As reviewer ccthemovieman-1 remarks, *Jumanji* is "a wild ride" which provides "a bunch of laughs and thrills."[19] Mediated by the roll of the die, ludic overturnings determine the narrative's progression. After beginning play, Alan Parrish is sucked into the world of the board game (and retained there for 26 years). When the die are rolled again, the fauna and flora of *Jumanji's* jungle world explode into the real world. As the board game continues after Alan's return, rhinoceri, elephants, and zebras stampede through the rooms and hallways of the old Parrish home before escaping and rampaging through the streets of downtown Brantford. Monkeys, called into being by the die, then "slow the expedition," by making off with a motorcycle and crashing Carl Bentley's (David Alan Grier) police car into a tree when the patrolman stops to help Alan search for his mother and father. Carl recovers his car only to have it later crushed and devoured by a jungle plant (produced in an earlier turn) while Sarah, Judy, and Peter create havoc in the hardware section of a Sir-Sav-A-Lot. Van Pelt, another denizen of the board game's jungle who appears in the real world, adds another layer of complexity to the game while stalking Alan. As Judy notes, those participating in the carnival that takes place in Brantford have no control over the nature of the play that happens. The players cannot stop the jungle and its inhabitants from escaping from the board game to upset everyday life in Brantford. Repeatedly unable to find the opportunity kill Alan, Van Pelt is particularly disruptive. When he appears, the board play must stop while Alan flees for his life. However, lacking the agency to stop the game, the players must continue. The carnival taking place in Brantford will end only when the pieces on the board reach the end of their designated path. Inscribed on its surface, the board game's caveat regarding this matter is perfectly clear: "Adventurers beware: do not begin unless you intend to finish. The exciting consequences of the game / will vanish only when a player has reached *Jumanji* and called out its name."

As Alan, Sarah, Judy, and Peter's adventures continue, each roll of the die creates another upending of order in the real world. Generally, play is considered to be an activity situated outside of the real or the ordinary, but, "the logic of board games and the attitude of play (the ludic) can permeate and encroach upon our experience of both the playful and the serious" the two, as Stoyanova notes, become "increasingly indistinguishable."[20] Overturned, the real becomes a venue in which to play. As Alan, Sarah, Judy, and Peter play, the boundaries between the real and the fantastic became more and more permeable. At first when Judy rolls the dice, nothing happens. Then, when Peter rolls a "five," Alan appears, released from the wild world in the game. As play continues, the board game is revealed to be an interface, (or avenue). Utilized by the real and the fantastic, the game serves as a conduit for both child and adult, mediating between the past and the present, and leveling hierarchical relationships between the child and the adult. As Alan, Sarah, Judy and Peter continue to play, Brantford, becomes a "gamic" space in which the real and the fantastic overlap and in which elements of the board game that have irrupted into the real world impede the players' progress. They must be avoided, outwitted, or defeated before the dice can be rolled again. After Alan, Sarah, Judy, and Peter rescue the board from a pesky pelican that flies off with it and elude Van Pelt, they return to the old Parrish house to end the game. Tellingly, they find that the interior of the old Parrish house has become a "gamic" jungle—their play takes place amid the huge trees and hanging vines.

In *Jumanji*, "play" is, as Huizinga asserts in his "Foreword" to *Homo Ludens*,[21] an innate characteristic of humanity that must be distinguished from the activity of "gaming," a highly specific form of organized play.[22] As Stoyanova points out, it is the "rule-bound and structured aspect of the game that allows for the convergence of gamespace and gamic space, as it is the specific structural logic of games that can be ported to non-game experiences…[and that] establishes the conditions for the phenomenological ambiguity between the game and the ordinary world made over as game."[23] In part, the central procedure of the game is to superimpose a linear narration on what is really extremely discontinuous material via the unicursal pattern of the board game. Playing *Jumanji* draws the film narrative on, because the game must be finished even though events, like a pelican making off with the board, occur, which interrupt the forward motion from start to finish. Throughout, binary oppositions between real and fantastic, present and past, adult and child unify Johnston's *bricolage*.[24] The corelations of "life" with staged fictive "play or gaming," in particular offers a metafictive gloss on reality rather than vice versa, as it is the roll of the die that determines what will happen next in *Jumanji*. Thus, throughout, the characters' narrative control is diminished, for Peter, Judy, Alan, and Sarah participate in a highly specific and organized type of play that celebrates random happenings. The arbitrary nature of their moves on the board signal their activity being, what Jacques Derrida would term, free play.

Structured in the same manner as Robin Williams's fast-paced improvisational, manic style of comedy, which draws heavily on associative and stream of consciousness techniques, *Jumanji* excels in demonstrating the activity of free play. The film's narrative is constantly re-constructed as Alan, Sarah, Judy, and Peter, decentered by each roll of the die, improvise when they are confronted with new dangers. Each time the roll of the die generates a new message from the board's center, agency is transferred from the players (who have just vanquished a predator or resolved a dangerous situation) to the new denizens of the jungle that emerge from the board game. Indeed, it may be said that the absence of the Williams's playful riffing is a trademark of his comedy in his performance as Alan Parrish is compensated for by the presence of the unpredictable gameplay that drives the film's narrative.

According to Derrida, in his 1966 essay, "Structure, Sign, and Play in the Discourse of the Human Sciences," free play occurs when the center of a structure is removed and the elements within that structure are no longer organized according to centralized references. Because the function of a center to orient, balance, and organize by placing limitations on the activities of the elements that take place within a structure, the removal of the center disrupts the coherence of the structure's system and frees the interaction of its elements. As Derrida notes, "[f]ree play is the disruption of presence,"[25] for the presence of an element is always a signifying and substitutive reference inscribed in a system of differences and the movement of a causal chain. This disruption of presence is an important aspect of free play in *Jumanji*, signalled by the return of Alan Parrish, whose presence is a constant reminder of his 26-year absence. The young Parrish's hauntingly horrifying disappearance into the world of the board game is also a prime example of the disruption of presence. As he is sucked into the vortex of the game's crystal, Alan's body becomes two-dimensional in order to enter the game he is about to inhabit. His absence in the real world disrupts his father's and mother's lives, causes the family business to fail, and redirects Carl's career trajectory. His return to the orderly world of the middle class, illustrated as Nora cleans and orders the old Parrish home into a bed and breakfast, upends his sad family history. When he ends the game and says, "Jumanji," order is restored as the present is erased and replaced with the past.

In children's films, adults who function as authority figures, fathers in particular, direct and control the lives of those around them. But as Stam points out, the logic of carnival is that of the world turned upside down in which those in power are mocked and "ridiculous kings are enthroned and then dethroned in an atmosphere of gay relativity."[26] In Brantford, the suburb's immaculately groomed lawns, gardens, and hedges are important expressions of the father's central position in the family, marking not only the economic but also the social respectability of the people living there, via man's ability to order and control the natural world. When Sarah rolls the die, this relationship between man and Nature is rudely overturned. Huge vines appear, to terrorize the players and then the town. They prove to be attached to plants not only as carnivorous, vigorous, and dangerous as John Wyndham's triffids, but also much faster moving. After Sarah rolls, the globe at the center of the board game warns the players, "They grow much faster than bamboo, take care or they'll come after you." When the first tendrils slither out of an electrical outlet to slide under a rug and around the dining table's chairs, Alan, who has become his group's paternal authority figure, warns, "Stay away from the walls, don't touch anything. No quick movements." He knows that the plant is not only investigating the dining room, it is looking for dinner. But, as he counsels his fellow players, "Stay away from the big yellow pods," a vine locates and wraps itself around Peter's leg. It then drags him toward a pod that bursts from the china cabinet. When the pod splits into four parts and opens its maw, it is evident that the tendril is acting like a tongue, drawing the boy into a cavernous mouth (that roars like a lion). Immediately upended again, the relationship between human and vegetable becomes humorous. Alan, acting as the *magister ludi*, finds a sword, and severs the vine from its pod, shouting "Harvest time!" to rescue Peter from being eaten. Then, an inversion that re-establishes the primacy of plant life over man occurs a few scenes later when the vine returns, having grown much bigger and far more aggressive. Having escaped the confines of the house, its brawny end snakes into Carl's police cruiser through an open window, folds the chase car in half and drags it off to be devoured in a bush where the pod is waiting. Lacking a sword, Carl, who is generally presented as heroic, can only shout impotently, "Fine, take it!!" Defeated by a vegetable, Brantford's emblem of male civic authority is reduced to dragging Nora down the street to safety while clutching his useless, holstered gun.

Another important carnival motif resides in the power inversions that frame the father and son relationships in *Jumanji*. Alan Parrish's boy-man status, in particular, resuscitates the perennial carnival trope of the *puer-rex* (boy-king) and *puer-senex* (child-man) At the age of ten, Alan Parrish appears to be a victim, bullied by a gang of his peers and decentered by his parents' decision to send him to a boarding school. When he returns home after surviving in the board game's jungle for 26 years, the first thing Alan does is run through the house looking for his parents. After learning they are dead, he discovers that his father had not been the all-powerful, uncaring figure he had thought him to be. Much to his surprise, Alan learns that he, not the Parrish Shoe Factory, had been the center of his father's life—and that when he disappeared, his father "put everything he had into finding him." The Parrish Shoe Factory failed, because no one "loved his boy more than Sam did." His relationship with his father upended, Alan realizes he has become like him. When Sarah asks Alan to comfort a sobbing Peter, Alan says to the boy. "What, are you crying?" You don't cry, all right? You keep your chin up.

Come on, keep your chin up. Crying never helped anybody do anything, okay? You have a problem? You face it like a man." It is only then that he realizes he has said to Peter what his father had said to him the day he disappeared into the board game: "Twenty-six years buried in the deepest darkest jungle, and I still became my father."

Throughout this sequence, Peter's increasingly simian appearance reminds the viewer of the permeability of boundaries in carnival as the high (a human) mingles with the low (an ape). When Peter attempts to win the game by cheating, the crystal informs the players that he "will be set back." Not only is his token set back; he himself is as he devolves, immediately growing monkey fur on the back of his hands. In subsequent scenes, his face also becomes furry, his nose changes into that of monkey, and he grows a tail (as noted above). When Alan takes the place of Peter's father, a comic *mèsalliance* also occurs. Alan obligingly stops Peter's crying by ripping open the back of the boy's pants. As Alan says, "Don't worry, we'll have you turned back into your old self in no time flat," Peter's freed, long prehensile tail swinging happily (and comfortably) behind him. When seen from behind, man and monkey walk back to the old Parrish home hand in hand.

This mingling of classical Apollonian order (human rationality) and the Dionysian carnivalesque (animality) is further developed as the game continues. Johnston immediately cuts to a mob of monkeys terrorizing a sidewalk in downtown Brantford. Stopping at the sight of flying monkeys in *The Wizard of Oz* (1939) shown on a portable television displayed in the storefront of the Ye Olde Beantiquated Discount Electronics Centre, these apes smash the windows of the store and make off with televisions and VHS players. At first, it seems that their behaviour contrasts sharply with that of the people attempting to re-establish order in the town. But as the town's inhabitants loot the contents of the Sir Sav-A-Lot and run off with bicycles, sports equipment, and children's toys, it is shown that human beings are capable of becoming apes too as they behave like a pack of wild animals (or the minions of the Wicked Witch in Oz).

Peter's attempted derailment of cause-effect logic to win and end the board game which begins this sequence reveals the importance of oxymoronic intertexts found in its carnival. The crystal warns that "A law of *Jumanji* having been broken / You will slip back even more than your token," but Peter ignores this warning and pays the consequences of attempting to drop rather than roll the die. However, as Stam points out, Bakhtin remarks that selfhood is achieved via a process of hybridization.[27] Shown in constant metamorphoses as he becomes a monkey-boy, Peter becomes a hybrid, embodying the carnivalesque. Part animal, part man, he is a creature "in which everything is pregnant with its opposite" and, in so doing, demonstrates the carnival's alternative logic of non-exclusivity. As reconstructions of the self take place in *Jumanji's* "wild zone," social polarities are upended, aesthetics of formal harmony and good taste are aggressively inverted, and barriers between man and animal are erased. This refashioning of self and Other not only demonstrates the permeability and the malleability of boundaries in carnival, it is also a deeply horrifying process. As Stam points out, the carnivalesque principle "abolishes hierarchies, levels social classes, and creates another life free from conventional rules and restrictions, all that is marginalized and excluded, the mad, the scandalous, the aleatory—[thereby taking] over the center in a liberating explosion of otherness."[28]

As Eisenbichler and Hüsken point out, carnival and its overturnings of authority are "inherently dangerous."[29] In carnival, acts of violence and murder are commonplace. Accordingly, in *Jumanji*, one discovers the Other found in horror movies to relocated to the board game's center. Alan says to Sarah, "You think that mosquitos, monkeys, and lions are bad? That is just the beginning. I've seen things you've only seen in your nightmares. Things you can't even imagine. Things you can't even see. There are things that hunt you in the night. Then something screams. Then you hear them eating, and you hope to God that you're not dessert. Afraid? You don't even know what afraid is. You would not last five minutes without me."

Here it is important to note that *Jumanji's* mashup of jungle action adventure and horror belongs to a subset of the action movie, set in "wild" places where the social logic of ordinary life is upended, that includes films like *The Naked Jungle* (1954), *Jungle Holocaust* (1977), *The Mountain of the Cannibal God* (1978), *Eaten Alive!* (1980), *Cannibal Ferox* (1981), *Predator* (1987), *Alive* (1993), *The Ghost and the Darkness* (1996), *Anaconda* (1997), *The Mummy* (1999), *Jurassic Park III* (2001), *Pirates of the Caribbean: The Curse of the Black Pearl* (2003), *Anacondas: The Hunt for the Blood Orchid* (2004), *and The Green Inferno* (2013). In these movies, "civilized" individuals find themselves relying on their instincts and animal drives to survive in tropical wildernesses that contain denizens representing the dark side of life. In the jungle, one finds what has been forbidden and strange and frightening events occur. A survival mashup made for children, *Jumanji*, like adventure serials from the 1930s and 1940s, features mini-episodes in which life-or-death experiences take place. Each of these survival narratives pit the players against what seem to be insurmountable odds presented by the typical elements of the jungle adventure—a hungry lion, man-eating plants, giant crocodiles, and the big game hunter. In these encounters, the players find resources within themselves and each other to overcome their merciless, relentless enemies. Like the survival movie, *Jumanji* is filled with terrifying predators and explores our primal fears, among them, the terror of vulnerability, alienation, loss of identity, dismemberment, and death.

As in all survival movies, Nature in *Jumanji* is Red in Tooth and Claw.

In the jungle survival movie, human beings are depicted as prey and as the victims of creatures or forces more numerous and powerful than themselves as their protection afforded by the modern, "civilized world" is stripped away. Accordingly, the threat that Nature represents to man in this film escalates as the game progresses. Judy and Peter, for instance, first ward off what appear to be pests—unnaturally large mosquitoes heralded by the game's warning that "a tiny bite can make you itch make you sneeze make you twitch." Next, the monkeys, who "slow the expedition" appear, smashing dishes in kitchen. It becomes evident that these amusing apes are dangerous only when they begin throwing knives at the children. Because the monkeys do not follow Judy and Peter upstairs, the threat their antics pose seems to be contained. Thus it is reasonable for the children believe that "there is no skill involved" in playing the game and, not wanting "Aunt Nora to pitch a fit" when she comes home to find smashed windows and crockery, they continue to follow the game's instructions. The lion, however, proves to be no harmless "hallu-cination." This big cat evokes modern man's most primal fear of death and dismemberment. As the game promises, "his fangs are sharp, he likes your taste, your party better move poste-haste." Tennis racquets had enabled the children to vanquish the mosquitoes; a locked door had protected them from the monkeys. But against the lion Judy and Peter prove to be completely vul-nerable. If Alan hadn't intervened at that moment in the game to lock the lion in a bedroom, they would have been killed and eaten.

Notably, every player involved in playing *Jumanji* suffers from the hor-rors of alienation and loss of identity. The game, for example, "ruined" both Sarah's and Alan's lives. She and Alan were "all alone" for 26 years—she, in Brantford, and he, in the jungles of *Jumanji*. As she tells Alan, everyone in Brantford has called her "crazy," since he disappeared, and she told them he had been "sucked into a board game." Orphaned, Judy and Peter are deeply alienated, unable to cope with their parents' untimely deaths. When intro-duced to others, Judy makes up fantastic stories about her father and mother's lives. She tells her aunt's real estate agent that she and her brother "barely even knew our parents. They were always away. Skiing, gambling in Monte Carlo, on safari in darkest Africa. We didn't even know if they loved us. But when the Sheik's yacht went down, they managed to write us a really beautiful goodbye note that was found floating in a champagne bottle amongst the debris." When Peter is introduced, he is so traumatized that he is unable to speak to anyone but his sister.

However, as the jungle survival movie's protagonists survive, the groups to which they belong, cut off from the orderliness of civilized life, become effective, functional units and the individuals which survive functional adults. Thus, playing *Jumanji* enables each individual to surmount his or her own terrors. As Alan, Sarah, Judy and Peter pool their resources to survive what each roll of the die brings, they become less and less alienated and more and more functional until their group becomes a functional unit. At the end of their adventures, they have formed a supportive "family" unit—what each player has lacked at the beginning of the game.

At base, *Jumanji* insists that family is necessary for one's personal growth, the metamorphosis of one's personality, maturation, and the discovery of self. Being part of a family allows for the individual's hybridization. When functioning in a supportive and "healthy" family, one cannot experience alienation and the loss of one's identity. Family is the means by which the self grows. An important part of this growth is the adoption *and* synthesis of the language of others. Stam points out that some languages, inscribed within the play of power, are "more equal than others."[30] In *Jumanji*, using the language of others guarantees success, for to be functional, the self must be a polyglot. Alan finally is able to end the game when he learns this life lesson. Finally incorporating his father's language into his vocabulary, he responds to Alan's challenge saying, "my father told me 'you should always face what you're afraid of.'" Van Pelt observes that Alan has become a "good lad" who is "finally acting like a man."

When Alan becomes "a man," the game ends, and he is able to say the word, "Jumanji." The carnival, which began when Alan rebelled against his father, concludes. As Alan uses his father's words (and follows his advice), Van Pelt and the other board game monsters are defeated, sucked back into the crystal via the vortex that first carried Alan away. In short order, *puer* becomes *senex*, and twenty-six years of history are altered. Order is restored to Brantford and to the Parrish family evidenced in Samuel Parrish's apology to his son. He tells Alan, "I'm sorry too. Look, you don't have to go to Cliffside if you don't want to. Let's talk it over tomorrow. Man to man." Alan, however, re-establishes order within his family by immediately asking, "How about father to son?" Having acknowledged his father's authority, Alan grows up to take over the family business, and he and Sarah marry; they hire Judy and Peter's parents and convince them not to go skiing in the Canadian Rockies (thereby averting their deaths). During the Christmas party scene at the end of the film, "Hark, the Herald Angels Sing" is played on the piano and sung by the guests as an homage to the closing scene in *It's a Wonderful Life* (1946) in which a fantastic journey also ends and the protagonist, like Alan Parrish, returns to reality, and order is restored to Brantford as it is to the community of Bedford Falls. In true carnival fashion, however, two girls walking on a beach in France discover the board game that Alan and Sarah threw into the river, and the jungle drums begin beating again. Clearly, the game is about to irrupt again … elsewhere. At the end of *Jumanji*, history itself is subject to parodic repetition suggesting that "the trope of marginality is Eurocentric misnomer," as Stam points out, since life "is lived centrally wherever there are human subjects."[31]

Stylized and hyperbolic, *Jumanji* upends and examines notions of high/
low, inferior/superior and even death/life, while creating a visual/textual
polyglossia, as Robin Williams, the *magister ludi*, generates a double-voiced
discourse throughout the game when counselling his fellow players, thereby
linking past and present with his own presence/absence. In final analysis,
Jumanji, a participatory spectacle that erases the boundaries between spectator and performer, remains a deeply disturbing family film. The permeability of the boundaries between the real and the fantastic guarantee no
protection for player or viewer when the die are rolled and monsters appear.
Becoming an adult, in *Jumanji*, is a horrifying process—for the child growing
up means surviving in a competitive jungle. Sony Pictures' 2017 reboot
directed by Jake Kasdan ensures, in true carnival fashion, the continuation
of this struggle for survival and the process of hybridization that accompanies
it. In *Jumanji: Welcome to the Jungle*, four teenagers are "sucked into *Jumanji's*
world" and "pitted against rhinos, black mambas and an endless variety of
jungle traps and puzzles."[32] Given three lives at the outset of the game and
upended, each teen plays as a character from the game, embracing his or her
opposite: "meek Spencer becomes a brave explorer (Dwayne Johnson); hulky
jock Fridge becomes a tiny genius (Kevin Hart); It-girl Bethany becomes a
bookworm professor (Jack Black); and unathletic Martha becomes an ama-
zonian warrior (Karen Gillan)."[33] In order to beat the game and return to the
real world, Spencer, Fridge, Bethany, and Martha, like Alan Parrish, "start
seeing things in an entirely different way,"[34] before any one of them can say
the magic word, "Jumanji." Remarkably, the carnival found in Kasdan's sequel
is not horrific, for the breaking of barriers results in diversity and inclusiv-
ity—and on their return to the orderly world of Brantford, New Hampshire,
the teens eschew their high school cliques and continue the friendships they
forged in the jungle.

NOTES

1. Janet Maslin, "FILM REVIEW; All Hairy and Scary After a Time of Rhyme" in *The New York Times*, December 15, 1995, http://www.nytimes.com/1995/12/15/movies/film-review-all-hairy-and-scary-after-a-time-of-rhyme.html.
2. Roger Ebert, "JUMANJI," RogerEbert.com, http://www.rogerebert.com/reviews/jumanji-1995.
3. Jack Matthews, "A Dangerous Game Shows It's a Jungle Out There" in *Los Angeles Times*, December 15, 1995, http://articles.latimes.com/1995–12–15/entertainment/ca-14298_1_board-game.
4. See "'Jumanji' Tops the Weekend and $500M Worldwide as 'Insidious 4' Scares Up Strong Debut" at Box Office Mojo, http://www.boxofficemojo.com/news/?id=4357&p=.htm. For information concerning box office grosses and summaries see *Jumanji: Welcome to the Jungle at Box Office Mojo*, http://www.boxofficemojo.com/movies/?id=jumanji2016.htm.
5. Dragon Antulov, "Jumanji (1995)" in *IMDb*, http://www.imdb.com/reviews/345/34594.html.
6. Mark Harrison, "Jumanji: revisiting the original film," http://www.denofgeek.com/uk/movies/jumanji/44363/jumanji-revisiting-the-original-film.

7. See children's reviews of *Jumanji* at *common sense media,* https://www.common sensemedia.org/movie-reviews/jumanji#.

8. Joel Chaston, "The 'Ozification' of American Children's Fantasy Films: *The Blue Bird, Alice and Wonderland* and *Jumanji,*" *Children's Literature Association Quarterly* 22, no. 1 (Spring 1997): 18.

9. Chaston, "The 'Ozification' of American Children's Fantasy Films: *The Blue Bird, Alice and Wonderland* and *Jumanji,*" 18.

10. Jyostana Kapru, *Coining For Capital: Movies, Marketing and The Transformation of Childhood* (New Brunswick, New Jersey: Rutgers University Press, 2005), 132.

11. Robert Stam, *Subversive Pleasures: Bakhtin, Cultural Criticism and Film* (Baltimore: Johns Hopkins University Press, 1989), 86.

12. *Ibid.,* 148.

13. Kapru, *Coining For Capital: Movies, Marketing and The Transformation of Childhood,* 132.

14. As Stam notes, carnival releases its participants from the restraints of social decorum. See his discussion about the freeing effect of carnival. See his discussion in *Subversive Pleasures,* 93–94.

15. Stam, *Subversive Pleasures,* 113.

16. Konrad Eisenbichler and Wim N.M. Hüsken, *Carnival and the Carnivalesque: The Fool, The Reformer, The Wildman and Others in Early Modern Theatre* (Amsterdam: Rodopi B.V., 1999), 105.

17. Jesper Juul, "Games Telling Stories?—A brief note on games and narratives," *Game Studies: the international journal of computer game research* 1 no.1 (July 2001), http://www.gamestudies.org/0101/juul-gts/.

18. Stam, *Subversive Pleasures,* 93–94.

19. See ccthemovieman-1's review in *IMDB's* "Reviews and Ratings for Jumanji," http://www.imdb.com/title/tt0113497/reviews.

20. Minka Stoyanova, "Gaming Systems: creative critiques of the ludic real," *APRJA 201,* http://www.aprja.net/?p=2549. Stoyanova notes that play theorists Johann Huizinga and Roger Caillois both situate play outside of the real or the ordinary.

21. Johan Huizinga. *Homo Ludens: A Study of the Play-Element in Culture* (Boston: Beacon Press, 1950), 1.

22. Here it should be noted that in *The Sociology of Fun,* Benjamin Fincham remarks that play, like fun, is "an end in itself" (53). Like play, which is a behavior that serves practical developmental functions, fun is pleasurable; but unlike play, fun is also "a mode of resistance to routine and regimentation" (6). In *Jumanji,* Alan and Sarah play for fun at the beginning of their adventure, and then discover that they must continue to play after the board game has ceased to be enjoyable.

23. Stoyanova, "Gaming systems: creative critiques of the ludic real," http://www.aprja.net/?p=2549.

24. Stam, *Subversive Pleasures,* 153.

25. Derrida, "Structure Sign and Play" in *Writing and Difference* (Chicago: University of Chicago Press, 1978), 294.

26. Stam, *Subversive Pleasures,* 148.

27. Stam notes on page 235 of *Subversive Pleasures* that hybridization is illustrated in the adoption and synthesis of various languages."

28. Stam, *Subversive Pleasures,* 86.

29. Eisenbichler and Hüsken, *Carnival and the Carnivalesque: The Fool, The Reformer, The Wildman and Others in Early Modern Theatre,* 8.

30. Stam, *Subversive Pleasures,* 76.

31. *Ibid.,* 155–56.

32. See the full summary of *Jumanji* (2017) at IMDB, http://www.imdb.com/title/tt2283362/?ref_=fn_al_tt_1.

33. For more information, see the full summary of *Jumanji* (2017) at IMDB, http://www.imdb.com/title/tt2283362/?ref_=fn_al_tt_1.

34. *Ibid.*

Bibliography

Brevet, Brad. "'Jumanji Tops the Weekend and $500M Worldwide as 'Insidious 4' Scares Up Strong Debut." *Box Office Mojo*, 7 January 2018. Accessed January 10, 2018. http://www.boxofficemojo.com/news/?id=4357&p=.htm.

ccthemovieman-1. "Review." *IMDB Reviews and Ratings for Jumanji*. Accessed January 2, 2017. http://www.imdb.com/title/tt0113497/reviews.

Chaston, Joel. "The 'Ozification' of American Children's Fantasy Films: *The Blue Bird, Alice in Wonderland* and *Jumanj*." *Children's Literature Association Quarterly* 22, no. 1. Spring 1997. 18.

Derrida, Jacques. "Structure Sign and Play" in *Writing and Difference*. Chicago: University of Chicago Press, 1978. 278–294.

Dragon Antulov, "Jumanji (1995)." *IMDb*. Accessed December 27, 2016. http://www.imdb.com/reviews/345/34594.html.

Ebert, Roger. "JUMANJI," Accessed December 27, 2016. RogerEbert.com. http://www.rogerebert.com/reviews/jumanji-1995.

Eisenbichler, Konrad and Hüsken, Wim N.M. *Carnival and the Carnivalesque: The Fool, The Reformer, The Wildman and Others in Early Modern Theatre*. Amsterdam: Rodopi B.V., 1999.

Fincham, Benjamin. *The Sociology of Fun*. New York: Palgrave Macmillan, 2016.

Harrison, Mark. "Jumanji: revisiting the original film." *Den of Geek*. Accessed December 29, 2016. http://www.denofgeek.com/uk/movies/jumanji/44363/jumanji-revisiting-the-original-film.

Huizinga, Johan. *Homo Ludens: A Study of the Play-Element in Culture*. Boston: Beacon Press, 1950.

Jesper, Juul. "Games Telling Stories?—A brief note on games and narratives," *Game Studies: the international journal of computer game research* 1 no.1. July 2001. http://www.gamestudies.org/0101/juul-gts/.

"*Jumanji: Welcome to the Jungle*." *Box Office Mojo*. Accessed January 10, 2018. http://www.boxofficemojo.com/movies/?id=jumanji2016.htm.

Kapru, Jyostana. *Coining for Capital: Movies, Marketing and The Transformation of Childhood*. New Brunswick, New Jersey: Rutgers University Press, 2005.

Kid, 11 years old. "Review." *common sense media*. Accessed December 28, 2016. https://www.commonsensemedia.org/movie-reviews/jumanji#.

Kid, 12 years old. "Review." *common sense media*. Accessed December 28, 2016. https://www.commonsensemedia.org/movie-reviews/jumanji#.

Maslin, Janet. "FILM REVIEW; All Hairy and Scary After a Time of Rhyme" in *The New York Times*, December 28, 1995, http://www.nytimes.com/1995/12/15/movies/film-review-all-hairy-and-scary-after-a-time-of-rhyme.html.

Matthews, Jack. "A Dangerous Game Shows It's a Jungle Out There." *Los Angeles Times*, December 30, 1995. http://articles.latimes.com/1995-12-15/entertainment/ca-14298_1_board-game.

Stam, Robert. *Subversive Pleasures: Bakhtin, Cultural Criticism and Film*. Baltimore: Johns Hopkins University Press, 1989.

Stoyanova, Minka. "Gaming Systems: creative critiques of the ludic real," *APRJA* 201, http://www.aprja.net/?p=2549.

"Summary." IMDB *Jumanji* (2017). Accessed at http://www.imdb.com/title/tt2283362/?ref_=fn_al_tt_1.

Transference and Translation

A Roosevelt/Williams Guide
to Museum Space

PRAJNA PARASHER

To some extent, *Night of the Living Dead* (1968) transformed filmic use of the institution as setting. Re-signifying the cemetery, and—in the next film—the mall, encouraged viewers to extrapolate through the conjunction of these familiars and the equally familiar but also different image of the zombie. Similarly, such conjunctions may also prepare an audience to read museum space in parallel time, using setting as metaphor. The profound dignity of these walls is the echo chamber for playful visual jokes whose rub is as solemn as an Ionic column. Robin Williams's unique genius was that he was technically a comic, but all his roles were Janus-faced in the classical sense; every grin a frown upended. Even his manic pacing, breathless and restless in another actor's performance, became for him a transparent screen for the tragedy just out of sight. This quality comes center stage in *Night at the Museum* (2006), where not only Williams but the other characters and the set itself investigate the museum as a container for history, critiquing the concept of history itself. Superficial gags, such as the Tyrannosaurus skeleton (dubbed "Rexy") at the fountain, metonymize lost, vivid events now made static by our need to name and thus own them. Early in the film, the fountain scene introduces the very magic space we have been warned was coming, and—as with any trip through the looking glass—we anticipate inversions. Predictable as the rustics in Shakespeare, we will be visited not by any actual artifacts, but by Hollywood clichés about them. These will jostle against one another with all the exuberant speed of Williams's Jonathan Winters-esque pink Pashmina performance improv from *Inside the Actor's Studio*. Anachronistic juxtapositions of centuries with cowboys reminds us that this is no

41

"history"—whatever that might have been—but the here-and-now: a text we are building for our current purposes.

It is 2006 New York City and in this world, destabilized image is more familiar than stasis and Shawn Levy's *Night at the Museum* interrogates such matters directly. An adult film based on a children's book, it posits "museum space" not directly as *questionable* so much as *malleable*, a fictive line which can be altered by the players, suggesting the notion that authorship itself is illusory. The tableaux and dioramas in museums with their handsome, sanitized representations of histories, we in the transitory, solid present, might forget these representations are almost exclusively legends over what is irretrievably lost.

In some respects, this film fits into the fantasy category, but because it is so full of textual questions, this would only loosely be the case. Much of this genre can be slotted into relatively fixed expectations about which elements can be modified and which maintained as consistent with general expectations (of the genre, of film, of star billing, of social values, et cetera), *Night at the Museum* uses our familiarity with the fantastic as a perspective parallax, as viewer turned inward. When embodied by Robin Williams, what we know of Teddy Roosevelt—as a self-made bully boy, a noisy, vigorous outdoorsman, an emblem of turn-of-the-century national pride—immediately contains its mirror space, the sickly, uncertain, grief-stricken rich child of Father Capitalism. Counterpointed by Larry Daley's (Ben Stiller) messy life in beyond-the-museum space, the flamboyant certitude of the ossified exhibits functions as a reminder that once we have identified anything as arbitrary, we are reinforcing the ultimate fluidity inherent in language, both verbally and visually.

Buried in the adventure quality of the plot is a more complex concern: value inherent in the purportedly "real," a substantive part of the 18th century, as European archaeological impulse behind museums is constantly challenged. As mediated experience (e.g., Facebook) increasingly supplants the direct, one scarcely notices that we speak of them as equal. For example, 9/11 was a television event for most of the country, and was/is a transgression against "us." The then-current violence of Roosevelt's print-era imperialist Presidency (1901–1909) can be eviscerated in its museumization, yet we can (and do) watch that second plane hit over and over (2001–present); an image remixed with multiple available others in service to whatever possible national narrative the current lexicographer is building. What was in the minds of those incinerated is not only gone with their bodies and work space, but also is no longer relevant. "I didn't do any of those things," Roosevelt whispers into Larry's ear. "I was made in a factory in Poughkeepsie." Similarly, the actual Sacajawea (whose museum-form is the love interest for museum-form Roosevelt), is only known by what was recorded by Lewis and Clark—

this is essentially all there is in terms of our known history of her. Thus, a conundrum of our time is that history itself has to become an image before it may even be acknowledged, even though making lived experience into an image is to capitalize on it, erasing as effluvia whatever the image-maker does not need.

To return to the uses of fantasy space to bridge this chasm, we may do a switchback to earlier "history." What we have of folk tales and origin myths can gesture toward how we contained history before it could be pickled in the saline of language or visual records. One of the things these traceries have in common is frequent forays into the magical, the superlative, the uncanny. How mighty Thor and cunning Odysseus were filtered and transformed into Batman is the subject for another paper; right now all I want to suggest is that while we are negotiating the obvious, some part of us recognizes these incarnations to only be that: a pale shadow of what once was there, in the flesh, as it were. Clear invention and improvisation are ways of accessing images the way we must look at the hand imprints of cave drawings. The fact of their survival impels us to imagine an origin. Any historic overview of the filmic depictions of Neanderthals would remind us how much these imaginaries reflect not any origin at all but the separate eras of their re-creation. *Night at the Museum* inserts itself here, not so much curatorial as the curator in a mania of representation's lost possibilities.

To its overt questions, Williams—already an independently iconic figure—brings his own Americana palimpsest, Mork, Garp, Popeye. (Films typically make use of actor layers without overt acknowledgment; subsequent narratives about the actors themselves reconfigure such layers to yet different purposes, thus becoming virtual human museums.) As in epics/origin stories, the supernatural becomes a way to suggest how much more there was than can be here evidenced. An interesting difference shows up in the way they are consumed. Consumers of enduring texts are frequently reminded that heroic days are gone forever. How different from the Ozymanian museum experience, itself oddly similar to genre fantasy's assumed elision of creator and viewer, one in which children or the otherwise inept have more power than authority figures. In this way the film nods toward its allied medium, computer gaming.

As in games, the film maintains formulaic conventions. Opening scenes reinforce an elite New York City location, an already mythic space to most of the world, with hapless Larry one of its lost. Early shots are not only of the museum building, but from angles that emphasize its archaic architecture and massive emptiness. Before we meet anyone important (beyond the love interest, (Carla Gugino), we are introduced to pudgy, fuss-pot museum director Dr. McPhee in his bad suit (Ricky Gervais), all clues for what we are to reject. The instantly-read codes are reinforced as we then meet the security staff, overtly insignificant in the basement but portrayed by famous actors (Dick Van Dyke, Mickey Rooney, Bill Cobbs). As Larry accepts his guard uniform, we understand that he will be transformed and become transformative within this magical space. The outcome is predictable; the plot is unimportant. We know it is the hero's quest, with Larry fighting a Trickster (a capuchin monkey dubbed Dexter) for the keys to a kingdom backlit by a motley of celebrities, with the horse-mounted Roosevelt, entirely at home in this Gilded Age space, clearly the spirit guide best able to identify both task and goal.

Blockbuster movies can be counted upon to include the monumental, the hyperreal not as snazzy bonus but as baseline expectation. With screens before us everywhere, we need particular inducement to go to the theater. It's made us novelty junkies. Each new film needs to be larger, more exciting, an event, something beyond whatever came before. Within the *Night at the Museum* trilogy this special effects addiction gets its fix, but additionally bends inward to disparage as inadequate the everyday museum, a dusty space outside Technicolor magic. The virtual competes with the tactile, the concrete, so ubiquitously in our lives that we've learned to see it as natural, not rupture, to move fluidly between them like a kid obsessing over a video game in his own bedroom. *Night at the Museum* may not intend to posit questions about this flexible reality but it cannot avoid them.

Computer graphics as well as predictable plot tensions within the film acknowledge its relationship to video games and unfolds another layer of meaning. Films are not interactive in the ways games appear to be (discounting that games are ultimately not interactive at all but multiply programmed). Interactivity in the film happens within the story line as we knew it would, when Dexter opens the window. The window itself, security grilled and old fashioned, reminds us that it guards a fusty museum space, the one outside dark and cold but from the point of view of the inmates, enchanting. In Darwinian progression, Dexter is followed by Neanderthals; it's interesting that what can be seen from here of the larger world is the bleak opposite of glamorized museum space, street people gathered around a burn barrel. This juxtaposition leads inevitably to general escape, the magical world loose in the "real" one.

The conventions of the hero's quest require that (1) his tasks appear insoluble and (2) gods intervene. These requirements are met in Central Park with a campy run through B level entertainment—stagecoach chases, police cars, boy hero—climaxed by the god using his superpowers to restore order. Whether we are experiencing one more fantasy film or something closer to magical reality is defined by Dr. McPhee, the voice of the past. He enters by scolding children for touching the artifacts and closes by forgiving all because the events of the night have made broadcast news and increased patronage, a successful advertising campaign. That the film finishes as an endorsement of contemporary museum practice, big on the touchable and small on the arcane, begs any larger issues about the museum as imperialist signifier. If it has become a confirmation of New York City values, we are indeed in magical reality, one where problems are solved in a short frame of time and mammoths can dance with children, a lá Sesame Street Live, coming to a town near you.

Fantasy differs from Magical Reality in the kind of disbelief we are willing to suspend, though they share space in the child mind where skeletons playing ball and animated dioramas are as likely as tomorrow. For the adult trying to make sense of this film, the kicker keeps coming back to Williams playing Roosevelt in 2006. His quality as an actor, a gallop across marble floors, suggests multiplicity and foolery well before he says he's made of wax. Teddy Roosevelt, President between the Spanish American War and World War I, flags the end of the kind of arrogance and certainty responsible for the museum in the first place. Who is better placed to show Larry the advantage of living in the emptied space between real and simulation? It can be replayed again and again, used in service to whatever claims it and at core as unreachable, unknowable, as Sacajawea behind her safety glass.

Magical Reality: severance from fact allows play to be possible. Williams breaks his Presidential pose when he admits to being wax and Rebecca breaks her scholar's pose when all she can say to her heroine is "You rock." We have been clowning here all along—Van Dyke as a feeble old man, Rooney as a thug, Attila as a PTSD sufferer—all of it rich with goofy entertainment and cultural connections. Why does the Easter Island head talk like Kunta Kente? Do the lions evoke Kimba? Is McPhee supposed to sound like the gecko of insurance ads? Noah is checking everyone in at the museum door. It's Hollywood hyperbolic from the starlet faces of academic grind and captive Indian guide to the monotonous Neanderthal grunts. Columbus, in copper and without his name (a pennyworth of credit?), stands silently in front of us, separated from acts a living person may once have done, or not done, but endlessly invoked over consequences any original figure? could never have imagined. The "real" is abolished, says Baudrillard.

Conjecture about reality in a product of mechanical reproduction lurks in the reality and reproducibility of the film itself. Within that product though there is another kind of "real," the one Benjamin would see in a piece of art. It's a good place for Ahkmenrah, doing his own dance on the tightrope of parody as he shakes a cloud of dust loose from his mummy wrap to disclose a Golden Globe heartthrob speaking Cambridge English. These are a fanzine series of jokes. Within the film's world though he owns the McGuffin that motors the plot, making it in that sense a "real" thing. It's also a real thing in that it is supposed to be an actual artifact, not taxidermy or facsimile, celebrity artifact too in that mummies and sarcophagi are consistent museum draws whenever displayed. Even without fictive superpower, it is presented as an original different from any reproduction, one we can play with though, immune from any awe its origins might have engendered.

As the series develops, we see more of the pharaoh's family weirdly displaying family values recognizable as 21st century contemporary cannot. A fixation on the "real" is also recognizable in the language of faith, all the more stridently in this era where multiple realities, religious and otherwise, are always before us. Fluidity as the rule makes our era different from the apparent constancy within museum exhibits. A fascination with Egyptian pyramids, way beyond any interest in the more nearby Mayan ones, is worth a thought. Is it the tracery of power, particularly that of gold, that makes them so intriguing? Is it easier to celebrate a dynasty we postcolonial don't feel any responsibility for trashing? The building of museums corresponds in time with 19th century European archeology expeditions specifically designed to gather up materials of other cultures and bring them back home for display, an ownership that implies kinship. Here is our Panopticon, index of who we are, are supposed to be. It's the predecessor, now usually thought of as archaic elite culture, that pop culture supplants. When a little girl today wants to be a princess, she's not thinking Sisi of the Hapsburgs, she's thinking Disney and her access is right there at Walmart. When *Night at the Museum* jumbles these up, it can't help but desanctify both, the dynamic at the core of comedy as tragedy's obverse.

Just as codified historical figures are used as signposts along this romp through national imagination, traditional family values are used to manage the plot; note that they are skewed family values since it is the father-son relationship, women scarcely mentioned. Rowdier and darker than the first of the series, *Night at the Museum III* (2014) extends its parenting theme to include the Pharaoh, Merenkahre. Even legendary bachelor Lancelot takes his turn at instructing the young. The knife-edge of parody turns on itself here where of the two few females present, Sacajawea appears as assistant to Larry, child minder to Dexter and love interest to Roosevelt, Tilly, the British museum guard, is a burlesque sex object and Rebecca the sidekick of 1940's screwball comedies.

The extent to which the film series is an inquiry into museum space per se becomes further complicated in *III*. While there has always been off-screen interplay between the roles and the actors, in this painfully final version, a segmentation of audience becomes obvious. Children's material that also offers something oblique to adults is not uncommon. In *Night at the Museum III* though, oldsters, scholars and aficionados are seeing a darker or perhaps even melodramatic story as supporting characters turn into museum pieces right before our eyes. There is a partial breakdown too, between the making of the film and the viewing of it. Possibly Williams's increasing fragility was evident to the cast and crew; Rooney's is unmistakable even on screen. To witness Andy Hardy as a weak old fellow in a wheelchair puts the lie to the internal legend, well-acted by geriatric Van Dyke, that magic can make us younger. Childish sub-text is overwritten by inevitability as the post mortem film is distributed and its cheery plot revealed as one more petrochemical illusion. By the time an audience sees Williams's final flourish of his sword, the zombie is already gobbling up that charming grin.

While it can be in the nature of a mass-distribution film to question its own legitimacy—common enough in a medium so dependent on innovation—the economics mean that these questions need to seem playful, not painful. A preoccupied copper Christopher Columbus, recognized by child but not father, toggles between Nickelodeon and political cartoon depending on the specular eye. Many of those paying eyes are there for the illusions, the special effects, the escape into action without consequence. Some may even reject the idea of a real museum not for its inherent dishonesty but because it is too much like reading (as different from viewing), requiring active participation to maintain interest. To the extent that these films *are* interrogative, one of the ways to focus its questions is to ask about the selection of shibboleths. Dinosaurs, Neanderthals, Mongolian Hordes, Roman legions, all the material of primary school world history, Modern America at its apex. Williams's ability to portray Roosevelt as an uncertain person destabilizes a museum narrative, but to supplant it with Hollywood romance narrative just as unsupportable. Big Stick with the hots for an Indian teenager? None of the plot conventions are to be taken seriously.

Colonial practice at its most obvious, Sacajawea, at first, can not move beyond the Plexiglas of her display case. Telling a truth it may not have meant to reveal, the museum confirms the cooptation of her story, of the culture she lived, so that its only trace is the version in service to Manifest Destiny. Similar to the Eskimos, she is little different from the stuffed seals and painted backgrounds that represent empty space into which English speaking people inserted themselves as they are in the film, active agents in a static space. She does eventually escape her diorama. Is this an effort to critique hegemonic history lines? It does not seem to be. Making use of her tracking skills is as cliché as her appealing appearance: she's Tonto, not Winona LaDuke. The argument of the film, if there is one, might be that the museum is not mausoleum space. In some respects the treatment of Sacajawea is successful as interrogation. While other exhibit figures can move around, talk or at least make themselves understood, she cannot hear or speak, instead paces back and forth as caged zoo animals do, to note a parallel imperialist institution. It's a moving trope for her cultural erasure (or would be were it not for the uncomfortable sexualization of Roosevelt's interest in her).

In its early days the Smithsonian was called "the nation's attic," accurate enough description of the oddment collection first housed there. Other museums though are national projects built to be imposing; the building visualizes its power relationship to what it encloses, and there is no effort to make any of the display items more than what the hegemonic text allows. Footnote Williams enters as a comedian, court jester, the one whose job it is to mention the unmentionable without making it unpalatable. Within *Night at the Museum III*, Lancelot, the most broadly played cartoon of them all, identifies Larry as such, an assignment Larry rejects. One of the ways to unpack this is to say that common man is unable to recognize himself as a joke; multiple threads snarl here in that Larry the Loser is a classic stock character, particularly as an inept father bumbling into competency. This particular Larry, lead actor, not commentator, hefts traditional Deus ex Machina material and leaves Williams to acknowledge the multiple lost narratives obfuscated by the obvious one, comedy's enduring task.

The self-consciousness that allows for a comic view in these films becomes a dangerous mode. The underlying source material is Hollywood pastiche so familiar to viewers that we scarcely note it. Magical events happen at night and cannot tolerate sunrise. Love and duty will be rewarded. Violence is frequent but nobody ever gets hurt. Families love one another. Wild animals feel affection toward people. All problems have convenient solutions and rewind is ever available. The ground the film stands on is this collection of conventions, shared hypothetical space separate from the life (or for some, death,) experiences of those on all sides of the camera. The spectacle lets us forget that it's ultimately a cheat. Williams is the Nestor we have for this epic, if not its organizing principle (plot) then its moral voice. His gradual elision into a wax facsimile is theoretically promising but unravels; Roosevelt's last moments are used to tease Larry about whether or not he's real. In many roles Robin Williams's hyperbolic portrayals allow a window into everything they do not contain but manages to remind us is there. This one, his last, risks being drained of that multiplicity, co-opting heterotopia as a topical, marketable concept and thus emptying it of meaning. If anything holds these raggedy ends in place it must be the portrayal itself, animating a silhouette from within so that the audience sees what the puppet master did not recognize was available.

Fantasy/adventure's appeal, whatever it might mean in the psychological realm, is largely escapist in that it fully follows the story conventions mentioned above. *Night at the Museum's* box office successes were a predictable if slightly unnerving echo of its advertising story lines and a reasonable prognosticator of increased interest in brick and mortar museums. By the time *III* arrived at the box office, reverberations abounded. The opening scene is a formal evening event, donor gala resplendent with moneyed guests and electronic astrology in addition to the familiar animated exhibits. Because of financial success, Larry is no longer the loser, one more Hollywood convention. Our internalized recognition lets us anticipate the disruption of the subscription party and, after further heroic adventures, magic restoration of equilibrium. Fantasy, as a form, is a carnival ride, promising thrills without actual risk. We follow the hero's trials avidly, knowing impossibilities will be overcome. Literary convention in fantasy is that whatever invented universe we inhabit; internal frameworks remain consistent. The beginning of *Museum III*, projections of constellations, fractures previous use of computer-generated effects; formerly an understood but covert part of the films, in *III* these manipulations not only enter the plot line but are specifically given to Larry. The popularity of the film could indicate that audiences were indifferent to a change-up. It could also include a mutual playfulness about following the rules, double dip at the end of the coaster ride. Such mutability is exciting but truly freeform possibility is another illusion; if some of us are out there having fun, somebody else is out of sight holding the edges of the known world together. It's not surprising that humor, like poetry, translates poorly. Each hopes to reach beyond its own structure toward the ephemeral that is as yet unnamed. Frightening territory indeed, space not often visited. The trickster, the jester, the comic, they are the ones able to throw a lasso around terror, allow us to glimpse it and still pass by safely.

A sophisticated sense of play is visualized by the chase scene inside an Escher drawing. Juvenile forms with aspects to intrigue adults must offer material which can be enjoyed exclusively for effect while experienced in a more complex and reflective way by those who recognize allusions. The museum setting offers multiple opportunities for broad jokes—Attilla PTSD, Pompeii saved by monkey pee—but the Escher segment is of a different order. The original prints are highly intellectual, beautiful and disturbing. As Larry, Lancelot and TR bounce in and out of crosshatch, there is an invisible reference point beyond the technology where viewers confront the nature of seeing, of being. To include Williams's character in this scene is significant. Surely Dexter would have been more engaging on the stairs. Lancelot in his armor does the pratfalls. Roosevelt, the one who is thrown out of the etching and blown back in again, is at once participant and narrator, audience guide to the message beyond the action. There is a distinction between an actor who can do comedy and the true comic with a personal voice rooted in universal despair. Williams is that in *Museum,* not so much out of fantasy as beyond it. He carries us through special effects slapstick into recognition of the ridiculous, unreconcilable human condition. In the fold upon fold that is film history, we cannot look into this recorded face without feeling that we see *into* it, owning the immanent death his public persona kept just beyond the frame.

BIBLIOGRAPHY

Baudrillard, Jean. *Simulacra and Simulation*. The University of Michigan Press, Ann Arbor. 1994.

_____. *The Spirit of Terrorism and Requiem for the Twin Towers*. Verso, London. 2002.

Bruchac, Joseph. *Sacajawea: The Story of Bird Woman and the Lewis and Clark Expedition*. San Diego, California: Silver Whistle, 2000.

Dubin, Steven C. *Displays of Power: Memory and Amnesia in the American Museum*. New York: New York University Press, 1999.

Foucault, Michel. *The Archaeology of Knowledge*. Trans. A. M. Sheridan Smith. London: Routledge, 2002.

_____. "Of Other Spaces." *The Visual Culture Reader*. N. Mirzoeff, Ed. London, NY: Routledge, 1998. 229–236.

_____. *The Order of Things*. Trans. Anon, London: Penguin, 1970.

Lefebvre, Henri. *The Production of Space*. London: Basil Blackwell, 1991.

Žižek, Slavoj. *The Parallax View*. The MIT Press, Cambridge, 2006.

_____. *Welcome to the Desert of the Real*. Verso, London, 2002.

Hot Flashes and Heroes

Mrs. Doubtfire as Threshold Figure

ELIZABETH LEIGH SCHERMAN

On August 12, 2014, a growing number of flowers, candles, and notes began to gather on the steps of a Victorian home on Steiner Street, San Francisco. The owner of the house was a craniofacial surgeon who told the media that he was fine with the makeshift, burgeoning memorial. "I turn boys' faces into girls' faces," he remarked to the press. "It seemed only natural."[1]

The house was featured in the 1993 film *Mrs. Doubtfire* (Columbus 1993),[2] which starred then 42-year-old Robin Williams in the titular role of the divorced father who impersonates an older female housekeeper in order to spend time with his children. The part required Williams's face and body to transform from that of San Francisco voice actor Daniel Hillard to Mrs. Euphegenia Doubtfire—housekeeper and nanny extraordinaire. Mrs. Doubtfire is extraordinary not only due to her inhabitation of a male body, but also because of the position she holds in the family. Strictly speaking, she is neither male nor female, neither family member nor servant, neither mother nor father. Mrs. Doubtfire functions as what Anne McClintock refers to as a *threshold figure*, "always between the house and the street, the family and lewdness,"[3] which Wanning Sun interprets as a person who is seen to be "negotiating a set of boundaries including gender, race, and class"[4]

Euphegenia Doubtfire's arrival on screen teases and lures us with a number of nuanced roles. She stands at the doorway of our lived experience as blended families, as trans people, and as parents negotiating social norms and expectations. Yet while some aspects of the role, such as Robin Williams's performance of gender have been widely analyzed,[5] the role of Euphegenia Doubtfire as a threshold figure further complicates that performance. Although McClintock places her use of the term "not in an [sic] universal

51

archetype, but in the class structure of the household,"[6] I will argue that there is merit in considering the role of Mrs. Doubtfire as a true threshold guardian in the archetypal sense. In *The Hero with a Thousand Faces,* mythologist Joseph Campbell describes the threshold as a point of no return, where the hero must prove himself worthy of passing through to the next stage of his journey. At this place of crossing over into a new realm, there is often a threshold guardian who poses questions or challenges to the hero.[7] In *Mrs. Doubtfire,* the hero—originally Daniel Hillard, the estranged father—must prove himself worthy of parenting his three children. To do so, he must pass through a threshold guarded by a woman with the strictest of standards: Euphegenia Doubtfire.

Guardian of the Threshold

Campbell observes that "the powers that watch the boundary are dangerous; to deal with them is risky; yet for anyone with competence and courage, the danger fades."[8] Mrs. Doubtfire is a risky person on more than one level. First, she is Daniel Hillard in disguise; should she be exposed, Daniel will pay the consequences. However, the risk goes beyond the mere unveiling of a female impersonator. If the ruse is exposed, Euphegenia Doubtfire herself may cease to exist, taking with her the lessons that she needs to teach Daniel, Miranda, and the children.

Anthropologist Arnold Van Gennep described rites of passage as having a three-part structure: first, the individual must experience a separation from the social position that he or she has previously occupied[9]—in Daniel Hillard's case, a husband and a full-time father who lived with his three children. Next, the individual must journey through a liminal period, where his or her status is "betwixt and between the positions assigned and arrayed by law, custom, convention, and ceremony"[10]—a state of limbo that Daniel must navigate as non-custodial father, ex-husband, and ersatz female nanny. Finally, the individual who has successfully negotiated the rite of passage will be reassimilated into society or family and given a new status. In order to clearly understand the situation in *Mrs. Doubtfire,* it is critical to see the character of Mrs. Doubtfire as separate from that of Daniel Hillard. While the spectatorial audience knows that Mrs. Doubtfire is Daniel in disguise, the diegetic (on-screen) family does not. She has her own agency and her own agenda, which with time will diverge from Daniel's original agenda.

In her examination of other "nanny" films, including *Mary Poppins* (Stevenson 1964) and *The Sound of Music* (Wise 1965), Anne McLeer argues that the role of the nanny is in fact that of a threshold figure.[11] In addition, the nanny is a "family interloper" and "the person responsible for reinstalling the father."[12] Mrs. Doubtfire performs each of these functions for the Hillard family, serving as a liminal figure who preserves boundaries but also challenges them. While such gatekeepers can be terrifying creatures such as Cerberus, the three-headed dog that guards the underworld, they may also be shape-shifters whose appearance changes according to the need. Mrs. Doubtfire is a shape-shifter. In this aspect she may be seen as a *Nanny McPhee* type: In the 2005 movie (Jones),[13] the character of Nanny McPhee takes on the appearance that is needed to establish order in the household. As the family learns to behave, her appearance changes. In like fashion, the cozy, grandmotherly Mrs. Doubtfire must take her place at the threshold to the next step in the family's journey, before her appearance changes to reveal the person within—the very father that Miranda judged unsuitable to raise the children.

From the beginning, protagonist and antagonist are clearly delineated. Underemployed actor Daniel Hillard is quickly set up as the hero: the fun-loving, noble, adoring father. He refuses to do the voice-over for a children's cartoon character who smokes, saying that to do so would be "morally irresponsible." As he quits, he channels Gandhi: "Then I've got to do what I've got to do." His children greet him with "Daddy! Daddy!" as he picks them up at school. He has planned an over-the-top birthday party for his son.

"I got off work early," he fibs to the children, to which his oldest daughter, Lydia (Lisa Jakub), replies, "You mean you got fired," then adds that her mother has forbidden parties. Thus, it is that even before we meet Miranda Hillard (Sally Field), we sense that she is at the very least a killjoy.

"Mom's not going to be home for four hours, will she?" retorts Daniel. If Miranda Hillard is not clearly the villain in the story, she's as close to it as one gets—even the humorless court liaison is, after all, only acting on Miranda's wishes that her ex-husband prove his fitness to be a father. *New York Times* film critic Janet Maslin notes that "the wife's job alone is enough to villainize her … [she] is seen doing something terribly important involving fabric swatches, while her sweet, helpless husband … can barely stay employed dubbing voices onto animated films."[14]

Miranda arrives home with a store-bought cake in hand to find her home filled with petting-zoo animals and her husband dancing on top of a table with the young guests. Miranda ends the festivity and argues vehemently with her husband while the children listen from the stairway. "Why do you always make me out to be the heavy?" she retorts to Daniel's accusation that her career is the problem.

"You do it to yourself!" he shouts back. She responds by demanding a divorce. The viewer is left wondering what the two ever saw in each other— and why neither of them seems to notice that their children are listening in, devastated by the argument. "I hate you!" each one of them tells the warring couple, before vanishing behind closed bedroom doors.

It's not enough for Daniel to simply meet the minimum requirements of the divorce court in order to share custody of the children; we are shown that despite his charm, he can be childish and combative. He has pulled his leery children into his plot to deceive Miranda, he blames her for their marital woes, and he even berates the children's grandmother, telling them that she smells of formaldehyde. Even little Natalie (Mara Wilson) calls him on his "teasing" that her mother might have amoebic dysentery, a potentially fatal disease.[15] "Why would you want mommy to die?" she asks him, and he shame-facedly backpedals. "I'll think good thoughts, okay?" he says, in what could be a reference to his character of Peter Pan in the movie *Hook*,[16] released just two years earlier.

Daniel Hillard, however, is the polar opposite of Robin Williams's character of Peter Banning from *Hook*. Banning is an uptight workaholic husband and humorless father whose task is to remember that he is actually Peter Pan. In contrast, Daniel Hillard is Peter Pan whose task it is to remember that he is also a father with responsibilities. The role of Daniel Hillard is among several father or father-trope roles that Williams has brought to the screen.

"How many times has Robin Williams played a father or father figure on screen?" asks *Variety*'s Justin Chang.[17] "He plays a mentor to the young and impressionable." Chang goes on to mention the gay dad in *The Birdcage* (1996), the therapeutic figures of Dr. Malcolm Sayer in *Awakenings* (1990), *Patch Adams* (1998), and therapist Sean Maguire in *Good Will Hunting* (1997). There are others—including the surrogate father figure of teacher John Keating in *Dead Poets Society* (1989), and the admittedly inadequate father in *World's Greatest Dad* (2009), in which a father tries and fails to save a brutish and unlovable son. In each incarnation of the father figure, Williams stumbles in his efforts to salvage and guide his vulnerable mentees. Perhaps it is this very brokenness that allows the audience to identify with the masks and guises that Williams invites us to witness—the masks and guises that each of us wear as we pretend to know the answers and as we perform in our roles as parents, when all the while we carry the wounds of our own childhoods within.

Amusing as he can be, Daniel must learn some lessons before he is allowed to cross the threshold into shared custody—and the very person to teach him those lessons is Euphegenia Doubtfire. It would be a mistake, however, to consider Mrs. Doubtfire as a threshold guardian for Daniel alone. Miranda Hillard clearly has a lot to learn. She doesn't appreciate Daniel's childlike playfulness—and while the spectator may understand her frustration, we are clearly expected to empathize with Daniel. She drops off the children late to his apartment, then rudely appears to pick them up early, asking "Are *my* children ready yet?" She looks at the dinner he has provided to the children and says, "Ugh," then tells them, "Let's get out of here. I would say use the bathroom but I don't think that's a good idea. Don't forget anything. I don't want to come back here." It's clear that the audience is expected to recoil at Miranda's snarkiness and to identify with Daniel. The truth is more complicated: they both need to cross over the threshold into a different way of parenting.

Enter the Interloper

Mrs. Doubtfire comes to the family by way of more deception on Daniel's part. He telephones Miranda pretending to respond to her ad for a housekeeper, and he uses his acting ability to pose as a number of undesirable applicants before clinching the job as a too-good-to-be-true matron with a gentle Scots accent. His portrayal of the undesirable applicants illuminates societal fear and prejudice: One of the "applicants" has just had a sex change (a bit ironic), another screams at her children, and another cannot speak a complete sentence in English. He clinches the job after meeting Miranda and the children, where he magically knows what interests the children, and he tells Miranda to sit down and relax while he fixes her a cup of tea—almost as much of a wife figure as a housekeeper figure. "Who needs a husband when I have you?" she gushes.

As an individual with access to the intimacies both of the household and its members, the role of the housekeeper or nanny/governess as an interloper has been found in literature for centuries. Mimi Matthews writes that the governess, for example, was "neither servant nor family member,"[18] an observation that places the nanny outside of both spheres, while McLeer inverts the sentiment and identifies the nanny as both "family and not-family."[19]

Miranda Hillard grows to consider her housekeeper the former. "You're family," she insists, when Mrs. Doubtfire tries to get out of attending Miranda's birthday celebration. Euphegenia Doubtfire, however, never hesitates in asserting her dominance over the domestic arena. She insists that the children eat only nutritious food and that they finish their homework before they watch TV—a policy that apparently neither of their parents enforced. When the three children test her on this, she punishes them by making them clean house. As with Mary Poppins and Maria in *The Sound of Music*, this results only in endearing her to both parent and child; She is a stable figure in a storm of change.

In addition, Mrs. Doubtfire is not timid about inserting herself into the custody battle. When Miranda begins to berate Daniel in front of the children, she interrupts. "Excuse me, but I'm sure you prefer the children step out of the room before you verbally bash their father," she snaps—ever so kindly.

Miranda responds flippantly. "Well, if I did that, I would never see them again." She laughs and waits for Mrs. Doubtfire to join her, but the interloper remains resolute, as do the three children. It is clear to Miranda that bad-mouthing the children's father is not acceptable. She quickly retreats.

The relinquishment of power to the household interloper has not always proved wise, historically. When *Mrs. Doubtfire* was released, news reports of nannies abusing their power appeared with some regularity in the press. One fear was that of the sexual predator who was out to steal the man of the house.[20] A deeper fear stemmed from a handful of sensational murder cases where nannies killed children in their care, a trope which goes back at least as far as the 1965 film *The Nanny*, where Bette Davis terrorizes her young charge.[21] In contrast to such horror stories, Mrs. Doubtfire joins the pantheon of magical and nearly-magical nannies and governesses who are, as Mary Poppins describes herself, "Practically Perfect in Every Way."[22] In fact, Mrs. Doubtfire literally saves a life by performing the Heimlich maneuver on Miranda's new boyfriend, who chokes on a piece of shrimp. She is a "safe" figure—old, overweight, and desexualized, not unlike the stereotyped "mammies" of old.[23]

The concern over sexuality, however, manifests itself as time goes on in the Hillard household. Unlike the plotline of the original children's book *Madame Doubtfire*, where the children are in on the ruse, the Hillard children are oblivious to their new housekeeper's disguise. When one evening Daniel a la Mrs. Doubtfire leaves the door the bathroom ajar, Chris sees "her" standing to urinate in the toilet. Chris is terrified. He runs from the scene of the atrocity, telling Lydia, "She's half man, half woman!" Lydia grabs a tennis racket as if she anticipates being assaulted by Mrs. Doubtfire—showcasing what may be described as the fear of cross-dressers or transgender people. Daniel rushes to calm the children. As Chris peers into his eyes, he recognizes his father.[24] His relief at the discovery is tempered by his concern about his father's appearance in drag. "You don't really like wearing that stuff, Dad?" he asks. Daniel assures him that he does not. "It's just a mask," Daniel says. "I didn't have any operations or anything." Even so, Chris declines his hug—another apparent allusion to the transphobia/homophobia expected of the "average" child at that time. Daniel plays along. "S'cool," Daniel nods. "It's a guy thing." He then pleads with the children to help him maintain the ploy and to keep it secret from the youngest child, Natalie.[25] The children agree, and Mrs. Doubtfire continues to mine Miranda for clues as to why she abandoned the marriage.

Mrs. Doubtfire asks Miranda why she married Daniel in the first place. Miranda replies that she fell in love with his spontaneity, energy, and humor—the very things that later irritated her. "He was romantic, passionate," she answers. "How was he on a scale of 1 to 10?" pushes Mrs. Doubtfire. Ignoring the inquiry, Miranda launches into the reasons she decided to leave him: He was always between jobs, the house would be wrecked and she'd have to clean it up, and she'd cry herself to sleep. "Daniel never liked to talk about anything serious," she adds. As the interloper and threshold figure in disguise, Mrs. Doubtfire is learning what makes Miranda tick—and what Daniel needs to do to be a better father.

Mrs. Doubtfire's lessons are not lost on Daniel. Soon, Daniel's bachelor apartment is a model of tidiness and comfort. He serves the children home-made spaghetti in a calm, happy, sit-down meal. "The place looks great," says Lydia. "The food is terrific. I'm really proud of you." Even Miranda, coming to fetch the children, notices the difference.

"I cook, I bake, I sew," says Daniel. "Give me a second chance." He is referring to the opportunity to watch the children in the afternoons, not to reconciliation. Miranda actually hesitates. "I can't get rid of Mrs. Doubtfire." Daniel nods. "Sounds like an amazing woman. Too good to be true."

She is amazing—even winning over Mr. Lundy (Robert Prosky), a children's television show executive who has seen Daniel perform as a man but who decides that Daniel as Mrs. Doubtfire is even better. When Daniel's ploy is finally revealed to Miranda, she is furious. Back in family court, the judge suggests that Daniel might even need to undergo psychological treatment for his "lifestyle" of the last three months. Privately, however, she joins the children in grieving the loss of Mrs. Doubtfire. The children miss her spaghetti, her jokes, her stories.

"There is nobody like her," Miranda admits. "Things were much nicer when she was around. But she isn't real! We have to stop referring to her as if she's a real person." No longer Mrs. Doubtfire, yet not yet a stable part of the family, Daniel enters a period of liminality. Miranda attempts to replace Mrs. Doubtfire, but the candidates, as in *Mary Poppins*, are all horrible. In *Mary Poppins*, a wind blows the horrid applicants all away. In *Mrs. Doubtfire*, the old lady herself will come to the rescue once more.

The Return of the Father

If the "nanny movie" was a genre, one certain trope would be that the nanny stays only until her task is accomplished. In most cases, including those of *Mary Poppins* and *Nanny McPhee*, the nanny has made this clear from the beginning. Her departure is swift and conclusive. In other cases, including *The Sound of Music* and *Mrs. Doubtfire*, the nanny disappears by transforming into a new role. In *The Sound of Music*, the governess Maria marries Baron Von Trapp and becomes the mother of the children. In *Mrs. Doubtfire*, the mask comes off to reveal Daniel Hillard. In all cases, however, the threshold figure's task is the same: the reinstallment of the father. McLeer argues that the nanny's ultimate service is to "restore family order by modernizing the father-child relationship" and explains that "the work they [nannies] carry out ... restores insecure patriarchal rule."[26] Although the nanny may have exhibited independence and acted as a strong female role model, the happy ending that she must bring, according to McLeer, is to reinstate the marginalized father. This is as true of *Mrs Doubtfire* as it is of the earlier "nanny" films.

Although Daniel and Miranda Hillard will share the duties of parenting, Daniel has been restored to his daily caregiving role in the children's lives, as well as the role of provider. In contrast to Mr. Banks and Mr. Panning, who are good providers but poor playmates, Daniel must learn to balance his playfulness with the responsibility of providing for his family. He succeeds magnificently, not only by landing a good job but also by displaying his mastery of Mrs. Doubtfire's cooking, cleaning, and child-rearing skills. He has absorbed the desirable traits of Mrs. Doubtfire and has made them his own. In this unveiling, he is not unlike the character of Michael Dorsey in *Tootsie*, who praises his alter ego Emily Kimberly. "I'm not mentally ill," declares Dorsey, echoing Daniel Hillard's insistence that his dressing in drag is nothing to fear. "But proud, and lucky, and strong enough to be the woman that was the best part of my manhood. The best part of myself."[27] After her initial shock and anger at Daniel's charade, Miranda confesses that she is grateful to have met Mrs. Doubtfire. "She brought out the best in them," she tells him, referring to their children. "She brought out the best in you." He responds, "And you."

Unlike Mary Poppins, however, Daniel needs his family. Miranda agrees to allow him to watch the children every afternoon, an arrangement that delights the children. In the children's book *Madame Doubtfire*, Miranda also relents in the end and allows Daniel to work afternoons at her house in the role of a gardener. In both versions, however, it is the mother who appears to hold the ultimate power; it is only by her largesse that the estranged father is allowed to return.

In her 1995 article "The Dubious Nature of *Mrs. Doubtfire*—Yet Another Case of Mal de Mère?"[28] Julie Harrower argues that such storylines expressed men's fear of being displaced in the modern family of the late twentieth century, when a number of films and television shows such as *Three Men and a Baby* (1987), *Mrs. Doubtfire* (1993), *Junior* (1994), *Parenthood* (1989), and *Full House* (1978–1995), addressed the role of the father. Although these stories are often couched in comedy, Harrower suggests that they reflect deeper issues, including "the supremacy of the father in a world where working women are seen to be deserting their responsibilities."[29] Indeed, early in Mrs. Doubtfire, Daniel Hillard criticizes his wife for spending too little time with the children, telling her, "Oh, *you* chose the career!" Adding fuel to the *mal de mère* (mother blaming) fire, McLeer claims that nanny movies illustrate "the dangers of absent mothers," and cites mid-century child raising texts that require a traditional, stay-at-home mother and a "dominant, bread-winning" father in order for children to grow up with healthy sexual self-identification. One can only wonder what Mrs. Doubtfire would say about that. Perhaps a hint of her position can be seen one of the final scenes of the movie, where Daniel Hillard appears in all his latex-ed, be-wigged splendor as host of the newly-created children's television show, "Euphegenia's House." Sitting in her doily-topped armchair before a fireplace, Euphegenia speaks gently to the camera, addressing a child whose parents are divorcing. She assures the child that there are many kinds of families; that both mummies and daddies love their children, and that ultimately, the "ties that bind" will win the day.

In the end, does it matter whether it is a woman or a man who saves the family? The magnificent thing about Euphegenia Doubtfire is her very liminality; a being who straddles the dichotomy and invites us to cross back and forth over the threshold as we question and construct new ways of being family.

NOTES

1. Dr. Douglas K. Ousterhout was the owner of the home at the time. Phaneuf, Whitney. "'Mrs. Doubtfire' House in Pac Heights Becomes Robin Williams Memorial." sfist.com. Last modified August 12, 2014. Accessed February 26, 2017. http://sfist.com/2014/08/12/mrs_doubtfire_house_in_pac_heights.php. Spontaneous memorials sprang up elsewhere, including the Mork & Mindy house in Boulder, Colorado.

2. *Mrs. Doubtfire*, directed by Chris Columbus, performed by Robin Williams, Sally Field, and Pierce Brosnan (1993; Los Angeles, CA: 20th Century Fox, 2007), DVD.

3. Anne McClintock, *Imperial Leather: Race, Gender and Sexuality in the Colonial Contest.* (New York/London, Routledge, 1995), 87.

4. Wanning, Sun, "Sex, City, and the Maid: Between Socialist Fantasies and Neoliberal Parables." *Journal of Current Chinese Affairs,* 39, 4, 39, no. 4 (2010): 53–69. Accessed February 26, 2017. https://www.researchgate.net/.

5. See, for example, Karen M. Odden, "Re-Visioning the 'Vision from a Fairer World than His': Women, Creativity, and Work in *East Lynne* and *Mrs. Doubtfire,*" (2007); also John Phillips, *Transgender on Screen.* (Basingstoke [England]: Palgrave) Macmillan (2010) http://public.eblib.com/choice/publicfullrecord.aspx?p=736433; and Kerry Mallan, "'Just a Boy in a Dress': Performing Gender in Male-to-Female Cross-dressing Narratives." *Turning the Page: Children's Literature in Performance and the Media* (2006).

6. McClintock, *Imperial Leather*, 87.

7. Joseph Campbell, *The Hero with a Thousand Faces.* (Princeton, N.J.: Princeton University Press, 1948).

8. Campbell, *Hero*, 77.

9. Arnold Van Gennep, *Les rites des passage.* (Chicago: University of Chicago Press, 1960).

10. See Victor Witter Turner, "Liminality and Communitas," *A Reader in the Anthropology of Religion.* (2002): 358–374.

11. Anne McLeer, "Practical Perfection? The Nanny Negotiates Gender, Class, and Family Contradictions in 1960s Popular Culture." *NWSA* 14, no. 2 (Summer 2002): 80–101. https://search.proquest.com/docview/233238661?, 1.

12. *Ibid.*

13. *Nanny McPhee*, dir. Dirk Jones. With Emma Thompson, Colin Firth, Angela Lansbury, Universal Pictures, 2005.

14. Janet Maslin, "A Wig, a Dress, and Voila! Dad Became the Nanny," review of *Mrs. Doubtfire*, 1993, *The New York Times* (New York), November 24, 1993.

15. This exchange is true to the children's book, in which Daniel's character is even more critical of his ex-wife, and in which the ex-wife (they are divorced when the book opens) is portrayed as a virtual witch.

16. *Hook*, dir. Steven Spielberg. With Dustin Hoffman, Robin Williams, and Julia Roberts (1991; Universal City, CA: Amblin Entertainment/Sony Pictures Home Entertainment, 2015), DVD.

17. Justin Chang. "Robin Williams Remembered: A Moviegoer's Greatest Dad." *Variety*, online, 2014.

18. Mimi Matthews, "The Literary Governess: Depictions in Austen, Bronte, Thackery, and Heyer." *Romance, Literature, History*. Last modified June 15, 2015, accessed March 11, 2017, https://mimimatthews.com/2015/06/15.

19. McLeer, 4.

20. Interestingly, Williams did in fact leave his wife for the nanny—Marsha Garces—who was employed as caregiver to his son.

21. *The Nanny*, dir. Seth Holt. London: Hammer Film Productions, 1965.

22. *Mary Poppins*, dir. Robert Stevenson. With Julie Andrews, et al. (1964; Burbank, CA: Walt Disney Studios, 2013), DVD.

23. Jim Pilgrim, "The Mammy Caricature." *Jim Crow Museum of Racist Memorabilia*. Last modified 2012. Accessed March 29, 2017. http://www.ferris.edu/htmls/news/jimcrow/mammies/.

24. This again may be seen to echo the moment in *Hook* when one of the Lost Boys recognizes the buried Peter Pan only by looking into the eyes of Peter Banning, played by Williams.

25. In contrast, the children in the book are in on the joke and share the hilarity of those who are not; the motion picture complicates the farce by, in effect, placing the children themselves in the role of victims or dupes.

26. McLeer, 11.

27. *Tootsie*, directed by Sidney Pollack, starring Dustin Hoffman and Jessica Lange (1982; Hollywood, CA: Columbia Pictures, 2008), DVD.

28. A pun on *mal de mer*, sea sickness—here meaning sickness of the mother.

29. Julie Harrower, "The Dubious Nature of *Mrs. Doubtfire*—Yet Another Case of Mal de Mere?," *Feminism & Psychology* 5, no. 3 (1995): [Page #], doi:10.1177%2F0959353595053022.

BIBLIOGRAPHY

Campbell, Joseph. *The Hero with a Thousand Faces*. Princeton, NJ: Princeton University Press, 1948.

Correa, Mariza. "Freud's nanny and other nannies." *Cadernos Pagu* 1, 2008: 1–14. Accessed February 26, 2017. http://socialsciences.scielo.org/scielo.php?script=sci_arttext&pid=S0104-83332008000100002.

Harrower, Julie. "The Dubious Nature of Mrs. Doubtfire—Yet Another Case of Mal de Mere?" *Feminism & Psychology* 5, no. 3, 1995. doi:10.1177%2F0959353595053022.

Hunt, Peter. "The Devil and Madame Doubtfire: Anne Fine and the Revolution in Contemporary British Children's Fiction." *The Lion and the Unicorn* 23, no. 1, January 1999: 12–21. https://search.proquest.com/docview/752002385?

Lockard, Robert. "9 Variations on the 'Nanny Fixes a Family' Movie Plot." *Deja Reviewer* (blog). Entry posted January 27, 2016. Accessed February 26, 2017. https://dejareviewer.com/2016/01/27/9-variations-on-the-nanny-fixes-a-family-movie-plot/.

Maslin, Janet. "A Wig, a Dress, and Voila! Dad Became the Nanny." Review of *Mrs. Doubtfire*, 1993. *The New York Times*. November 24, 1993.

Matthews, Mimi. "The Literary Governess: Depictions in Austen, Bronte, Thackery, and

Heyer." Romance, Literature, History. Last modified June 15, 2015. Accessed March 11, 2017. https://mimimatthews.com/2015/06/15.

McClintock, Anne. *Imperial Leather: Race, Gender and Sexuality in the Colonial Contest.* New York/London: Routledge, 1995.

McLeer, Anne. "Practical Perfection? The Nanny Negotiates Gender, Class, and Family Contradictions in 1960s Popular Culture." *NWSA* 14, no. 2, Summer 2002: 80–101. https://search.proquest.com/docview/233238661?

Nayar, Sheila. "'Dreams, Dharma, and Mrs. Doubtfire; Exploring Hindi Popular Cinema Via its 'Chutneyed' Western Scripts.'" *Journal of Popular Film & Television* 31, no. 2, Summer 2003: 73. https://search.proquest.com/docview/199485237?

Palmer, John. "'Mrs. Doubtfire' House Becomes a Robin Williams Memorial." Boston.com. https://www.boston.com/culture/celebs/2014/08/13/mrs-doubtfire-house-becomes-robin-williams-memorial.

Phaneuf, Whitney. "'Mrs. Doubtfire's House in Pac Heights Becomes Robin Williams Memorial.'" sfist.com. Last modified August 12, 2014. Accessed February 26, 2017. http://sfist.com/2014/08/12/mrs_doubtfire_house_in_pac_heights.php.

Pilgrim, Jim, ed. "The Mammy Caricature." *Jim Crow Museum of Racist Memorabilia.* Last modified 2012. Accessed March 29, 2017. http://www.ferris.edu/htmls/news/jimcrow/mammies/.

Sun, Wanning. "Sex, City, and the Maid: Between Socialist Fantasies and Neoliberal Parables." *Journal of Current Chinese Affairs,* 39, 4, 39, no. 4, 2010: 53–69. Accessed February 26, 2017. https://www.researchgate.net/publication/48292865_Sex_City_and_the_Maid_Between_Socialist_Fantasies_and_Neoliberal_Parables/fulltext/00b05ce70cf22e1822 5819fc/48292865_Sex_City_and_the_Maid_Between_Socialist_Fantasies_and_Neoliberal_Parables.pdf?origin=publication_detail.

Turner, Victor Witter. Liminality and Communitas to *A Reader in the Anthropology of Religion,* 358–74. N.p., 2002.

Van Gennep, Arnold. *Les rites des passage.* Chicago: University of Chicago Press, 1965.

Generations of Men and Masculinity in *Dead Poets Society*

ANDREW SLADE

Since its opening in 1989, *Dead Poets Society* has enjoyed enduring success. Perhaps the great success of *Dead Poets Society* comes from how the film reminds its spectators what it feels like to have had a great teacher—a teacher who has, through some seeming magic, managed to change them. Robin Williams's performance of John Keating—a prep school graduate who returns to his alma mater as a teacher—covers familiar ground in teacher-student genre films. He puts his misunderstood students on a path to their freedom and passions; he leads them from ignorance into knowledge, from oppression to empowerment. If this were all that *Dead Poets Society* and its performances had on offer, the film would have been quickly and rightly forgotten. Classroom melodrama sells; it captures the nostalgia for youth of the old and the exuberance, anxiety, and hope for the future of the young. Yet great teaching has to have substance. What does Keating teach?

By recalling for its audience what it is like to have had a great teacher, *Dead Poets Society* screens the way one generation of boys takes on the masculinity that has been left to them by their fathers and the drama and struggle that their inheritance requires of them. To hook its audience, the film depends on what that audience knows about teachers and teaching and the pleasurable pay-off of having had an excellent teacher. In this sense, the film depends on its spectators' experiences of their very best teachers. Of course, the very best teachers are not objectively so, but are the very best for very specific students. Anyone who has taught for any length of time will understand the experience—sometimes baffling—of having had, in the very same class, a profound impact on one student or group of students, and nearly none on others. Stu-

62

dents will surely know one person who is inspired by one professor whose peers just cannot see how it could be. Encountering a great teacher is never about the teacher, but about the student for whom the teacher has become great.

The substance of the film is only poetry on its surface. Poetry is the mechanism that helps the white boys becoming white men. Academics have largely rejected the film on the grounds that it misrepresents teaching and the difficulties of teaching well. These critics misconstrue the film's point— to show the struggle of these boys to become men while avoiding the pitfalls of repeating their fathers' lives. Unlike their fathers, they want to become what Mr. Keating wants for them, as he says, to become a man "who can— through words—change the world." Robin Williams's performance of poetry and pedagogy is not a primer in teaching but a performance of the struggle to become a particular kind of man.

The film is full of teachers and their students even if most of the screen time has nothing to do with teachers teaching and students learning. The fact does not stop educators from lamenting about the model of teaching that they see in Williams's performance of John Keating. Writing in *English Journal* in 1989, Mark Collins declares, "But does the teaching style portrayed by Williams as Keating offer a convincing model for students whose aim is to change their lives for the better? I have my doubts"[1] *Dead Poets Society* fails Collins's hopes for a complex look at the relations between students and teachers in the late 1980s cinema.

Robert Heilman hopes to debunk the "myth of the great" teacher by taking his reader through a series of observations on the "Keatings" that he has known in the university over his career. He is annoyed by the film's attack on a poetry textbook, an actual textbook, *Understanding Poetry*, whose authors, "would not be caught dead saying … anything faintly resembling the passage that the instructor … so spectacularly takes off against."[2] Heilman delights in his annoyance at the film: "When one starts putting into specific words the general annoyance aroused by the film, one warms to the task."[3] Of course, who has not delighted in the raucous critique of something about which so one is absolutely certain? The movie is terrible, let us count the ways!

Heilman is annoyed by the Keating type who, "trades respect from his equals in for adulation by a more populous world."[4] The horror, people like him! Heilman distinguishes between two kinds of teachers—the good and the great: the good teacher is a humble servant of knowledge who works to speak on behalf of a field, he (are there any women?) speaks to those who are on the field and part of it. This is a small group—much smaller, alas, than the totality of students the good teacher will have taught. The good teacher is known by his work as "a cool expositor."[5] Heilman invests considerable energy in the difference between the "cool expositor" whose work speaks from and for a field and the "striking figure" of the Great Teacher who, like Keating, lives on in students' memory. The Great Teacher is made great by recognition from an audience of students rather than of peers and because of that, it would seem, Heilman distrusts them.

Heilman ends his attack on the great teacher myth, and on the film, with a story about a dinner conversation with his grandchildren: "one set ordered me to leave the table. The other set, more mindful of the infirmities of age, sentenced me only to the loss of dessert."[6] Yet for all this, the Keatings of the world have a particular value in education—to satisfy the need for a hero. *Dead Poets Society* gives a mass culture audience a hero in the guise of a great teacher. If the film is about teaching and the best ways to do that, then, indeed it is a bad film. If it is, as Heilman suggests, a film about the wish for a hero, then *The Avengers* or *Iron Man* or any of the other more recent spate of comic book hero films would share much with *Dead Poets Society* and probably be more effective. Why should the film continue to be as popular as it is, even being reworked for the stage in 2016?

Psychoanalytic accounts of masculinity argue that the ultimate limit of masculine identity is the rejection of femininity. In "Analysis Terminable and Interminable," Freud introduces this notion as the concept of "bedrock."[7] It is a geological metaphor that signifies the ultimate limit of psychoanalytical work. In "Men and Their Bedrock: Repudiation of Femininity," the Argentine psychoanalyst, Alcira Miriam Alizade observes that "the struggle against femininity oscillates between fascination and vehement rejection"[8] and "has its root in the difference between the sexes." In the clinical sense, masculinity is established in its relation to the bedrock, which is itself a defense. What, then, is the threat that the repudiation of the feminine defends against? Alizade answers: femininity is bound with life and death, with the dynamics of regeneration and decay that is itself tied up with the changeable feminine body. Against the fear of change that the feminine principle entails, the masculine position aims to stabilize itself in and through the setting aside of femininity through repudiation.[9] From this point of view, masculinity will always be attached to fears of death and the various fantasies that accompany it. It should be no surprise then that a death is the real central event in *Dead Poets Society*.

Masculinity is the repudiation of femininity rather than a distinct, positive, thing in itself. There is no masculinity, only the not-feminine. The setting of *Dead Poets Society*, Welton Academy, is the social embodiment of the repudiation of femininity. The all boys school facilitates the process that will make the boys into men. Repudiation is at work in the opening sequences of the film when the boys are moving in for another school year. The older boys know the script, having been through it already, while two younger boys cry to their mothers. The ritual of the beginning of the school year concludes with the younger boys leaving their mothers, taking their place among the other boys, and reciting the "Four Pillars"—Discipline, Honor, Tradition, Excellence—of the school. These pillars rule over the boys and militate against any intrusions of the feminine order that would allow them to cry—there are no tears in the pillars. The boys are shown crying only when shot with their mothers. The pillars are the structural support that repudiates femininity at Welton. The pillars are the province of the men and the boys who recite them and which become the common language of masculinity.

Becoming a man at Welton Academy is a process in which race is unmentioned and where class structures are reproduced. The race and class structures of the United States and at Welton are reproduced as a way to maintain the tradition represented by the four pillars. That is, the adoption of masculinity by one generation from the older one preserves tradition. The tradition that dominates Welton is a way of understanding time without change. Tradition, honor, discipline, and excellence keep the powerful just the way they are: they hold up the social structures that have brought all of them to the school in the first place—to gain access to the elite of U.S. society or to maintain their place in it. Repudiation of femininity is ultimately the repudiation of the black, of the poor, and of women.

Dead Poets Society is a white world. The question of race only enters the film when the boys of the Dead Poets Society chant from Vachel Lindsay's "Congo": "Then I saw the Congo creeping through the black/Cutting through the forest on a golden track."[10] The boys chant these lines as they run from the cave in the woods where they hold their meetings to the main house at Welton. There is no indication that they have any understanding of the poem or what it is about. They revel in its music and its effects. The question of race is not erased—the film does not even raise the issue. It would not have been difficult to acknowledge that Lindsay's poem raised the question of racism from its first publication in the early twentieth-century, with contemporaries such as W.E.B. Du Bois noting the poem's racist images and cadences, even as Lindsay would not see how the poem was anything other than celebratory. The film reproduces Lindsay's own blindness to how others might have seen his work.

The racial politics of seize the day and suck the marrow of life appear in the film as if they are without context or history, as if they can and should be taken up as the slogans of a life well lived. That may be the case for the boys of Welton Academy whose institutional mission is to secure for its graduates a place among the elites. Mr. Keating presents his slogans as subversive repudiations of Welton's aims and values. When have the elites not seized whatever they want? When have they not feasted on marrow? One way to understand their exuberance at the discovery of poetry is to understand it as the recognition and delight of their privilege which they at once denounce and embrace. The boys get to be like their fathers without having to be like them. White masculinity, and the privilege that attaches to it, is both repudiated and preserved.

Donald Moss describes the transmission of masculinity from one generation to the next as a process of repudiation of repudiations.[11] Whereas Alizade emphasizes the clinical quality of repudiation of femininity, Moss emphasizes an existential process whereby generations of men individuate themselves. He describes "emergent masculinities" as they seek to differentiate themselves from the men and masculinities that have come before them. More than resistance to the demands on behavior and thinking from their elders, the repudiations that Moss describes create space for the younger men and boys to create a masculinity of their own. Moss writes that as emerging masculinity,

> Takes one step forward, it leaves behind a repudiating predecessor. This predecessor, of course, had itself once left behind a repudiating predecessor of its own. Emerging masculinities, then, looking back over their own shoulders, will spot the traces of ever receding, ever surpassed, always anachronistic, old-fashioned masculinities; a historical trail, each advance marked by a repudiation of a predecessor. No longer repudiating what their predecessors had to repudiate, emerging masculinities will necessarily claim that they are, by self-definition, freer, stronger masculinities, in fact, more masculine masculinities.[12]

In *Dead Poets Society*, after the opening assembly of the year, the boys return to their room and begin to plan their studies for the year. Here they give their first, collective, act of repudiation. They create from the four pillars, their own version: Travesty, Horror, Decadence, Excrement. They exult in the chant and the minor rebellion it entails. They know the four pillars are a sham and, at the same time, they know that they can navigate through those pillars and still get what they want. No repudiation, however, will come for free. Just as they are celebrating with their chant about excrement and smoking their cigarettes, Neil's father (Kurtwood Smith), enters the room. He tells Neil that, in going over his schedule with Mr. Nolan, he has decided that he is too involved in extra-curricular activities. So, he takes him out of his role in producing the school's yearbook. Neil protests; it won't be fair, he says, the others are counting on him. His father recognizes the protest and, in response, asserts his power over him—do not ever disobey me in public, the father insists. The role of the father is to keep his son from doing what he enjoys. The father, it turns out, can be repudiated in his absence but in his return to the scene, he becomes stronger. Just when they think that the fathers are gone and departed, they return with stronger prohibitions than any of them expected.

The father, is of course, Neil's father, believes it's all for the good. What father does not believe that he is out for what's good for his children! The actual repudiation of the father far exceeds the aggressive unconscious wishes of childhood even as the tasks of repudiation sound their echo. What had been done will be repeated. Emergent masculinity seeks a way to differ from the older masculine models even as the hallmark of repudiation is a certain degree of repetition. Repudiation retains a core of the model and exaggerates its differences. The repudiation of the feminine makes the repudiation of the models of masculinity an existential and imaginative possibility. Repudiation is the echo of repetition. The boys will become like their fathers—Welton is designed to ensure it happens.

If the boys in Mr. Keating's class are experiencing the very best that there is in teaching, what else would they do than seek his approval? Two sequences illustrate this point. First, when the boys read aloud from their textbook, *Understanding Poetry*, they earn Keating's approval through tearing out the book's pages. Destroying a textbook in the name of learning and at the behest of the teacher is an act of rebellion against the role of the teacher as such and is especially pleasurable when coordinated by the teacher himself. The boys find a model for their masculine rebellion; they repudiate a feminine position which would turn them as readers into containers of knowledge—the knowledge of poetry, hence passive recipients rather than active producers. Of course, their repudiation is limited because they are not at ease with their own activity. While repudiation may have been thrilling; it is also frightening. Rebelling against their fathers and the conventions of knowledge that they represent earns the boys the recognition of their new master. The ripping out of the introduction signals a rejection of the pillars transmitted at Welton. Mr. Keating describes the passage that they read aloud as "excrement." He echoes the boys' revision of the pillars. In using "excrement" to describe the language of the introduction, Mr. Keating situates himself on the side of the students against the establishment teachers and their distant and irrelevant masculinity.

In a second instance, Charlie (Gale Hansen), gets into considerable trouble when he publishes a demand in the school newspaper for Welton to admit girls. He signs the demand in the name of the Dead Poets. The entire school is assembled in the main hall and Mr. Nolan insists that the guilty student come forward. In a spectacular ploy of rebellion, Charlie answers a ringing telephone, stands, and says, "Mr. Nolan! It's God. He says we should have girls at Welton!" The act unleashes the headmaster's anger and Charlie is brought to the office where he is paddled, counting aloud, and ordered to disclose the members of the Dead Poets Society. Later, Mr. Keating comes to the boys as they are studying and instead of praising Charlie, he chastises him. Getting expelled does not help him or anyone. Instead of gaining Keating's praise, he gets his criticism. It amounts to the same thing, however, when Keating remarks: had the call been collect, it would have been daring.

The criticism is coupled with praise. This sequence is a pedagogical moment, but the object of the teaching is not poetry, but masculinity. He illustrates the limit of repudiation—too much repudiation and emergent masculinity risks exclusion from the emergent community of men.

In describing how repudiation of masculine models works, Moss describes a Jack Black character, Nacho Libre, who dresses as a Mexican wrestler in order to have fun "playing in stretchy pants."[13] To play in stretchy pants becomes one of the ways that Moss thinks about how emerging masculinities engage with the models that are trying to repudiate. For the playful model of repudiation to work, the models have to be pliable. That means that there will have been space for the emerging men to play and that the models are available for destruction or revision. Moss's playful account of masculinity as it emerges against another generation works as long as the fathers that came before are willing to play according to the rules that allow the sons to craft their own version of what it might mean to be a man. *Dead Poets Society* shows what might happen when they refuse to be repudiated.

In 1913's *Totem and Taboo*, Freud tells a similar story of a father who does not yield even in death.[14] Freud imagines a primal community where the father controls access to all of the goods of the world. In this work, the son's rebellion takes the form of murder. The sons think that if they kill the father, then they will have access to his great power, to wives, and to wealth. Instead, they find that in death, the father has become more powerful than when he was alive. The brothers are consumed by guilt for what they have done and fear that they may meet the same fate as their father. Guilt and fear of the father and of each other becomes the tie that binds them. In *Dead Poets Society*, the sons are not trying to murder the father in the literal sense. Yet, when the boys engage in the slightest deviations from the fathers' desires, they are met with a violent response. Neil's father's threat: Don't you ever defy me in public. He does not state what the consequence will be. What does the child fear: the withdrawal of the father's love and recognition.

The risk of violence is everywhere in *Dead Poets Society*. The main conflict in the film is mediated through a suicide. Knox Overstreet, (Josh Charles) is the first to mention suicide; if he doesn't have Chris, he's going to kill himself. This declaration moves him to call her on the phone which gets him what he believes is an invitation to a party. "I've only met her once and she's already thinking about me," he declares. Knox's declaration is not a real threat. The second suicide is the central conflict in the film and comes after Neil's father retrieves him from the opening night performance of *A Midsummer Night's Dream*.

Neil Perry's suicide on the opening night of his performance as Puck in *A Midsummer Night's Dream* is the event that the plot moves toward. Neil did not start out as an actor, but a boy under his father's strict control. From the beginning of the film his life is orchestrated by his father. In an act of rebellion and repudiation, Neil auditions and takes the lead role in the play. Through a chance encounter with an acquaintance, Neil's father discovers his son's act and tries to forbid him from carrying through his plan. Neil does it anyway and on opening night, his father arrives and takes him home. Mr. Parry views Neil's act an open and willing betrayal. Neil regards his father's demands as uncaring and capricious. The conflict between generations of men is inevitable. Neil turns to his mother who is incapable of saving him from his father's demands. The last person to whom he can turn can do nothing for him. That he was good is irrelevant. In the night, Mr. Perry is awakened by a noise that only he has heard and he discovers his dead son in his study.

How did Neil arrive in that despairing place where the best future is one where he is not in it? The film aims to answer the question by showing an inquiry that seeks to assign blame and responsibility. The school and the family align as two institutions that have been harmed: Mr. Keating has disrupted the order of things and he must be expelled to preserve tradition and order. Before the boys's lives were disrupted by this insider who is an outsider, everything was working well—75% of Welton graduates went to the Ivy League, after all!

Neil's friends respond to this inquiry as they are able. One of the weaker boys sides with the school; the others with Keating as if their friend's death by his own hand were an argument between sides. Neil's father is easy to blame; unyielding and controlling as he is. Even after the play performance when Neil asks that his father listen to how he feels, Kurtwood Smith's performance captures the duality of Neil's father's love—tell me how you feel, he says, yet the message is that Neil can feel exactly as his father says he can feel. The father's demand cannot be fulfilled by his son. There is no space, in this house, for more than one desire. His father says as much: you can do anything you like when you are on your own.

Between the fullness of Neil's despair and the future that his father imagines for him, there is no reconciliation. Neil moves from the present of his father's desire to a present in which the future never comes, a present where the power and the reach of the father never ends, a perpetual present of abject disappointment where being good is irrelevant and where this is only pain. Neil is left with a fantasy—the plea at the end of *A Midsummer Night's Dream* when Puck begs the audience their pardon is shot as Neil trying to reconcile with his father. Neil's father refuses the reconciliation and Neil is left alone, dejected, and rejected. The bedrock of femininity is the last defense; his mother, as I noted, cannot help him. Neil is stuck between paternal rejection and bedrock; suicide is the defense against that terror. Neil commits suicide in his father's study with his father's gun. Neil becomes the literal presence of his actual absence in his father's universe. In his father's world the son is an extension, undifferentiated, of his own future.

We are left, then, with the impeccable logic of the suicide against which there is no argument: *since there is no place for my desire now, there is no place for me in your future. Since there is no place for me in your future, there is no place for me.* The suicide's defenses cease to function and the full expression of the death drive as violence against the self takes over. In a double rejection, Neil committed suicide not as Neil, but in the costume of his character, Puck. Even in his death, the father will not permit Neil to be Neil.

The terror of suicide is, in part, the way that the act negates the future. Unlike other deaths that are contextualized by the ongoing continuity of life around us, by the rites and rituals that give meaning to the person we've lost and to our survival, the suicide erases all of that. The future that was anticipated has disappeared through the dead ones deliberate act. Those of us who survive the suicide's death have lost a future that we thought was ours. In this sense, Neil takes his life from his father. But he also takes it from his mother who cries out in desperation that he's not dead. Of course, he takes all of those fantasies about the future—which remain always fantasies—and extinguishes them with his dead, wounded, body. The materiality of suicide coincides with the materiality of gender.

In 1917's "Mourning and Melancholia," Freud discusses two responses to loss.[15] There is no doubt that Neil has lost something profound. When he decides to audition he is adamant to his roommate, Todd: "I found it. What I want to do right now. It's really, really inside me." Neil has expressed what he wants to do before; he's involved in the annual among other extracurriculars that his father has controlled, but he has not shown such excitement for it before on screen. This is inside him. This thing in him is what he will lose.

Loss is typical; everyone loses something or someone who matters to them. In mourning losses, we find ways to separate the lost person or object from how we think and feel about ourselves. Mourning is the name of this process. "Mourning is commonly the reaction to the loss of a beloved person or an abstraction taking the place of the person."[16] Mourning is a process that brings us to acknowledge the loss of the person and allows us to separate from the lost one whom we loved.[17] Mourning separates us from our loss. When we mourn, we continue to live our lives.

Melancholia is also a response to the loss of a person, but, Freud notes, "that it may be possible to recognize that the loss is more notional in nature."[18] The more "notional loss" may be of a whole range of ideas. What has Neil lost? His desire to act—yes, but since he has actually carried it out, that cannot be what he has really lost. What he has lost is the recognition of his father. After the performance, he is acknowledged and congratulated by all of his friends and by Mr. Keating. All of his partners in repudiation of the four pillars recognize him in his act and yet, the act is ineffective in repudiating the father's desire. His father's desire is not weakened by his act, but becomes stronger. Neil's suicide is the melancholic response to the loss of what is inside him which is made concrete by the non-recognition of his father. His melancholic logic might run like this: Father, if you don't recognize me, I'm not your son. If I'm not your son, then I am dead. The suicide occupies the most radical melancholic position.

The conception of masculinity that is represented by the fathers—Mr. Perry, Mr. Nolan, the four pillars of Welton—is in itself melancholic. In part is it melancholic because of the inability to recognize what is lost as integral to identity; white, melancholic masculinity refuses to yield to the demands of the other. If the story of masculinity is a story of losses through repudiation over generations, then masculinity, as much as it might successfully move from generation to generation, must be mourned. In such a story, the son would detach from the fathers. We would lose something in making that separation—painful and necessary as it is. In fact, in "Family Romances," Freud notes that, "The separation of the individual, as he grows up, from the authority of his parents is one of the most necessary achievements of his development, yet at the same time one of the most painful."[19] The intergenerational story of masculinity is as painful as it is necessary. We might say, that fathers must mourn their sons; that each must separate his life from his children's who are no longer children. The parent mourns the loss of the child as the child separates—painfully and necessarily—from the parents. In *Dead Poets Society*, the loss in repudiation is not mourned but clutched melancholically. Welton is the mechanism that aims to guarantee the repetition of race, class, and gender identities of the white elite in the U.S. Masculinity in the world of *Dead Poets Society* is a melancholic one. The time of melancholia is the time of repetition. Time as repetition is time that does not change. If Mr. Keating is dangerous, it's not because of what he teaches and it's not because of poetry. If students continue to love the film, it's not because of what it teaches about literature or what they learn about teaching and teachers from it. Students of all ages know what they want in a teacher.

In the last moments of the film, the boys pass through some difficult transitions. They endure the death of their friend. They have to learn to live without him; they witness the firing of their beloved teacher and have then to navigate their loss without a key ally. Mr. Keating has a difficult transition; he just lost a student to suicide and got fired from his alma mater. In the final exuberant sequence of rebellion, the boys stand on their desks and declare, "Oh Captain my Captain!" and then wait for Keating to respond. He says, "thank you, boys."

We might point to this sequence and say that Mr. Keating has been successful in his teaching, the students learned to seize the day, to see the world from a different perspective and now he can go. In this reading, the tragic end is redeemed by the students' recognition of their teacher. If the film is about having had a great teacher, what has been its lesson? Perhaps, the lesson is that the great teacher makes the separation of the individual from the father less painful. In this claim, perhaps, Robert Heilman, who found the film so annoying, is correct. The film is about the need for a hero. What is heroic in this end? What has the great teacher accomplished with the students? At best, perhaps, they acknowledge the loss of something that is in them that is no longer there—their friend Neil. The school and the father are looking to blame, to find responsibility, to preserve discipline, to preserve their traditions, their excellence, their honor. Unwilling to be put aside, the fathers have created a place and a space where the future they seek is their own immortality. The boys may repeat their fathers' lives, but they may not repudiate them, set them aside, or push them over. Masculinity in *Dead Poets Society* is melancholic and desperate. Hope for tomorrow, for what is to come, relegated to moments of escape that are unsustainable over time. The end of the film augurs a generation of men who have not been able to separate from their parents, as Freud describes in "Family Romances," so they become them. They become the same white men who cannot see how their experience is anything other than typical, normal, universal, and true. Where the four pillars of Welton are equally true as their ironic reversal—where "Discipline, Honor, Tradition, Excellence" and "Travesty, Horror, Decadence, Excrement" are echoes of the same masculinity.

NOTES

1. Mark Collins, "Make Believe in *Dead Poets Society*," *The English Journal* 78.8 (1989), 74.
2. Heilman, "The Great-Teacher Myth," *The American Scholar* 60.3 (Summer1991), 417.
3. *Ibid.*
4. *Ibid.*, 419.
5. *Ibid.*
6. *Ibid.*, 423.
7. Sigmund Freud, "Analysis Terminable and Interminable," *Totem and Taboo* in *On Murder, Mourning, and Melancholia*. Shaun Whiteside, trans. The New Penguin Freud. Adam Phillips, Ed. London: Penguin, 2005, 252.
8. Alcira Miriam Alizade, "Men and Their Bedrock," *Masculine Scenarios*, Alcira Mariam Alizade, ed. London: Karnac, 2003, 14.
9. *Ibid.*, 15–16.
10. Vachel Lindsay, "The Congo: A Study of the Negro Race," 432–3.
11. Donald Moss, *Thirteen Ways of Looking at a Man*. New York and London: Routledge, 2012, 1–2.
12. *Ibid.*
13. *Ibid.*
14. Freud, "Totem and Taboo," *Totem and Taboo* in *On Murder, Mourning, and Melancholia*. Shaun Whiteside, trans. The New Penguin Freud. Adam Phillips, Ed. London: Penguin, 2005, 140–143.
15. Freud, "Mourning and Melancholia," *Totem and Taboo* in *On Murder, Mourning,*

and Melancholia. Shaun Whiteside, trans. The New Penguin Freud. Adam Phillips, Ed. London: Penguin, 2005, 203.
  16. *Ibid.*
  17. *Ibid.*, 204.
  18. *Ibid.*, 205.
  19. *Ibid.*, 37.

BIBLIOGRAPHY

Alizade, Alcira Mariam. "Men and Their Bedrock: 'Repudiation of Femininity.'" *Masculine Scenarios,* Alcim Mariam Alizade, ed. London: Karnac, 2003. 43–72.
Brantley, Ben. "Seizing the Day, Hankie in Hand." *New York Times* 18 Nov. 2016: C1+. *Academic Search Complete.* Web. 15 December 2016.
Collins, Mark. "Make Believe in *Dead Poets Society.*" *The English Journal* 78.8, 1989: 74–75.
Delia, Mary Alice. "*Dead Poets Society*: Uncritically Acclaimed." *Works and Days* 9.1, 1991: 91–96.
Farhi, Adam. "Hollywood Goes to School: Recognizing the Superteacher Myth in Film." *The Clearing House* 72.3, 1999: 157–159.
Freud, Sigmund. *Totem and Taboo* in *On Murder, Mourning, and Melancholia.* Shaun Whiteside, trans. The New Penguin Freud. Adam Phillips, Ed. London: Penguin, 2005.
Gale, Trevor and Kathleen Densmore. "Questions of (re)production and Legitimation: A Second Screening of Three Films on Teacher-Student Relations." *Journal of Curriculum Studies* 33.5, 2001: 601–619.
Heilman, Robert B. "The Great-Teacher Myth." *The American Scholar* 60.3, Summer 1991: 417–423.
McLaren, Peter and Zeus Lombardo. "Deconstructing Surveillance Pedagogy: *Dead Poets Society.*" *Studies in the Literary Imagination* 31.1, 1998: 127–147.
Moss, Donald. *Thirteen Ways of Looking at a Man: Psychoanalysis and Masculinity.* New York and London: Routledge, 2012.

Cold War Culture in the Films of Robin Williams

MICHELLE CATHERINE IDEN

When Ronald Reagan took office in 1981 the Cold War was still in full swing and Robin Williams was already a household name. Williams was a well-known comic from his stand-up routine, 1980 Grammy award winning album *Reality.... What a Concept*, and popular television show *Mork & Mindy* (1978–1982). By the end of the 1980s Williams grew into a movie star with two Oscar nominations [*Good Morning, Vietnam* (1987) and *Dead Poets Society* (1989)], the Cold War was coming to a crashing end, and Reagan was so influential that the decade came to be known as the Reagan Era. The intertwining of these developments played themselves out in two of Williams's films: *Moscow on the Hudson* (1984) and the aforementioned *Good Morning, Vietnam*. Both films were a product of, and therefore provide commentary on, the Cold War Era they were created in. They simultaneously critique and celebrate American society and history, but in a palatable way that is possible because of their combination of comedy and drama, seen in Williams's comedy being used as a foil to the dramatic backdrop of each film.

Movies dealing with the Cold War were nothing new to American audiences. Since World War II movies dealing with defection, freedom, and the Cold War were thought to be important because they could "consolidate consensus, woo neutrals, and divide opponents."[1] As authors Tony Shaw and Denise J. Youngblood point out, "The truth is that American film ... has always been political in one way or another."[2] American audiences of the 1980s were primed to understand the language of the Cold War when they saw it in film because it was a part of the political dialogue of the time. President Reagan, a well-known ardent Cold War warrior, made sure the nation continued to focus on the Cold War when he took a tough stance publicly against the Soviet Union. In a speech given June 8, 1982, he stated the Soviet Union, "runs against the tides of history by denying human freedom and human dignity to its citizens." He spoke of a plan that would lead "the march of freedom and democracy which will leave Marxism-Leninism on the ash-heap of history, as it has left other tyrannies which stifle the freedom and muzzle the self-expression of the people."[3] The Soviet Union, or perhaps more broadly communism, was clearly an enemy "Other" that represented the opposite of celebrated American freedom. This enemy could easily be written in to the plot of Hollywood films.

Robin Williams entered this world of Cold War cinema when he starred in *Moscow on the Hudson* in 1984. The movie tells the fictional story of Vladimir Ivanoff, a Russian saxophonist (Robin Williams) who defects to the United States while shopping in Bloomingdales when the circus troop he performs with visits New York City. While telling the story of Ivanoff's adjustment to living in America, the Paul Mazursky directed film provides what author Philip Gianos describes as "détente on a personal scale."[4] The reference to the political term applied to the easing of tensions during the Cold War is apt as the movie includes scenes from Moscow and New York to allow for the juxtaposition of the differences between the two superpowers in the Cold War. While it is true that by the end of the film the United States is portrayed as a land of opportunity while Russia is a place with too much state control, the Russians are also humanized so that the audience can identify with the "enemy" and the faults of the United States are not overlooked.

We first encounter Ivanoff riding a bus in New York City helping someone else navigate the bus system, showcasing he has fully adjusted to life in the United States. Ivanoff's transformation is highlighted as we are then brought back to his time in Moscow with scenes that criticize the state of life there and demonstrate the absurdity of the conditions the Cold War has created. For example, frequent jokes are made about the inability to obtain goods, as seen in the need to wait in a long line for toilet paper or shoes.[5] The critique of the absurdity of the circumstances created by the Cold War continues beyond what happens in Moscow. When Ivanoff first defects while in New York the media is quickly alerted to what has happened and he is hounded in Bloomingdales as a media circus starts to develop around the performer. Williams's comedic talents are visible as he leads the KGB agents on a chase throughout the store. Underlining this, however, is his ability to add dramatic elements to the developments. He is never over the top so that the intensity of the decision to defect for the Ivanoff character is still always evident, acting as a foil to the comedic scene while calling attention to the absurdities of the Cold War.

The scenes at Bloomingdales also provide for a comparison of capitalism and communism, ultimately allowing for a celebration of American capitalism. For instance, while people wait in long lines for things in Moscow they have numerous options to buy a variety of products in New York City. While Ivanoff had to settle for shoes that didn't fit him in Moscow, he later shops for shoes in NYC and has so many varieties in color and shape to try on that he is overwhelmed with the choices. This celebration of consumerism is what leads writer Tim Cavanaugh to describe the film as a "benchmark anti–Soviet film" because Ivanoff "learns that the pains of U.S. life (unsolved crimes, general indifference to your existence) are outweighed by the pleasures (overflowing supermarkets, a pepper-pot girlfriend)."[6]

Other scenes contribute to audience expectations of what "the enemy" of the Cold War is like. When Ivanoff is in Moscow he runs into someone he knows who was sent to a mental institution for being crazy after having protested Soviet involvement in Afghanistan. This scene is minor in the entire context of the film, but it provides a major critique of Soviet repression and Soviet involvement in Afghanistan.[7] This type of repression presents a stark contrast to a later diner scene in NYC when Ivanoff rants against the United States. He is disillusioned with the United States as he has recently been robbed. Sitting with his Cuban immigrant lawyer as they wait for their order of the quintessentially American iconic food of apple pie, he yells, "In Russia I knew who the enemy was, here it's so confusing … this is false liberty." He is able to loudly make this claim without fear of any secret police attacking him. The complexity of the situation is noted when his lawyer replies, "What do you want the perfect place to live? It doesn't exist."

This critique doesn't overshadow the celebratory nature of the film as America is portrayed as the country where you may be able to get close to that perfect place to live. The multiculturalism of NYC is showcased as Ivanoff and his lawyer interact with the workers and patrons at the diner: another Russian immigrant, a Chinese speaking immigrant, a white waitress of undetermined background, and a Spanish speaking worker. The patriotic celebration of this diversity is hit home when the diner patrons recognize that it is Independence Day and together recite the preamble to the Declaration of Independence.

The celebration of multicultural diversity is also evident in the personal relationships Ivanoff develops with others in NYC. He has a romantic relationship with the character Lucia Lombardo, an Italian immigrant portrayed by Maria Conchita Alonso. He also develops a close friendship with Lionel Witherspoon, a black security guard at Bloomingdales originally from Alabama, (Cleavant Derricks.) While coming from very different backgrounds, the three bond over their experiences of trying to make their way in New York. For Lucia, that includes becoming an American citizen. In the courtroom scene that features this, Ivanoff and Lionel look on as immigrants of various nationalities take the oath of allegiance to become citizens. Diversity is highlighted as the camera pauses on people of varying ethnicities and ages.

This celebration of diversity as compared to the repression of Russia is not done while shying away from showing the complexity of the experience of immigrating to the United States. At the party for Lucia after her citizenship ceremony Ivanoff and Lucia sit on a boat discussing their future. We find out that Lucia's uncle doesn't like Ivanoff because he thinks he is a communist since he is Russian. Despite the emotional nature of the scene we are reminded as viewers that communism is the enemy. Lucia and Ivanoff then fight because she implies that as a new citizen she would prefer to date an American. She starts yelling in Italian and as the noise escalates we hear a neighbor say, "There goes the neighborhood." We are reminded of the fear or dislike of immigrants that can exist, just as we are symbolically reminded of the long history of immigration of the nation. The houses where all of this occurs are located on the water, symbolically showing how these immigrants and Americans from different parts of the world came together. This patriotism with a critique is the only kind that might be accepted by a nation that has been through the upheavals of Vietnam, Watergate, and the resignation of President Nixon.

Clearly the movie does not shy away from showing both the cultural diversity and economic opportunities of the United States that can be celebrated, and the real consequences the individuals caught in this larger Cold War ideological divide can suffer. Ivanoff gets to experience freedom when he successfully defects, yet when he does so he leaves behind his family and friends. It is then difficult to keep in touch with them because of the ever present threat of the Russian secret police: the KGB. Some of the letters he does send are narrated by Williams to demonstrate the contradictions between reality and what is written. When Ivanoff writes that he has gotten a sales job we see one of the strongest comedic moments of the film as we see Williams hocking cheap goods from a cart on the streets of New York. He then talks of opening his own small restaurant, but we see that he means a hotdog cart. The deadpan delivery of the lines of the letter help highlight the contradictions between what is written and what is seen. Scenes like this act as a foil to the dramatic elements of the film. Ivanoff is, ultimately, an immigrant who finds life in the United States difficult at times, but he tries to portray that life as the land of opportunity expected.

Even as he gets to enjoy the land of opportunity we see the repression of the Soviet Union continues to have an impact. Williams's acting helps emphasize the troubles Ivanoff experiences when he receives a letter from home with bad news. Ivanoff finds out that his grandfather has died. Their close relationship is seen in the opening scenes when comedic family banter provides a foil and relief to an otherwise drab Moscow. The scenes resulting from the news of his death could, therefore, lend themselves to creating overly melodramatic moments, but it is Williams's subtlety in showing Ivanoff's struggle with this loss that creates a credible viewing as he poignantly plays "Take the A Train" on his saxophone—the song that he and his grandfather joyously sang together near the beginning of the film. The difficulty in leaving a life behind when immigrating is highlighted, while also emphasizing that this could all be avoided if the Soviet Union wasn't so repressive.

The freedom available in America that contrasts this Cold War Era repression is emphasized in the closing scenes of the film. Here we can return to the hot dog cart. Ivanoff runs into one of the circus troops' former KGB handlers, who is now running his own hot dog cart in the city. The agent's entire demeanor has changed. He smiles more and his body language is much more relaxed than he ever before. The two men get their start in America by working at a hot dog cart, a restaurant without walls that invites and welcomes its owner to interact with the diverse population of New York and symbolizes what can be accomplished when living in a land that cherishes freedom. The interaction of these two specific characters shows how much one has already adapted to the United States, while the other is closer to starting his journey. Ultimately, the Soviet Union is so repressive even one of its government workers wanted to defect.

The scene that is perhaps the heaviest-handed in its celebration of freedom and diversity comes shortly after this interaction. Ivanoff is seen playing his saxophone to a culturally diverse crowd in New York City while a song about freedom plays when the credits start to roll. If any viewer had missed the message of the celebration of freedom in America throughout the course of the film this scene makes sure it isn't lost on them. The attempt at portraying complex issues like freedom, immigration, and diversity in a Cold War context may have been too much for the film had it not been for Williams helping prevent it from caving in on its own grandness through the combination of his comedic and dramatic talents.[8]

Building on that experience, Williams then starred in the film that garnered him his first Academy Award nomination for best actor: *Good Morning, Vietnam* (1987). Critic Vincent Canby noted in *The New York Times* that each of Williams's other well-known films up to that point, "had its endearing moments, but there was always the feeling that an oddball natural resource was being inefficiently used."[9] *Good Morning, Vietnam* changed this while presenting a meaningful portrayal of the Vietnam War as it was understood in the Cold War period.

The movie tells the story of Adrian Cronauer, a radio disc jockey assigned to the Armed Forces Radio Service in Saigon in 1965. His comedic style is a hit with the troops, but gets him in trouble with some of the officers stationed at his location. His antics eventually get him sent back to the United States. As we watch this story unfold we see the relationships he develops within the military and with the local population. While telling these stories director Barry Levinson capitalizes on Williams's ability to shift from comedic to dramatic scenes, thereby successfully challenging viewers of the film to consider several larger issues of the war, including the complexity of the Vietnamese as enemy. Once again we see both the critique and celebration of American society and culture, exemplified by comedy as foil to a dramatic backdrop.

As with *Moscow on the Hudson*, *Good Morning, Vietnam* was a product of the Cold War culture in which it was created. Reagan was still in office, but much had changed since *Moscow* came out. While it wasn't yet clear that the Cold War would soon come to an end, a thaw had certainly occurred.[10] At the same time the relationship between the United States and Vietnam had evolved. By the time the movie was released the people of the United States had already watched the fall of Saigon, the capital city of the formerly U.S. backed South Vietnamese government, in 1975.[11] They saw the nation so divided about the war that by August of 1980 Reagan spoke of the "Vietnam Syndrome" on the campaign trail, arguing at a speech given at a Veterans of Foreign Wars convention in Chicago that Americans had been misled through propaganda to think they couldn't win the war and that the government had limited the success of the military. He stated, "It is time we recognized that ours was, in truth, a noble cause."[12] These ideas were the salve many felt was needed to "heal" the nation from the divisive nature of the Vietnam War as the debate over it continued to rage on.

Even though a language of healing was being used to a great extent when Vietnam was discussed in the 1980s, there was still contention. Diplomatic relations weren't normalized with Vietnam until 1995.[13] Some Americans still so adamantly believed that prisoners of war and those missing in action were still in Vietnam that historian George C. Herring wrote that the "issue took on the power and mystique of a religion."[14] That belief meant that Vietnam was still an ongoing issue for many Americans and that the Vietnamese could be portrayed as the "Cold War enemy" in films about the war.

This was done to varying extents in films of the late 1970s and the 1980s. Heavy hitters like *The Deer Hunter* (1979) and *Apocalypse Now* (1979) dealt with moral issues connected to the war, while films like *Missing in Action* (1984) and *Rambo: First Blood Part II* (1985) allowed for an escape into thinking that some men missing in action were in fact prisoners of war who could be saved.[15] In the year before the Robin Williams driven film came out *Platoon* was released and in the same year as *Good Morning, Vietnam* the intense dramas *Full Metal Jacket*, and *Hamburger Hill* came out. Director Barry Levinson stated, "We've already seen the combat stuff in *Platoon* and *Full Metal Jacket*. So I wanted to give a sense of what it was like in 1965. This movie is on the train tracks heading for the wreck. We're still at the point where we're seeing scenery along the way."[16] Indeed, here Levinson touches on one of the key aspects of the film: as a result of the timing of when it was released and the time period it covers, the audience is well aware of the chaos that is about to erupt on a larger scale as the war divides the nation. The film can then safely deal with controversial issues regarding the war because it looks back at a time of relative innocence, while also clueing the reader in to the loss of innocence that they know is about to come.

This worked so well because it fit audience expectations of Williams as both an actor and a comic. Reviewing the film upon its release Roger Ebert described it as "the best work Williams has ever done in a movie" because "his own tactics are turned against him."[17] Williams's time in front of the mic as a deejay provides the setting that is the rationality for Cronauer being in Vietnam in the first place, essentially allowing him to present his comedy routine between the more dramatic elements. Director Levinson famously allowed Williams to improvise as much as possible in those scenes, and Williams used that to great effect. He presents jokes about the demilitarized zone, fighting in the jungle, the heat, and more. They are so memorable that Richard Schickel of *Time* wrote of Williams, "Up to now, his genius has not fit any known film format. Narrative obligations and the implicit demand that leading characters be sane, likable and consistent have always constrained him."[18] Yet it is *Good Morning, Vietnam* that allows for his genius to be on full display.

Just as the radio station was the perfect vehicle for Williams's comedic talents, it also allowed for the presentation of controversial issues related to the war. For example, American leadership is criticized. As Cronauer is first shown around the station we see a news item coming in over the wire. It mentions that President Johnson held a press conference noting that the troop commitment in Vietnam will go up. As viewers we know that this is just the beginning in the increase in the number of troops that is to occur over the next few years. Later, as the group of deejays meet with their superior officer after Cronauer's first performance on the radio a visit by former vice-president Richard Nixon is discussed. While there is no dialogue within the scene that disparages the former VP, when Edward Garlick, (Forrest Whitaker) states that "The former VP is a delight" the audience is certainly aware of the humor in this given his forthcoming scandals, resignation, and unpopularity.

Criticisms of the handling of the dissemination of information during the war also create a complex view of who the enemy is. Garlick shows Cronauer the newsroom and states, "Regardless of what you read here the Department of Defense wants final say." Cronauer eventually gets in trouble because he reads a news story that hasn't been approved out of a desire to share information about what is really happening in Saigon (in this case an explosion at a café he and the other deejays frequent).

Connected to this is the critique of the military structure. There is a clear divide between members of the military who are friendly and relatable in the film and those who are maligned because they always do as ordered without questioning. Lt. Steven Hauk, (Bruno Kirby) and Sgt Major Dickerson (J.T. Walsh) do not like Cronauer's loose style on the radio, which they find dangerous, and they ultimately succeed in getting him removed from the broadcast. This is a common trope in Vietnam War films as it addresses the divisions within the military that existed during the war itself. The critique of the military is softened, however, in the likeable character of General Taylor (Noble Willingham) who finds Cronauer funny, but ultimately can't cover for him when it's found out that one of his Vietnamese friends is a Viet Cong terrorist with sympathies to the North Vietnamese, enemies of the U.S. allies, the South Vietnamese.

The setting of the radio station also allows for critiques of the war as we witness it escalate. It is as though the impending crisis of an escalating war becomes the enemy. When we initially see Cronauer as a deejay the first song played is "Nowhere to Run" by Martha and the Vandellas. As it plays the scene cuts from Cronauer in the radio station to troops lounging on a Patrol Boat River, then troops training, and Hauk upset at the modern music being played. The juxtaposition of the song with the visual of troops training is a clear commentary on the Vietnam War. The soldiers are the ones who have nowhere to run or nowhere to hide. And since the film is set in 1965 the audience knows just what this means for the troops who are there: an escalation of the conflict and a further loss of life. Indeed, this is clearly evident for viewers because every time we return to the radio station montage set up the war developing outside has escalated: there is an increasing number of troops, then eventually villages on fire and protests in the streets.

In the film these scenes allow for a complex view of the Cold War enemy presented. While the Vietnamese are the Cold War era enemy, there is a complexity to war that means lines are often blurred. After Martha and the Vandellas play we quickly then move to scenes of the streets of Saigon as the Beach Boys' "I Get Around" is played. We see an American soldier walking with a Vietnamese woman, Vietnamese children playing in the street, then later some Vietnamese working in a rice paddy. These scenes humanize the Vietnamese so that while they are still discussed as the Cold War enemy in parts of the film by people like Hauk, they are also people whom Americans interact with. Director Barry Levinson noted that he wanted to show "the Vietnamese people as just people."[19]

The complexity of who the enemy is becomes clear as the film progresses. In the beginning of the film Cronauer quickly lusts after Vietnamese women and implies that they all look alike. He chases one woman to an English class she is taking. Here we find Williams's comedic acting helps again as he jokes with a group of Vietnamese who he is teaching English to. But the folly presented soon acts as a foil to the serious backdrop of the war. As the film develops Cronauer befriends the woman's brother, Tuan. This ultimately allows for a critique on the nature of the guerrilla style warfare of the conflict. Cronauer is caught off guard when he learns that Tuan was a VC sympathizer. As we watch Williams react to the news we see the innocence and jovialness of his demeanor immediately turn to confusion and disappointment. When he confronts Tuan the audience is reminded by Tuan that, to the Vietnamese, the United States is the enemy, "You killing my own people so many miles from your home." Cronauer is upset that he was used by Tuan to unwittingly help with the bombing that killed two people, but Tuan is quick to point out to Cronauer that these are just two deaths among the many the Vietnamese have suffered. We are left wondering: who is the real enemy in a Cold War conflict? Are the lines drawn between friend and enemy as clear as we might think?

One could argue that the stakes were raised in *Good Morning, Vietnam* because Adrian Cronauer was a real deejay in Vietnam, but the movie doesn't have much overlap with the real Cronauer's experiences aside from his name and job. Undeniably, some criticized the movie for its historical inaccuracies and for not dealing with the serious scenes well enough.[20] However, these assessments fail to account for the nuances and historical context of the film. At a time when the subject of the Vietnam War was still very contentious Levinson and Williams were able to pull off a critique of the war with comedic elements that could get viewers to contemplate large theoretical issues. Schickel wrote in *Time* that "You may be out on the sidewalk before you realize that these are not just broadcasters. They represent the confused voices of all America registering shock as solid-seeming ground turns to quagmire."[21] While the movie strays from the historical circumstances of Cronauer's life, it accurately reflects the time in which it was produced: a Cold War American landscape still dealing with the long-term consequences of the divisive Vietnam War.

In the end, *Moscow on the Hudson* and *Good Morning, Vietnam* highlight Robin Williams's acting abilities while demonstrating that the right casting can make a difference in how successfully the characters on screen are portrayed. Williams went on to a film career which counted movies that were both successes and failures at the box office. Yet since he began his film career in the 1980s Williams's early works are indelibly a part of the Cold War culture. Evaluations of *Moscow on the Hudson* and *Good Morning, Vietnam* allow viewers to see just how much the films were a product of the culture in which they were produced, each ultimately reflecting the historical and social culture in which it was made. Indeed, one might question whether these films could be made in the post–Cold War world. The nebulous nature of the relationship between the United States and Russia and the language of healing that still surrounds portrayals of the Vietnam War warrant the consideration that *Moscow on the Hudson* and *Good Morning, Vietnam* demonstrate that changing historical circumstances necessitate that a film fit into its particular cultural climate.

NOTES

1. Tony Shaw and Denise J. Youngblood, *Cinematic Cold War: The American and Soviet Struggle for Hearts and Minds* (Lawrence, KS: University Press of Kansas, 2010), 215.

2. *Ibid.*, 17.

3. Ronald Reagan, "Address to the Members of British Parliament," *Ronald Reagan Presidential Library and Museum*, National Archives and Records Administration, Accessed Oct. 9, 2016, https://reaganlibrary.gov/archives/speeches/30-archives/speeches/1982/1349-60882a.

4. Phillip L. Gianos, *Politics and Politicians in American Film* (Westport, CT: Praeger, 1998), 158.

5. The film, then, built upon the history of other well-known films that already dealt with the absurdity of the conditions of the Cold War, while also dealing with larger issues of nuclear warfare and the heightened geo-political climate. Perhaps the best known film to do this was Stanley Kubrick's *Dr. Strangelove or: How I Learned to Stop Worrying and Love the Bomb* (1964), a satirical black comedy that dealt with issues regarding nuclear weapons.

6. Tim Cavanaugh, "Hollywood Comrades," *Reason*, 41, no. 6 (Nov. 2009), http://reason.com/archives/2009/10/30/hollywood-comrades.

7. Walter A. McDougall, *Promised Land, Crusader State: The American Encounter with the World Since 1776* (Boston: Hougton Mifflin Company, 1997), 197.

8. As *Variety* magazine suggested when the movie came out, "Moscow would be in a lot of trouble without a superbly sensitive portrayal by Robin Williams of a gentle Russian circus musician." From: "Review: Moscow on the Hudson," *Variety*, December 31, 1983, Accessed August 25, 2016, http://variety.com/1983/film/reviews/moscow-on-the-hudson-1200426042/.

9. Vincent Canby, "Film: Good Morning, Vietnam," *New York Times*, December 23, 1987, Accessed September 20, 2016, http://www.nytimes.com/movie/review?res=9B0DE0D8173FF930A15751C1A961948260

10. Mikhail Gorbachev became general secretary of the Community Party in 1985 and promoted his ideas of glasnost and perestroika, openness and reform politically and economically. In October of 1986 Gorbachev and Reagan proposed a ban on nuclear weapons.

11. George C. Herring, *America's Longest War: The United States and Vietnam, 1950–1975* (New York: McGraw-Hill Education), 348–50.

12. Ronald Reagan, "Veterans of Foreign Wars Convention," *Ronald Reagan Presidential Library and Museum*, National Archives and Records Administration, August 18, 1980, Accessed Oct. 1, 2016, https://reaganlibrary.archives.gov/archives/reference/8.18.80.html.

13. Herring, 373.

14. *Ibid.*, 370.

15. Author Jeremy Divine argues that by the time *Good Morning, Vietnam* (1987) came out far more films were willing to tackle the difficult subject of Vietnam because, "The passage of time had finally blunted some of the pain...the soldier was a sentimental hero once again in films, and he, like the country itself, would somehow survive the trauma." From Jeremy Devine, *Vietnam at 24 Frames a Second* (Austin: University of Texas Press, 1999), 274.

16. Lawrence H. Suid, *Guts & Glory: The Making of the American Military Image in Film* (Lexington, KY: University of Kentucky Press, 2002), 536.

17. Roger Ebert, "Good Morning, Vietnam," RogerEbert.com, Accessed Oct. 2, 2016, http://www.rogerebert.com/reviews/good-morning-vietnam-1988.

18. Richard Schickel, "Motormouth in Saigon," *Time*, December 28, 1987, 130, no. 26, http://content.time.com/time/magazine/article/0,9171,966337,00.html.

19. "Production notes," *Good Morning, Vietnam*, directed by Barry Levinson (1988; Burbank, CA: Buena Vista Home Entertainment, 2006), DVD.

20. Hal Hinson of *The Washington Post* criticized Williams's performance when writing in 1988 that "the film's tone shifts from irreverent to serious and suddenly the subject becomes 'How I went to Vietnam and Had my Consciousness Raised.'" His assessment is that, "All of this feels compulsory and condescending." From Hal Hinson, "Good Morning, Vietnam," *The Washington Post*, January 15, 1988, Accessed September 28, 2016, http://www.washington post.com/wp-srv/style/longterm/movies/videos/goodmorningvietnam.htm

21. Schickel, "Motormouth in Saigon."

BIBLIOGRAPHY

Canby, Vincent. "Film: Good Morning, Vietnam." *The New York Times*. December 23, 1987. Accessed October 2, 2016. http://www.nytimes.com/movie/review?res=9B0DE0D8173FF 930A15751C1A961948260.

Canby, Vincent. "Film: Paul Mazursky's Moscow on the Hudson." *The New York Times*. April 6, 1984. Accessed October 5, 2016. http://www.nytimes.com/movie/review?res=9A02 E2DD1638F935A35757C0A962948260

Cavanaugh, Tim. "Hollywood Comrades." *Reason* 41, no. 6, 2009. http://reason.com/archiv es/2009/10/30/hollywood-comrades.

Devine, Jeremy M. *Vietnam at 24 Frames a Second*. Austin: University of Texas Press, 1999.

Ebert, Roger. "Good Morning, Vietnam." RogerEbert.com. January 15, 1988. Accessed October 2, 2016. http://www.rogerebert.com/reviews/good-morning-vietnam-1988.

Ebert, Roger. "Moscow on the Hudson." RogerEbert.com. January 1, 1984. Accessed October 2, 2016. http://www.rogerebert.com/reviews/moscow-on-the-hudson-1984.

Gianos, Phillip L. *Politics and Politicians in American Film*. Westport, CT: Praeger, 1998.

Herring, George C. *America's Longest War: The United States and Vietnam, 1950–1975*. New York: McGraw-Hill Education, 2002.

Hinson, Hal. "Good Morning, Vietnam." *The Washington Post*. January 15, 1988. Accessed September 28, 2016. http://www.washingtonpost.com/wp-srv/style/longterm/movies/ videos/goodmorningvietnam.htm.

McDougall, Walter A. *Promised Land, Crusader State: The American Encounter with the World Since 1776*. Boston: Houghton Mifflin Company, 1997.

Reagan, Ronald. "Address to Members of British Parliament." *Ronald Reagan Presidential Library & Museum*. National Archives and Records Administration. June 8, 1982. Accessed October 9, 2016. https://reaganlibrary.gov/archives/speeches/30-archives/spe eches/1982/1349–60882a.

Reagan, Ronald. "Veterans of Foreign Wars Convention." *Ronald Reagan Presidential Library and Museum*. National Archives and Records Administration. August 18, 1980. Accessed Oct. 1, 2016. https://reaganlibrary.archives.gov/archives/reference/8.18.80.html.

"Remembering Robin Williams." *The Julliard Journal*. September 2014. Accessed September 20, 2016. http://www.juilliard.edu/journal/1409/obituary-robin-williams.

"Review: Moscow on the Hudson." *Variety*. December 31, 1983. Accessed August 25, 2016. http://variety.com/1983/film/reviews/moscow-on-the-hudson-1200426042/.

Schickel, Richard. "Motormouth in Saigon." *Time*, December 28, 1987: 130, no. 26. http://con tent.time.com/time/magazine/article/0,9171,966337,00.html.

Shaw, Tony. *Hollywood's Cold War*. Amherst: University of Massachusetts Press, 2007.

Shaw, Tony, and Denise J. Youngblood. *Cinematic Cold War: The American and Soviet Struggle for Hearts and Minds*. Lawrence, Kansas: University Press of Kansas, 2010.

Suid, Lawrence H. *Guts & Glory: The Making of the American Military Image in Film*. Lexington, KY: University Press of Kentucky, 2002.

Toplin, Robert Brent. *Reel History: In Defense of Hollywood*. Lawrence, KS: University Press of Kansas, 2002.

Williams, Robin. *Good Morning, Vietnam*. Directed by Barry Levinson, 1987. Burbank, CA: Buena Vista Home Entertainment, 2006. DVD.

Williams, Robin. *Moscow on the Hudson*. Directed by Paul Mazursky, 1984. Minnentonka, MN: Mill Creek Entertainment, 2014. DVD.

"Fosse! Fosse! Fosse!"

Robin Williams's Queer Performances

GAEL SWEENEY

With his outsized, over-the-top stand-up routines and comic perform-ances, Robin Williams was never afraid to veer into camp and even overtly queer portrayals, especially in his film roles. His skewed comic sensibilities invite queer readings of many of his 'straight' roles and inform his openly gay ones. Williams was one of the few A-List actors who never hesitated to take on overly queer characters, both comic and dramatic. I'd like to look at the development of his queer personas on film, examining his campy per-formances in *Mrs. Doubtfire* and *The Birdcage*, and his later, more serious portrayals of troubled gay and closeted men in *The Night Listener*, and his final filmed role, *Boulevard*.

The Flamboyant Body

In his early stand-up routines and his first sitcom, *Mork & Mindy,* Robin Williams brought a camp sensibility to mainstream audiences. Camp is a flamboyant, and highly referential style of queer performance, but the straight Williams adapted the most outrageous aspects of camp to his highly individ-ualistic comic persona. Williams's stand-up act was characterized by an improvisational style that featured free-flowing wordplay, manic movement, constantly changing voices and impressions, and rapid-fire pop culture ref-erences, both iconic and obscure.

Playing the off-the-wall alien Mork from Ork (who first appeared in a guest role on *Happy Days* in 1978 before starring in the sitcom *Mork & Mindy* from 1978 to 1982) gave Williams the opportunity to indulge his frenetic performance style and introduce it to a national television audience. Mork is a creature of pure id who says anything that comes into his head and acts upon every impulse. Because he is not human, he has agency that ordinarily would be denied to a heterosexual white male in the 1970s. He has the uninhibited and flamboyant body and voice usually connected in mid–20th century culture with gay men. In this way Mork is queer, if not recognizably a "fag": he's an alien, literally from another world that is far removed from mainstream America. His body is uncensored and his language full of double-entendres that would not have made it to broadcast if said by any other straight, white, male character. Mork, in his end-of-the-episode talks with his Orkan superior, the unseen Orson, critiques the actions of Earthlings as the ultimate outsider: human foibles and prejudices are revealed, as well as the ominous condition of a backward backwater of a planet. Mork, as an alien, also uses his body in a non-straight manner. He takes queer pleasure in using his body-parts in ways for which they weren't intended, such as drinking through his finger, sitting in a chair head first, or wearing his clothes backwards. This backwards trope is expanded on in the show's final season when Mork demonstrates (sort of!) his heterosexuality by marrying roommate Mindy and having a child. But Mork and not Mindy is the one who lays the egg that hatches into baby Mearth (played by Williams's comedic idol, Jonathan Winters), revealing that Orkans are born old and their bodies then age backwards into childhood. It's not surprising that Williams revered Winters, an improvisational comedian from the 1960s whose decidedly "wacky" and flamboyant style included portrayals of effeminate men, obstinate children, and his most famous character, the drag performance of foul-mouthed old lady Maude Frikert. Winters used these stock characters, a range of voices, and random objects handed up from audience members to create surreal and often subversive bits that critiqued society and authority figures, a tactic that got him labeled as difficult and even crazy for his non-conformity, often making it hard for him to find work. Winters, who was bipolar and institutionalized a number of times (which he referred to as time spent in "The Zoo"), inspired Williams, who carried on this radical improvisational style, but found that much more success as attitudes towards nonconformity, sexuality, and the role of masculinity changed in the 1970s and beyond. Williams was able to take much of Winters's comic sensibility and flamboyance and carry it further than Winters had ever dared

Throughout his film career, Robin Williams played a number of "queer"— or "queerish"—characters. The title character in *Popeye* (1980), while enamored of Olive Oyl, is literally a living cartoon with more in common with the polymorphously perverse Genie of *Aladdin* (1992) or the penguin characters of *Happy Feet* (2006) than with any "straight" character in his film canon. The manic-depressive Parry of *The Fisher King* (1991) and the painfully inhibited Dr. Malcolm Sayer (based on gay writer and physician Oliver Sacks) are also outside the norms of traditional heterosexual masculinity, as are gay—coded cameo characters such as the Mime in *Shakes the Clown* (1991), John Jacob Jingleheimer Schmidt in *To Wong Foo, Thanks for Everything, Julie Newmar* (1995), or Osric in Kenneth Branagh's *Hamlet* (1996). But in four films Williams takes his flamboyant stand-up persona directly into roles that are either openly gay, or steeped in queerness.

Mrs. Doubtfire *(1993)*

Robin Williams's highest grossing starring role, with a box office of $411 million worldwide,[1] was also the film in which the flamboyant body is not simply displayed, but is the center of the narrative: *Mrs. Doubtfire*. Daniel Hillard is an actor and voice-over artist, his manic vocal style drawing on Williams's voices in successful animated films such as the Genie in Disney's *Aladdin*. But Daniel also difficult to work with, quitting his job after he's reprimanded for refusing to stick to the script in voicing a parrot who is shown smoking. Of course, Williams himself was infamous for going off-script in his animated roles, something that was actually built into his turns as the Genie in *Aladdin* and the *Happy Feet* films. Daniel's estranged wife, Miranda (Sally Field, in a thankless role of "straight woman" to Williams's uncontrolled antics), is a high-powered career woman, which means she's a humorless, stressed-out bitch for the majority of the film. After separating from Daniel, she begins a relationship with Stuart Dunmeyer (Pierce Brosnan) is in his best James Bondian romantic lead mode here, but he's also the unintentional "villain": he's uptight and represents the traditional masculine, but he's not at all a bad guy and he's good to Miranda and the children. He's also another "alien": like the Scottish-accented "Mrs. Doubtfire," he's from Great Britain, but with all the connotations of upper class privilege: Stu drives a Mercedes, belongs to exclusive clubs, and eats at expensive restaurants, all of which are beyond Daniel's means. As a rival for Miranda's affections, Stu is Daniel's worst nightmare.

But even more than the wish to win back his wife, is Daniel's desire to stay close to his children. Portrayed as an over-grown child himself, Daniel's immaturity and inability to control his impulses has separated him from his kids; as a father, he's a failure. Of course, this being a Robin Williams comedy, his solution to this separation is not to prove his fitness as a father in any mundane (i.e., "normal") way, but to transform himself into the female nanny his ex-wife is seeking to hire. And, of course, Daniel's gay brother, "Uncle" Frank (Harvey Fierstein), and his partner, "Aunt" Jack (Scott Capurro), are brilliant make-up artists, able to accomplish this overnight, making two gay men the chief allies in Daniel's transformation. "Make me a woman!" Daniel pleads, and Frank and Jack are only too happy to oblige. In the first of the many set-pieces that allow Williams to demonstrate his flamboyant body, Frank and Jack turn Daniel into various musical comedy divas, including Barbra Streisand, as they search for the perfect drag persona. The straight Daniel has no qualms about this transformation—his flamboyant body, the film suggests, can become a woman as easily as a man, all it takes is the right voice, the right dress, and the right make-up. In this masquerade, Daniel literally wears a latex mask that Frank crafts to convert him into Euphegenia Doubtfire.

But a funny thing happens when Mrs. Doubtfire takes over the household: Daniel seems to become a different person in drag—he becomes "Mrs. Doubtfire." "I know you're used to loosey goosey, but when I'm in the house, I'm in charge," she says, laying down the law. And unlike the "loosey goosey" and unreliable Daniel, the new nanny is a martinet, banning television, making the children mind their manners, do their homework, and share in household chores. This is the opposite of the "fun" style of parenting Daniel has always espoused, but is gratefully embraced by the uptight, controlling, and exhausted working mother, Miranda. The flamboyant Daniel and his philosophy is subsumed by the proper Euphegenia Doubtfire.

Williams's drag scenes are punctuated by pop songs that reference gender reversal or change, such as Frank Sinatra's "Luck Be a Lady" (during Daniel's "transition"), James Brown's "Papa's Got a Brand New Bag" ("Ain't no drag"), the Four Seasons' "Walk Like a Man," and the predictable "Dude Looks Like a Lady," by Aerosmith, during a montage that shows Mrs. Doubtfire displaying her "new" female body in various comic situations: playing soccer, cleaning the house, dancing, cooking lobsters like her role model, Julia Child (who she awkwardly resembles), playing air guitar with a broom, and beating up a purse-snatcher with her handbag. These montages aren't necessary scenes, but they show the audience what they came for: Robin Williams using his improvisational skills to indulge the flamboyant body outside of the film's actual narrative.

When Daniel finally "comes out" as Mrs. Doubtfire to the two older children, Lydia (Lisa Jakub) and Chris (Matthew Lawrence) they are shocked. They tell him that "I wish dad was here," to which Daniel replies: "I'm here, guys. Well … in some form." But they also worry that their father is cross-dressing for his own pleasure. He reassures them that it's all for their benefit and that "I don't go to Little Old Lady bars after work." Even in full drag, Daniel must reassure his children of his heterosexuality, even if we never see it demonstrated. Although Miranda is given a new love interest in Stuart, Daniel is not. Daniel even seems to lose interest in winning back Miranda once Stuart is firmly in her life. In *Mrs. Doubtfire*, Daniel's only enduring love affair is with his children.

Mrs. Doubtfire in general treats "real" (cisgendered) women (Miranda,

Daniel's two daughters, his landlady) as problematic, but Daniel in drag as Mrs. Doubtfire especially comes in for comic abuse. The female body as grotesque is central to the slapstick set pieces that anchor this picture: Mrs. Doubtfire's boobs catch on fire ("My first day as a woman and I'm getting hot flashes"), her face is covered with whipped cream, her body pummeled and pounded as if the forces of nature (or Daniel's maleness) were rebelling against her, especially in the "tea scene" where Mrs. Doubtfire is explained away to Daniel's nosy landlady, Mrs. Cheney (Polly Holliday) as his sister "Priscilla." In the restaurant scene that is the comic climax of the film, Daniel attempts to go back and forth from himself to Mrs. Doubtfire while having dinner with Miranda, Stu, and the kids, as well as with his new boss, television executive Jonathan Lundy (Robert Prosky), as the masquerade unravels.

When the truth of Daniel's masquerade is fully revealed, Miranda is furious at the deception and initiates a custody battle. The judge sides with traditional values and the Hillard family, as imperfect as it was pre–Mrs. Doubtfire. Clearly, the judge sees such "normal" families as under threat by queer forces. San Francisco might be a gay mecca in popular culture, but in court the nuclear heterosexual family prevails. "You've been able to fool a lot of people," says the judge, pointing out that Daniel's masquerade has been a "terrific performance by a very gifted actor," which is a perfect description of Robin Williams's own performance. But in the diegesis of *Mrs. Doubtfire*, the flamboyance and the success of his performance damns Daniel as a father in the eyes of the court and society: "Your lifestyle over the past few months has been very unorthodox, and I refuse to further subject three innocent children to your peculiar and potentially harmful behavior." Regardless of the fact that the children have benefited greatly not only from Mrs. Doubtfire's parenting skills, but from reconnecting with their father, the judge awards Miranda full custody, with Daniel allowed only supervised visitation, "Like I'm some sort of deviant." But flamboyant men who cross-dress, no matter what the reason, are "deviants" in straight society, even minutes away from the Castro.

Fortunately for the film's family-friendly narrative, Daniel's new job redeems and recuperates for normality both him and Mrs. Doubtfire. Daniel becomes the host of a new children's show, *Euphegenia's House*, which features a no-nonsense, but lovable nanny who offers children—and parents practical advice about how to navigate a difficult and often confusing world (with the help of a chimp puppet named "Kovacs"—an obvious Williams inside joke), Daniel uses his alter-ego not only to become a successful father himself, but to revive his acting career. It's the "*Tootsie* Effect" revisited: a man masquerading as a woman, even for a short time, learns how to become a better man. *Mrs. Doubtfire* suggests that the trappings of femininity—fake breasts, girdles, wigs, stockings, and high heels—are what makes a "true" woman, and that the best function of the feminine (and the flamboyant body) is to aid and guide straight men. As the reconciled Miranda tells Daniel, Mrs. Doubtfire "brought out the best in them—she brought out the best in you."

The reunion that closes the film is not the typical romantic comedy ending, with the separated couple seeing the error of their ways and happily reuniting. Instead, the ending is much queerer and also more realistic. Divorce is a fact of life for modern couples and modern children, as Euphegenia makes clear to sidekick Kovacs, but that doesn't mean love isn't there. Daniel and Miranda go on with their separate lives, but Daniel is allowed to see his children and take over some of the duties of his "predecessor," Euphegenia Doubtfire.

The Birdcage *(1996)*

The Birdcage is Mike Nichols's remake of the French hit of the late 1970s, *La Cage aux Folles*. The premise is pure farce, with a gay couple who own a drag club in South Beach attempting to pass as straight to assuage their son, who is engaged to the daughter of a homophobic politician. Robin Williams plays Armand Goldman, the biological father of Val (Dan Futterman), and the partner of Albert (Nathan Lane), the drag diva Starina, who has raised Val in the place of his long-absent biological mother, Katherine (Christine Baranski). Nichols originally envisioned Steve Martin as Armand and Williams as Albert/Starina, but when Martin dropped out of the project Williams switched to Armand because, according to writer Sarah Karlan, "having... starred in the film *Mrs. Doubtfire*, he decided he would rather play the more subdued role."[2] Of course, whether Armand is "subdued" remains to be seen, but it seems that Williams did not want *The Birdcage* to be viewed as a re-hash of his drag turn in the earlier film.

With Armand, Williams takes on his first fully gay character in a leading role, which in the mid-nineties was still seen as a risky move for a star, even a comic actor like Williams, although the relationship between Armand and Albert is filmed as overtly non-sexual, with their twenty-year bond demonstrated mainly by discreet hand-holding. Even so, Williams manages to use his flamboyant body and improvisational style to give Armand, the "straight-acting" partner, a distinctly queer sensibility. In Williams's performance, Armand tries to contain himself in acting as the "normalized" gay man to Albert/Starina's hysterical drag queen, but he fails constantly, letting the flamboyant body escape in moments of comic display. Armand thinks he can "pass" as straight, but his son Val shows him that he's as transparent in his way as Albert: he wears make-up, florid Hawaiian shirts, and gaudy gold jewelry tangled in his profuse chest hair, which might be acceptable in South Beach, but never to the right-wing father of his son's fiancée, Republican Senator Kevin Keeley (Gene Hackman). Armand might be "straight-acting," but only in the context of the over-the-top Miami culture of drag queens, Art Deco, and kitsch. He's also a Jew, which is yet another thing that separates Armand Goldman from Keeley and his ultra-conservative, intolerant ilk, the Coalition for Moral Order. Of course, the Coalition prove to be hypocrites when their founder turns up dead in the bed of an underage African-American prostitute. But to please his son for one night, Armand redecorates his house (removing all the penis statuary), changes his name to "Coleman," reinvents himself as the "Cultural Attaché to Greece," and even tries to banish his partner, who is a failure at acting even the least bit "normal," replacing him with Val's biological mother, all to impress the homophobic Keeleys.

Director Mike Nichols was well aware that in order to get the comic performances necessary for this kind of farce, he would have to allow both Williams and Nathan Lane (a gay actor also noted for his improvisational style) a certain amount of on-set experimentation, but with one caveat: he "required that Nathan Lane and Robin Williams film at least one take of each scene sticking to the script before he would allow them to improvise."[3] In these slapstick scenes, especially those involving Armand, Albert and their campy Guatemalan "maid" Agador (Hank Azaria), in the famous set-piece "toast scene," in which Armand instructs the even more flamboyant and flighty Albert how to act like "a man" and walk like John Wayne, and in the disastrous dinner with Senator Keeley and his wife (Dianne Wiest), where Albert, in "Barbara Bush" drag, attempts to pass himself off as Val's "mother," Williams's usually unfettered talents take a backseat/ There's great irony—but also great comedy—in watching Armand, a normally uninhibited gay man, desperately trying to suppress every instinct and play it "straight," which is exactly what Williams is doing himself.

But Williams's most notable turn in *The Birdcage*, and the one where his personal style is most evident, is the scene where he demonstrates "The History of Dance in Thirty Seconds,"[4] otherwise known as "Fosse! Fosse! Fosse!" When there is difficulty with Albert/Starina's stage show, Armand is called in to defuse the situation between Starina and her dance partner, a good-looking but dim hustler-type ("22 and hung") who chews bubble gum during rehearsal and is clueless about the true meaning of "Art."

"What do I do? Do I just stand there like an object?" he pouts, "You do an eclectic celebration of the dance!" says Armand, stepping into the void, "You do Fosse, Fosse, Fosse!" (slithering hips). "You do Martha Graham, Martha Graham, Martha Graham!" (extravagant gestures). "Or Twyla, Twyla, Twyla!" (dipping and thrusting) Or Michael Kidd, Michael Kidd, Michael Kidd, Michael Kidd!" (cowboy galloping). Or Madonna, Madonna, Madonna!" (Vogueing all the way). Then he adds, "But you keep it all inside...."

Thus Williams encapsulates contemporary dance in this "hilarious and now infamous"[5] moment. This short segment is the most popular *Birdcage* excerpt on YouTube, with over 70,000 viewings of the longest clip, as well as the most quoted of all the lines in the film.

While The "Fosse" dance is often referenced as one of the best examples of Williams's improvisational film style, it was unscripted, but not unchoreographed. Vincent Paterson, who had choreographed Madonna's "Vogue" performance on the MTV Music Awards and her Blond Ambition Tour, as well as numerous Michael Jackson videos, was brought in to do the drag dances in the club scenes, but was then called upon by Williams. Says Paterson:

> I had choreographed for Robin, Whoopi Goldberg and Billy Crystal for *Comic Relief* … (and) I had directed him in a Turner documentary on Dr. Seuss…. So during shooting, Robin pulled me aside and he said, "I'm so tired of playing the straight man. Everyone is getting laughs. It's driving me crazy"…. So on the next break we went behind the set wall and I said, "What about: The History of Dance in Thirty Seconds?"[6]

Mike Nichols was dubious about the bit, even though the crew was laughing, and told Williams that they should move on, Williams insisted he be allowed to do a few more takes, with no promise from Nichols, But the dance did make the final cut, "We never thought it would become what it has," says Paterson, "It's iconic." By honing in on the dance in the context of the drag show and calling out and imitating the icons of musical theater (Martha Graham! Bob Fosse! Twyla Tharp! Michael Kidd!) and video culture (Madonna!), Williams as Armand validates his credentials as a gay man and allows him to play the "gay" straight man, stealing the show in the manner expected by his fans.

The Night Listener *(2006) and* Boulevard *(2014)*

In the late films *The Night Listener* and *Boulevard*, his final on-screen starring role, Williams plays gay men, one out and one deeply closeted. These are dark films, both literally and thematically: they take place mainly at night and in the shadows and deal with the protagonists' late-in-life crises. In these two films Williams's flamboyant body and typical camp humor are nowhere to be to found. Instead, we see older, troubled, and searching characters.

The Night Listener's Gabriel Noone is based on writer Armistead Maupin and an actual experience he had with a fan, Anthony Godby Johnson who turned out to be something other than claimed. Noone, who hosts an all-night radio talk show, "No one at Night," is facing the break-up of his long-term relationship and re-examining his life as a gay man. He becomes obsessed with a caller to his show, a young boy who has suffered unspeakable sexual abuse and is now dying of AIDS. The film is described as a psychological thriller, but even more it seems to be about the internal struggle of an ageing gay man facing the loss of his sexual power and the choices he's made in his life. Gabriel reaches out to his late-night listeners in ways he cannot in his real life, and especially not with his estranged partner, Jess (Bobby Cannavale), Pete Logand, a 14-year-old boy with AIDS represents all of Gabriel's fears and hopes: he's suffered hideous damage to his body and psyche, yet he's smart (he's written a memoir about his abuse), funny and resilient, exactly the kind of heroic survivor Gabriel needs to believe in at this point in his life. Unfortunately, it seems that Pete is also imaginary, the creation of a deeply disturbed woman, Donna (Toni Collette) who craves the attention "Pete" brings her.

Gabriel decides to find Pete and prove that he really exists, especially to prove it to Jess and his personal assistant, Anna (Sandra Oh), which leads him to a small Wisconsin town and increasing paranoia. Donna, who is blind (perhaps), plays on Gabriel's expectations and desperate desire to believe that Pete is real, leading to Gabriel being arrested. But except in shadowy calls and video tapes, Pete (Rory Culkin) remains elusive, always out of Gabriel's sight and reach, In the end, the only way Gabriel can make sense of "Pete" is to recreate his story for his "night listeners" and move on with his life, alone.

Williams's performance style in this film is the opposite of flamboyant; the only thing queer about his characterization of Gabriel Noone is the presence of his lover, Jess, and even then their relationship is distant and non-physical. Rather than the initiator of the action, Gabriel is a passive figure, frantically chasing phantoms through dark woodlands and being manipulated, both on the radio and in person, by Donna, whose motives remain inexplicable. The film is unsettling, not because of Gabriel's sexuality or Williams's performance, but because it lacks a center: Pete. We never understand exactly why Gabriel is so obsessed with this ghost-boy, to the detriment of his real-life relationship––Jess believes Pete is a fake almost from the start— only that he seems a manifestation of Gabriel's late-life crisis. Williams's flamboyant body seems exhausted, literally running in circles, to no particular end except to perpetuate the story and the mystery.

If the flamboyant body is exhausted in *The Night Listener*, in *Boulevard*, it's completely played out and beaten down. Nolan Mack works in a bank and is in a childless marriage with Joy (Kathy Baker), a woman whose only dream is to go on a luxury cruise, with or without her diffident husband. What Nolan's dream is isn't certain, but he cruises the city streets at night, looking for … something else. He finally finds that something in Leo (Roberto Aguire), a skinny street hustler badly in need of rescuing, mainly from his abusive pimp, Eddie (Giles Mathey), who calls him "Princess" and demands more and more money from him, and, eventually, from Nolan. Leo is the object of Nolan's desire, but only through the gaze: Nolan hires Leo and takes him to a motel, but only to look at and talk to, never to touch.

Nolan's father (Gary Gardner) is semi-comatose, dying in a nursing home, so Nolan feels safe in confiding in him about his sexuality and confessing that although he knew he was gay when he was 12 years old, now, in his 60s, he still can't admit it. He can't be honest to his wife Joy: she's distant and puzzled by him, especially after his encounters with Leo cause him to stay out late and become erratic at work, something he's never done before. They watch television together, but Nolan constantly checks his Blackberry, looking for messages from Leo. He attempts to establish a relationship with the hustler, apparently unaware that he's not only a prostitute, but also a drug addict. He takes Leo out to dinner at an expensive restaurant, but has to explain him away to his boss. Nolan is also beaten by Leo's pimp when he attempts to come to his rescue once again, leading to more questions from Joy and his boss, who understand that something troubling is happening to Nolan, but are unsure of what to do about it.

"How come we don't do more?" Leo asks, mystified about his benefactor's intentions. Nolan recoils from Leo's attempts to have sex, telling him that "Sometimes it's nice to be somewhere else." But where is that "somewhere else"? The film, like Leo, seems unsure of what Nolan really wants. Leo disappears, Nolan and Joy separate, and we see Nolan meeting someone who might be a new relationship, but that air of uncertainty and melancholy remains. In the final scene of *Boulevard*, Williams speaks his last words on screen as an actor: "I drove down a street one night, a street I didn't know. That's the way life goes sometimes. Drive down this one, and another. And now ... another."

The journeys of Gabriel and Nolan follow similar paths. Both men are in denial about their lives and find that as they age they can no longer continue the way they are. Their sexuality is in crisis: Gabriel with the breakup of his relationship and Nolan with coming to terms with his homosexuality and the breakdown of his marriage. Both chase an idealized connection with a younger character who is a projection of everything they desire and have suppressed. Both are also physically abused in their quest: Gabriel is beaten by police who mistake him for a dangerous stalker, while Nolan is beaten by Leo's pimp. These assault force the men to understand the depths their own delusions and to face the consequences of reality; Gabriel must admit that Pete is a hoax and go on without his partner, while Nolan must give up the ideal of Leo and learn to live the rest of his life as a gay man.

In these late films Robin Williams's body is no longer pliant and unpredictable, no longer full of exuberant joy. He's older and heavier, his characters weighed down with grief and confusion. The flamboyant body of most of Williams's career has been tamed and subdued. These gay men are at the end of their familiar lives, but both films also promise new beginnings and new understandings of their own natures, with Gabriel realizing that he can move on without his partner, and Nolan leaving his marriage and job to explore his late-in-life coming out.

Gabriel and Nolan are looking for impossible human connections, in *The Night Listener* with a dying child, in *Boulevard* with the young hustler; both are lost, imaginary figures, boys who represent wasted chances and unfulfilled desires. While the younger men of *Mrs. Doubtfire* and *The Birdcage* are both biological fathers who must find a way to deal with their roles as parents outside the conventional rules of society, the older men of *The Night Listener* and *Boulevard* look for a different connection with "sons" who are unavailable, elusive figures of fantasy *Mrs. Doubtfire* and *The Birdcage*, as family-oriented comedies, end with the reconciliation of Daniel and Armand with their children and the hope of renewed and redefined relationships. But *The Night Listener* and *Boulevard* have much more somber resolutions. Thwarted dreams have forced the ageing Gabriel and Nolan to reinvent themselves in ways that are painful, but necessary, in a world in which the lives of gay men are changing swiftly and inevitably.

NOTES

1. Julia Boorstin and Matthew J. Belvedere, "Robin Williams—The $5B Man at the Box Office," *CNBC*, August 12, 2014. http://www.cnbc.com/2014/08/12/robin-williamsthe-5b-man-at-the-box-office.html

2. Sarah Karlan, "19 Things You Didn't Know About *The Birdcage*," *BuzzFeed*, January 13, 2014. http://www.buzzfeed.com/skarlan/19-things-you-didnt-know-about-the-movie-the-birdcage#.ppLKXmNxGV

3. *Ibid.*

4. Debra Levine, "How *Birdcage* Choreographer Vince Paterson Created 'Fosse Fosse Fosse' Number," *arts meme*, November 24, 2014. http://artsmeme.com/2014/11/24/vince-pa terson-birdcage-choreographer-remembers-mike-nichols-robin-williams/

5. *Ibid.*

6. *Ibid.*

BIBLIOGRAPHY

Allen, Mark. "Bruce LaBruce's New Take on Susan Sontag's 1964 Essay 'Notes on Camp,'" *Gay Voices: Huffington Post*, May 13, 2013. http://www.huffingtonpost.com/mark-allen/bruce-labruce-camp_b_3230251.html

Babuscio, Jack. "Camp and the Gay Sensibility," in *Camp Grounds: Style and Homosexuality*, David Bergman, ed., Amherst: University of Massachusetts, 1993.

Boorstin, Julia, and Matthew J. Belvedere. "Robin Williams—The $5B Man at the Box Office," *CNBC*, August 12, 2014. http://www.cnbc.com/2014/08/12/robin-williamsthe-5b-man-at-the-box-office.html

Bradley, Bill. "Robin Williams' Deleted *Mrs. Doubtfire* Scenes Will Make You Cry," *Huffington Post*, February 11, 2016. http://www.huffingtonpost.com/entry/robin-williams-mrs-doubtfire-deleted-scenes_us_56bc9fd8e4b08ffac12408b5

Breznican, Anthony. "Remembering Robin Williams: The *Mrs. Doubtfire* Sequel That Almost Was," *Entertainment Weekly*, August 11, 2015. http://www.ew.com/article/2015/08/11/remembering-robin-williams-mrs-doubtfire-sequel-almost-was

Coates, Tyler. "Was It Good for the Gays?: *The Birdcage*," *Decider*, November 5, 2014 http://decider.com/2014/11/05/was-it-good-for-the-gays-the-birdcage/

Cormier, Roger. "16 Sure Facts About *Mrs. Doubtfire*," *Mental Floss*, September 17, 2016. http://mentalfloss.com/article/71451/16-sure-facts-about-mrs-doubtfire

Dunning, Jennifer. "*The Birdcage*: Reaping a Robin Williams Whirlwind," *New York Times*, March 31, 1996. http://www.nytimes.com/1996/03/31/movies/film-reaping-a-robin-williams-whirlwind.html

Emerson, Jim. "Movie Review: *The Night Listener* (2006)," RogerEbert.com, August 3, 2006. http://www.rogerebert.com/reviews/the-night-listener-2006

Emery, Mark. "*Mrs. Doubtfire*: 10 Fun Facts about the Robin Williams Hit 22 Years After Its Release," *New York Daily News*, November 24, 2015. http://www.nydailynews.com/entertainment/movies/10-fun-mrs-doubtfire-facts-22-years-release-article-1.2445526

Fairfax-Owen, Shyla. "10 of the Highest Grossing Robin Williams Films," *The Richest*, August 20, 2014. http://www.therichest.com/expensive-lifestyle/entertainment/10-of-the-highest-grossing-robin-williams-films/

Farmer, Jim. "Robin Williams Plays Gay in Final On-screen Film Role," *Georgia Voice: Gay & LGBT Atlanta*, July 23, 2014. http://thegavoice.com/robin-williams-plays-gay-in-final-on-screen-film-role/

Goodman, Elyssa. "How *The Birdcage* Married Jewish and Civil Rights," *The Forward*, January 29, 2016. http://forward.com/culture/film-tv/332144/how-the-birdcage-married-jewish-and-gay-civil-rights/

Hartl, John. "*Boulevard*: Robin Williams' Portrait of a Repressed Man," *Seattle Times*, July 30, 2015. http://www.seattletimes.com/entertainment/movies/boulevard-robin-williams-portrait-of-a-repressed-man/

Hollywood.com Staff. "The Bizarre True Story Behind the Plot of *The Night Listener*," Hollywood.com, 2006. http://www.hollywood.com/general/the-bizarre-true-story-behind-the-plot-of-the-night-listener-57171900/

Jean, Eric, and Daniel J. Rowe. "And Robin Williams as Osric. Wait. Who Is Osric?" *The Bard Brawl*, August 13, 2014. https://bardbrawl.com/2014/08/13/and-robin-williams-as-osric-wait-who-is-osric/

Juzwiak, Rich. "*Boulevard*, Robin Williams's Bittersweet Final Onscreen Role," *Defamer*, July 8, 2015. http://defamer.gawker.com/boulevard-robin-williamss-bittersweet-final-onscreen-r-1716477260

Karlan, Sarah. "19 Things You Didn't Know About *The Birdcage*," *BuzzFeed*, January 13, 2014. http://www.buzzfeed.com/skarlan/19-things-you-didnt-know-about-the-movie-the-birdcage#.ppLKXmNxGV

Kauffmann, Stanley. "*Awakenings*: This Was Robin Williams' Best Non-Comic Performance," *The New Republic*, August 12, 2014. http://www.newrepublic.com/article/119054/robin-williams-dead-63-stanley-kauffman-awakenings-review

K.J. "Who Killed Osric in Kenneth Branagh's *Hamlet*?" *Bardfilm*, March 24, 2010. http://bardfilm.blogspot.com/2010/03/who-killed-osric-in-branaghs-hamlet.html

Kohn, Mitch. "Op-Ed: The Amazing Story Behind *To Wong Foo*," *The Advocate*, August 13, 2015. http://www.advocate.com/commentary/2015/08/13/op-ed-amazing-story-behind-wong-foo

LaBruce, Bruce. "Notes on Camp/Anti-Camp," NatBrut.com, 2012. http://www.natbrut.com/essay-notes-on-campanti-camp-by-bruce-labruce.html

Lambe, Stacy. "Robin Williams Struggles with Being Gay in One of His Final Roles," Out.com, August 8, 2014. http://www.out.com/entertainment/movies/2014/08/19/robin-williams-struggles-being-gay-one-his-final-roles

Lang, Nico. "After *The Birdcage*, Hollywood Shoved Gay Comedies Back in the Closet," *The A.V. Club*, May 9, 2016. http://www.avclub.com/article/after-birdcage-hollywood-shoved-gay-comedies-back-234273

Larsen, Sarah. "Robin Williams: The Best Weirdo," *The New Yorker*, August 12, 2014. http://www.newyorker.com/culture-desk/sarah-larson/robin-williams-best-weirdo

Levine, Debra. "How *Birdcage* Choreographer Vince Paterson Created 'Fosse Fosse Fosse' Number," *arts meme*, November 24, 2014. http://artsmeme.com/2014/11/24/vince-paterson-birdcage-choreographer-remembers-mike-nichols-robin-williams/

_____. "Robin Williams' 'Eclectic Celebration of the Dance' in *The Birdcage*," *arts meme*, May 6, 2012. http://artsmeme.com/2012/05/06/robin-williams-eclectic-celebration-of-the-dance-in-the-birdcage/

Linden, Sheri. "In His Final Lead Role, Robin Williams Boldly Underplays the Timid Tale of *Boulevard*," *Los Angeles Times*, July 16, 2015. http://www.latimes.com/entertainment/movies/la-et-mn-boulevard-movie-review-20150717-story.html

Lowder, J. Bryan. "The Missed Opportunity of *Boulevard*," *Slate Outward*, July 22, 2015. http://www.slate.com/blogs/outward/2015/07/22/robin_williams_final_film_boulevard_reviewed.html

_____. "Postcards from Camp: Is Camp Just for Gay Men?" *Slate*, April 18, 2013. http://www.slate.com/articles/arts/culturebox/features/2013/postcards_from_camp/is_camp_just_for_gay_men.html

_____. "Postcards from Camp: There's a Big Difference Between Camp and Campy," *Slate*, April 1, 2013. http://www.slate.com/articles/arts/culturebox/features/2013/postcards_from_camp/camp_and_campy_there_s_a_big_difference.html

Marfil, Hannah Raissa. "Robin Williams Played Closeted Gay Man in Final Film *Boulevard*," *International Business Times*, July 16, 2015. http://www.ibtimes.com/robin-williams-played-closeted-gay-man-final-film-boulevard-2011812

May, Elaine, Foreword by Mike Nichols. *The Birdcage: The Shooting Script*. New York: The Newmarket Press, 1997.

Meyer, Moe, ed. *The Politics and Poetics of Camp*. New York: Routledge, 1994.

Miller, Richard. "Q&A: Armistead Maupin: The Author Discusses *The Night Listener*," ArmisteadMaupin.com, August 7, 2006. http://armisteadmaupin.com/blog/?p=338

Murray, Rebecca. "Exclusive Interview with Critically Acclaimed Author Armistead Maupin," *About Entertainment*, 2006. http://movies.about.com/od/thenightlistener/a/maupin080206.htm

O'Hehir, Andrew. "*Boulevard*: In Robin Williams' Tormented Final Role, the Beloved Star Still Doesn't Know What He's Looking For," Salon.com, July 8, 2015. http://www.salon.com/2015/07/08/boulevard_in_robin_williams_tormented_final_role_the_beloved_star_still_doesnt_know_what_hes_looking_for/

_____. "Robin Williams' inexhaustible comic force: An eccentric, electric performer who fought his demons on-screen," Salon.com, August 12, 2014. http://www.salon.com/2014/08/12/rip_robin_williams_an_eccentric_electric_performer_who_fought_his_demons_onscreen/

Peeples, Jase. "Final Film Starring Robin Williams as a Gay Man May Not Be Released," *The Advocate*, October 24, 2014. http://www.advocate.com/arts-entertainment/film/2014/10/26/final-film-starring-robin-williams-gay-man-may-not-be-released

Phillips, Michael. "Truth Obscured by Shadow in Engaging *Night Listener*," *Chicago Tribune*, August 4, 2006. http://articles.chicagotribune.com/2006-08-04/entertainment/0608040230_1_night-listener-well-acted-picture-anthony-godby-johnson

"Remembering Robin Williams: His Best LGBT Roles," *Pink News*, August 11, 2015. http://www.pinknews.co.uk/2015/08/11/remembering-robin-williams-his-best-lgbt-roles/

"Robin Williams Box Office," *Box Office Mojo*, December 13, 2016. http://www.boxofficemojo.com/people/chart/?id=robinwilliams.htm

Ross, Andrew. *No Respect: Intellectuals and Popular Culture*. New York: Routledge, 1989.

Sontag, Susan. "Notes on Camp (1964)," *A Susan Sontag Reader*. New York: Vintage, 1983: 105–19. (Reprinted from *Against Interpretation*.)

Tracer, Dan. "Irreplaceable: A Look Back at Robin Williams' Gayest Moments," *Qweerty*, August 12, 2014. https://www.queerty.com/a-look-back-at-robin-williams-gayest-moments-20140812

Tucker, Karen Iris. "Celebrating the Birdcage, 20 Years Later," *Slate Outward*, March 7, 2016. http://www.slate.com/blogs/outward/2016/03/07/revisiting_the_birdcage_on_its_20th_anniversary.html

Zuckerman, Esther. "*The Birdcage* Then and Now: How Much Has Changed Since *The Birdcage* Came Out?" *Refinery 29*, March 8, 2016. http://www.refinery29.com/2016/03/105324/the-birdcage-then-and-now#slide

PART 2

Dark Spirits

Essays on Politics, Everyman and the Universe

"Watch out for the terrible, the ugly undertoad"

The World's End According to Garp

PHILIP L. SIMPSON

The World According to Garp (1982), directed by George Roy Hill and based on John Irving's best-selling 1978 novel, is an early starring vehicle and first dramatic role for Robin Williams as the titular Garp, an Everyman figure on a picaresque journey through a funhouse-mirror version of the American cultural scene of the 1970s and early 1980s. *The World According to Garp* (hereinafter referred to as *Garp* for brevity's sake) as film is critical in any understanding of Williams's journey from comedian to an actor who could inhabit both comic and dramatic worlds effortlessly, often simultaneously in the same film. T.S. Garp is the role that set Williams on this journey. It is hard to imagine how any other of Williams's contemporaries could have pulled off Hill's darkly comic vision so well.

Critics who were otherwise lukewarm to, if not outright dismissive of, the film found depth in Williams they were not expecting, even if they found his performance uneven. Typical is Janet Maslin, who writes that "Mr. Williams is at his most affecting with the children; he makes a fond, playful father…. His performance is engaging but erratic, more effective in the clownier, busier scenes than in those that ask him to recite lines or stand still."[1] For what it's worth, John Irving is on record as approving of Williams's casting, even if Irving's words imply some initial doubt about the decision and include the following humorous anecdote about the suspension of disbelief required to accept Williams as a teenager in the earlier part of the film: "George [Roy Hill] was right to have faith in Robin Williams; Robin was an excellent Garp."[2] The actor's origins as a West Coast stand-up comedian, including his starring role in the highly rated *Mork & Mindy* (1978–1982) television series, serve

100

him well in capturing the dark humor director Hill was known for in earlier films such as *Butch Cassidy and the Sundance Kid* (1969), which also went against type in a different direction by casting "serious" actors Paul Newman and Robert Redford in essentially comic roles. Indeed, Wes D. Gehring, in drawing a parallel between *Butch Cassidy* and *Garp*, notes that Hill "seems drawn to empathetic characters fated to die in dark comedies" and argues that Garp's philosophy of the tragicomic nature of life as stated in Irving's novel—"people's problems are often funny and that the people are often and nonetheless sad"—summarizes Hill's brand of dark comedy as well.[3] Andrew Horton argues that, in spite of some controversy attending Hill's selection of Williams, this selection demonstrates how "Hill was purposely lightening up the character of Garp while simultaneously holding Williams down from his usual comic antics and drawing forth from him a performance of substance."[4] The story's various tragedies allow Williams to restrain his over-the-top comic persona and show the dramatic chops that would later be put to such good use in dramas (or dramedies) such as *Good Morning, Vietnam* (1987) and *Dead Poets Society* (1989).

Williams's death by suicide in 2014 compelled a critical reexamination of his roles both dramatic and comic, not the least of which is a search for possible clues as to why such a beloved figure would take his own life. During the week following Williams's death, for example, blogger Lois Alter Mark immediately turned to Williams's role in *Garp* and singled out the Undertoad, an imaginary man-eating sea monster in Garp's son's imagination, as the movie's prime metaphor for a free-floating sense of anxiety or even danger in one's daily life.[5] The violent events of the movie, in the form of vicious dogs or vehicle crashes or mutilation or assassins or the undertow that Garp's youngest son Walt (Ian MacGregor) mishears as "Undertoad," threaten (and in some cases claim) the lives of Garp and his family at practically every step. This kind of extreme violence as encapsulated in the Undertoad is emblematic of the more quotidian hazards facing Garp and his family, and thus by implication all of us in the modern American age: war, social or political conflict, misogyny, alienation, obscurity, anger, resentment, depression, illness, random accidents, unchecked lust, and infidelity. Any or all of these elements can at any moment shatter, if not destabilize, the artifice of normality (stable family life, for example) so painstakingly constructed over time, a fate which befalls both Garp and Williams. The Undertoad eventually claims all.

Within the context of both Irving's novel and the film, the Undertoad becomes the harbinger of doom in Garp's world, a devouring beast of the apocalypse specifically cited by name by his sons just before Walt's death by car accident—the most cataclysmic event in the Garp family life and one wrought by the cumulative infidelities of Garp and his wife, Helen Holm Garp (Mary Beth Hurt). But as tragic as this disaster is, it ushers in a new familial understanding and reconciliation between Garp, Helen, and their surviving son Duncan (Nathan Babcock). The apocalypse is not meaningless, or if it is, the irrepressibly optimistic Garp invests it with meaning anyway. In the sense that the landmark violent events in Garp's life accompany or unveil heretofore hidden (and typically unpleasant) truths and presage the passing of one era of his life into another new and more enlightened age, one can say that the violence is personally apocalyptic. With apologies to John Irving for taking an instructive liberty with his title, one may, from this perspective, think of the movie as telling the story of *The World's End According to Garp*.

If *Garp* is a text that incorporates apocalyptic ideas, then it is necessary to define what is meant by "apocalyptic." In the words of John J. Collins, apocalypse as a literary (or cinematic) genre must be distinguished from "apocalypticism as a social ideology, and apocalyptic eschatology as a set of ideas and motifs that may also be found in other literary genres and social settings."[6] In other words, as Klaus Koch is among the first to argue, one must differentiate between the "apocalyptic as a literary type" and the "apocalyptic as a historical movement."[7] For scholars, the apocalyptic genre, as well as other apocalyptic movements in culture and history, arises from the attempt of humanity to, as Stephen D. O'Leary puts it, "imagine and predict the end of time. Every culture that has developed a myth of its divine and cosmological origin has sought to peer ahead toward its own ending."[8] O'Leary further argues that the human tendency to view history in terms of inevitable decline (in morals, particularly) from some imagined previous high point is a manifestation of the apocalyptic mindset imagining humanity's own end.[9] The word "apocalypse" itself, according to O'Leary, is "a Greek word meaning revelation or unveiling," so the apocalyptic tradition in Judeo-Christian culture is "discourse that reveals or makes manifest a vision of ultimate destiny, rendering immediate to human audiences the ultimate End of the cosmos in the Last Judgement."[10] As the last part of O'Leary's definition makes clear, the Western apocalyptic tradition is rooted in religious imagery and language.

However, scholars have also noted in the more recent apocalyptic tradition a movement away from notions of divine intervention in human affairs. This reconceptualization is what enables us to think of a secular twentieth-century text such as *Garp* as apocalyptic. Contemporary scholars typically approach this problem of apocalyptic ontology from somewhere on a spectrum between a religiously based understanding of apocalypse and a more secular one. A scholar such as John J. Collins, for instance, belongs in the former camp, with his insistence that supernatural forces, divine intervention in human affairs, and a punishment/reward system in the afterlife must be present in the text for it to be called truly apocalyptic. He succinctly argues that "If we say that a work is apocalyptic we encourage the reader to expect that it frames its message within the view of the world that is characteristic of the genre."[11] Somewhere in the middle of the spectrum is Conrad E. Ostwalt, who argues that in modern culture the ancient legacy of apocalyptic themes and elements still resonates, albeit in a form typically stripped down if not entirely scrubbed of its supernatural, other-worldly trappings and evincing a contemporary secular sensibility even in the face of global or localized catastrophe. In other words, he contends, "popular culture has co-opted what was the religious business of apocalyptic thinking.... Popular movies have taken up the charge and created an alternative secular apocalyptic imagination in which the end is less threatening and can even be avoided."[12] The cataclysm, or the End, loses its more metaphysical dimension to become a secularized or societal cataclysm, in which the world or a society (or even an individual) representative of that world either ends or is threatened with an end. Elizabeth K. Rosen, noting the enduring fascination of apocalyptic fantasy in our collective (and desperate) attempt to glean meaning from a world that "sometimes appears to be coming apart at its economic, political, and social seams," concludes that apocalyptic literature brings comfort to "people whose lives are, or who perceive their lives to be, overwhelmed by historical or social disruption."[13] It is this notion of apocalyptic disruption which most clearly applies to a work such as *Garp*.

First, *Garp* explores the anxieties of late twentieth century America, particularly those related to rapidly changing conceptions of gender and identity. Garp as a character negotiates a life-long treacherous path through a tumultuously shifting societal landscape in which traditional categories of masculinity and femininity are in flux and the world as men and women know it is ending, though an inchoate new world whose contours can just be seen through a glass darkly is on the rise from the ruins of the old.[14] Each violent or dangerous event in Garp's life is in one way or another predicated upon the tensions between the women in his life and himself reaching the boiling point. A few representative examples include: When Garp as a boy (James McCall) nearly falls from the dorm roof, he has just told his mother he needs a father, which his mother flatly denies. Garp is attacked by the dog Bonkers during his first sexual encounter with his neighbor Cushie (Jillian Ross as "Young Cushie" and Jenny Wright as "Grown Cushie"). When a later sexual encounter with Cushie creates the first relationship crisis between Garp and Helen, Garp attacks Bonkers. At the lowest point of the marriage between Garp and Helen, a car crash nearly kills them. These events serve as the crucible through which Garp advances to not only a new phase of his life (childhood, adolescence, young single adulthood, marriage and fatherhood, early death) but a new understanding. In this sense, then, the apocalypse is relocated from some metaphysical judgment or world-ending calamity to the contested site of the fraught relationships between men and women. The Garpian apocalypse, if you will, is an example of what in another context Andrew Hewitt calls the "practical apocalypse, physical and partial rather than totalizing and transcendent."[15] The specter of a personally violent, limited apocalypse in fictional texts such as *Garp* may be considered as a way of culturally constructing an imaginative experimental space in which not only to dramatize signature concerns of the contemporary historical moment but also to show their violent, world-reshaping (if not world-ending) consequences upon the individual during an age of societal upheaval.

From this perspective, then, the apocalypse in *Garp* illuminates much about the otherwise unexpressed or secret longings, anxieties, and terrors in the larger culture. Implicit in the concept of apocalypse, at least as it is commonly understood today, is a blasting away or leveling of social artifice and constructions to lay bare certain essential truths. One of those truths is that civilization, as much as the individual life, is fragile beyond one's worst imaginings. In the story of *Garp*, for instance, Garp begins his life as literally the last act of a dying World War II tail gunner, Technical Sergeant Garp. All that remains following his terrible injury (the first of many such mutilations in the story) is his remaining instinctual drive to mate, a war-inflicted priapism that Jenny Fields (Glenn Close) exploits to conceive Garp in the only way open to her to have a child without being burdened by a man who will be around to lay claim to either her body or her baby. Arguably, then, the world of Garp the future writer is one conceived in one of the most cataclysmic events in human history. Through the circumstances of Garp's life, sexual reproduction and art and death are inseparable for him. The positive life of artistic creation he attempts to construct for himself, though seemingly far removed from war and death, is perennially threatened by violence because in its very DNA it is bitter fruit borne from a truly global conflict. Even Garp's name—T.S. Garp—is not just the name of his father, but also an allusion to the poet T.S. Eliot, whose modernist (and apocalyptic) poem "The Wasteland" (1922) provides a thematic template for many of *Garp*'s central concerns: rape, dead fathers, a blighted modern world wrecked by war, and a country full of the wounded who can never heal.

The world of Garp, so spontaneously joyous and zestful on the surface, is a sublimely terrifying, dangerous wasteland ever poised to obliterate Garp. As Andrew Horton puts it, what director Walter Hill "has managed to capture in his version of Garp even more convincingly than in Irving's novel is the intensity between the security Garp seeks and the flux and danger of the world and society around him…. The world according to Garp is drowned out by other worlds pressing in on the environment he would like to stake out and inhabit."[16] Drowning, or the potential for it, pervades the narrative. The sounds of the ocean waves on the shores of Jenny's property drown out the dialogue in the opening scene when Jenny tells her parents how Garp was conceived. Many shots of the ocean waves washing onto the beach punctuate the most symbolically poignant of the scenes, notably when Garp's doomed son Walt, replicating his father's journey into that same ocean, enters the water. A few scenes later, on a rainy night which makes Walt feel like he is underwater, he dies in the car crash. In a later scene, Garp stares apprehensively over that same ocean vista, sensing that his mother's appearance at a political rally will result in her death. The ocean, home of the Undertoad, is the film's ubiquitous signifier of death.

Even flying, a source of great comfort to Garp because of his romanticized vision of his dead father, is associated with disaster. Probably the best scene illustrative of that point occurs when the newly married Garp and Helen, inspecting a house for sale with a realtor who does not recognize him as an author in his own right but as "the bastard son of Jenny Fields," have to duck to avoid being killed by an out-of-control small airplane that crashes into the side of the house. Garp, far from being shaken by the experience, exclaims to Helen and the realtor that this is going to be his and Helen's home: "The odds of another plane hitting this house are astronomical. It's been pre-disastered. We'll be safe here." His pronouncement of safety proves to be tragically naïve, given that disaster will indeed strike the house later in the form of the car crash that kills Walt.

In that Garp's personal world is inundated and ultimately destroyed by larger social forces, which the out-of-control crashing plane symbolizes, his personal doomsday is representative of the fate of all those who strive to establish their own lasting space and identity in a rapidly changing late twentieth century America. As the film changes its tone from the lighter mood of Garp's childhood to the darker hues of his adulthood, and even as Williams the most childlike of actors conveys something childlike and innocent about the grown Garp, we, as audience, witness one catastrophe after another violently disrupt Garp's passage through existence. The final tragedy for Garp is when he is shot by Pooh Percy (Brenda Currin), the youngest sister of his childhood girlfriend Cushie, just when he has reached a degree of peace with himself and his family and re-established himself as a wrestling coach in his hometown. Thus his words to Helen during their first courtship prove lamentably prophetic: "We haven't got much time. Men die young in my family, Helen!" Irving's novel concludes with the sentence "In the world according to Garp, we are all terminal cases," which could also well serve as the film's coda.

The latent danger of Garp's world is implicit from the beginning in the imagery of the opening credits sequence. The naked infant Garp, smiling beatifically and looking around in wonder, rises and falls in slow motion, seemingly weightless and untethered, through the film frame against a bright blue sky lightly brushed with white clouds. In other words, we first see Garp in cherubic form floating through an iconic image of Heaven, an image that will be recycled at the film's end as the medical helicopter bears away the mortally wounded Garp to that same cloud-streaked Heaven. Andrew Horton says this image "sets both the tone and theme" for the film—an image that is "both pleasant and disorienting in the opening (we are up in the air whereas the rest of the film will be grounded in Garp's life) and disturbing at the close as Hill ends with a freeze-frame of the smiling baby's face." The image is fraught with ambivalence, Horton concludes, because "We respond to the innocence of the baby's smile, but we know that Garp is dying."[17]

The rest of the opening scene is carefully constructed to wring the maximum impact from this ambivalence. The Beatles's sprightly, bouncy song "When I'm 64" plays over the credits, its lyrics capturing both the innocence and limitless potential of youth but hint at the inevitability of decline and death. As the opening credits end, the film reveals that Jenny has been tossing the naked infant into the air and catching him, a spontaneous act of joy but a potentially dangerous one as well. She stands in front of the ocean vista which we will later learn is the home of the sinister Undertoad, further reinforcing the grim fate awaiting both characters. This first action we see of Jenny's is in keeping with her eccentric character; she defies all conventional expectations of parenthood and is to all appearances fearless, not so much reckless as unintimidated by possible negative consequences. Baby Garp himself is visibly unafraid; indeed, he seems right at home floating among the clouds, as fits his origin as an airman's son, and utterly trusting of his mother's ability to keep him from harm. By film's end, however, it has become clear that this idyllic scene, playing out on the Undertoad's front porch, so to speak, also foreshadows how Jenny's own strong will to defy convention and Garp's maternal attachment leads to both their deaths.

Garp's relationship to Jenny is one of the structural linchpins of the story, the key to understanding its apocalyptic trajectory, and one of its most critically complicated aspects to address. Both the novel's and film's depiction of the state of twentieth-century feminism, as a social force advocating an apocalyptic destruction of the existing order, is ambivalent at best. Jenny is the story's central feminist character, one whose iconoclastic views of sexuality and parenthood put her at odds with a patriarchal culture, first glimpsed in her wealthy, conservative parents' shocked, angry reaction to her having a child out of wedlock. Her parents' anger, however, is nothing compared to the predictable gender wars backlash that ultimately kills both her and her son. Had Jenny lived a private life as the eccentric mother who "raped a dying man," in Dean Bodger's words, to conceive a bastard son, she would have encountered little more than the disapproval and gossip of those in her town. No, Jenny's real transgression is to pen what her publisher deems "a political manifesto.... dangerous stuff."

She begins writing her autobiographical book, *Sexual Suspect*, after her impulsive interview with a street prostitute (whose services she purchases for Garp) leads her to an epiphany that no matter what a woman chooses to do sexually, a woman should have her own agency in that decision and not be subject to the domination of men. Therefore her book opens with this line: "In this dirty-minded world you are either somebody's wife or somebody's whore or fast on your way to becoming one or the other." Her subsequent publishing success establishes her, in the words of her publisher, as a cult who becomes a beacon to what one reviewer of the film calls "waves of radical feminist pilgrims to the author's New England seaside house." This same reviewer identifies Jenny's undoing as her "boundless tolerance and at times excess naiveté" that gets "in the way of realizing precisely what furies her seminal work has unleashed and how dangerous she now appears to those who would do her great harm."[18] One can't say Jenny remains ignorant of her peril for long. In a blatant foreshadowing of her ultimate fate, her first promotional rally is ended abruptly when police shoot and kill a potential assassin. In spite of the danger, she continues to carry out her role as healer (signified by her donning of her nurse's whites) of the women in flight from a repressive, abusive society who gather around her at her seaside haven. These women view her as their nurse, defender, confidante, protector, guardian, consoler, counselor, and deliverer all in one. Though Jenny undeniably loves her son and does what she thinks is best in raising him, her dedication to her self-created feminist utopian community, which she wants to expand outward into the larger society by supporting a woman gubernatorial candidate, eventually dominates her life and leads inexorably to her and her son's deaths.

This tragic end is foreshadowed by the narrative's negative stance toward the Ellen Jamesian Society, a group of women who take radical feminist sisterhood to a whole other level by cutting off their tongues out of solidarity with Ellen James, an eleven-year-old girl whose rapists cut out her tongue to silence her. This self-mutilation is not portrayed in much of a sympathetic light in either Irving's novel or the movie. Rather it dramatizes a grotesque manifestation of complete avoidance of and hatred toward all men, an attitude further out but on the same spectrum as Jenny's own belief that men are helpless to control their own lust. From this perspective, her autobiography's title, *Sexual Suspect*, may ambiguously refer either to her as a suspect in the conflicted sexual dynamic between men and women—a suspect because of her self-imposed exile from the society of men and her negative attitude toward sex—or any man as suspect in his potential to harm women either emotionally and/or physically because of his uncontrollable desires. While Jenny provides a safe place to all women in search of one, her home becomes a particular draw for the Ellen Jamesians, who see in Jenny a kindred spirit in their mutual antipathy toward men, the patriarchal society through which they control women and men alike, and the violence that a lethal brew of masculine will to dominate and unbridled sexual appetites engenders. Garp clearly finds the Ellen Jamesians to be a source of vexation. On the one hand, he sympathizes with the histories of exploitation and violence many of them have suffered; on the other, he detests how they have mutilated themselves out of some misguided sense of solidarity with Ellen James and fears that their form of protest will continue to catch on (go viral, if you will) and lead more women to self-harm.

On the periphery of this insular society of women stands Garp, a representative of the male sex that Jenny dismisses in both her personal life and writer's life as driven by lust more than any other motivating force. Whereas Jenny is rather formal, if not distant in her relationships with people (even those damaged women she is trying to help), Garp is portrayed as spontaneous and true to his emotions. The various women at the Fields compound who regard Garp with fright, suspicion, and hostility—a sexual suspect, if you will—fare even worse by comparison with the openly expressive Garp. Clearly the film "takes" Garp's side against Jenny and the women she shelters, more evidence of its problematic sexual dynamics but nevertheless a partisan endorsement of Garp that the film's viewers must contend with. Unlike his more intellectually and mission-driven mother, he answers primarily to his passions—for life, writing, love, and yes, even lust. For being true to his passions, the narrative tends to exonerate Garp of culpability in the consequences of his excesses, depicting him as a twentieth-century "American Adam," to use R.W.B. Lewis's famous idea of masculine innocence standing self-reliantly apart from history,[19] defining the world in his own terms ("the world according to Garp"), yet tragically fated to suffer and die in a personal apocalypse resulting from the inevitable forward movement of history which stirs up passions far more lethal than Garp's own.[20]

Garp and Jenny symbolize the forces of radical feminist woman and postfeminist man seeking some kind of reconciliation that ultimately eludes them as they are consumed by the apocalyptic forces they have unleashed through their writing. Andrew Horton makes the point that Garp and Jenny in "almost every way contrast with each other, even though they are mother and son.... Garp ... longs to be everything his mother is not: a sharing lover, parent, husband, friend."[21] For Sally Robinson, however, the film has a more troubling agenda than what Horton identifies. According to Robinson, the film repeatedly "beats" feminism through rigging the narrative against Jenny and in favor of Garp: "Jenny is represented as not only asexual but violently antisexual, while Garp's desire to sleep with any woman who happens along is represented as 'natural.' ... The human is opposed to the feminist, and feminist ideology is caricatured as a single-minded and life-denying obsession with rooting out lust, sex, and happiness wherever it grows."[22] For Robinson, Irving's novel is a complex if problematic attempt to reconstitute white masculinity in crisis in a postfeminist world, whereas the film "sanctifies" Garp in comparison to his mother and his wife, whose own affair with graduate student Michael Milton (Mark Soper) is a far more calculated endeavor than Garp's own "natural," spontaneous, and one-time dalliance with the babysitter (Sabrina Lee Moore). The sexual encounter with the babysitter, in a darkened car pulled over on the side of the road, is the only infidelity he engages in the film, whereas he has other affairs in the novel. He also repudiates the film's representation of radical feminism when as a man he reclaims feminism by writing the book *Ellen James* after his son's death, an action which is specifically "blessed" by the grown Ellen James herself (Amanda Plummer) when she shows up to thank him for publicly denouncing the movement that took her name and endlessly replicates her mutilation against her express wishes. Whatever one makes of Garp and his function in the film as postfeminist man, his spontaneous life force is clearly represented as antithetical to Jenny's mission-driven, clinical approach to life. In the end, however, their self-created personal apocalypse burns them both up.

Spared the worst of the inferno is Roberta Muldoon (John Lithgow), the transsexual ex-football player who becomes a loving confidante to both Jenny and Garp. Through Roberta's character and how she serves to unify the family split, one can observe the dilemma in play for Hill as director, who wants to show a society in apocalyptic transformation but also sentimentally wants, given the dark source material, to give its suffering characters some peace before the bloody end. Roberta is arguably the most sympathetic and empathetic character in the story. At first glance one is taken aback at how positively (and openly) the film represents transsexualism during the 1980s era of triumphant resurgence of cultural conservatism. Roberta as liminal figure, liberated of the rigidly binary orthodoxy of maleness and femaleness of conservative America, seemingly represents a negotiated identity with one foot planted in the "sensitive" masculinist world of Garp and the other in the radical feminist world of Jenny. Through Roberta's kindly and nurturing presence, Garp noticeably softens in his hostile attitude toward the women who flock to his mother's house, particularly after Roberta explains to Garp that everyone at Jenny's house "has something missing, or some wound that won't heal. Your mother tries to nurse them back to health." He and Roberta forge a loving, platonic friendship in which she is also a playful aunt to the Garp children.

Yet this alternative model of domesticity is undercut by the film's visual portrayal of Roberta as more humorously masculine than feminine and actor John Lithgow's overly mannered performance of a burly, formerly hypermasculine male (signified by his prowess in that most testosterone-drenched of male occupations, professional football) transitioning into womanhood.[23] As a character, Roberta falls into the cinematic category of what Julia Serano calls "pathetic transsexuals," who while attempting to live as female often still behave in stereotypically male fashion. Roberta's sheer size, her frequent playing of volleyball and football at the Fields compound, her serving as bodyguard for Jenny in her public appearances, and her punching of a woman attacking Garp at Jenny's memorial service all code her as still essentially male in spite of lacking a male appendage, undergoing hormone treatments, developing female intuition, taking male lovers, and adopting the outer appearance of a woman. According to Serano, the net result of an "extreme combination of masculinity and femininity does not seem designed to challenge audiences' assumptions about maleness and femaleness,"[24] but rather to reinforce the commonly accepted attributes of both, none too subtly point to the absurdity of trying to transition from one to the other, and reassure conventional audiences at a time of conservative backlash to profound social reconfigurations that trans women are really still men, even if they do have their penises amputated.

Indeed, the castration complex that pervades the story, most dramatically represented in Helen's accidentally biting off most of Michael's penis during an act of fellatio, is reinforced through the character of Roberta, whose own penis has also been removed. Through this act of mutilation, both characters are rendered harmless, freakish outsiders. The more conventional gender and social roles embodied by Garp and Helen are restored in another of Hill's sentimental flourishes. The thematic link between Roberta's voluntary castration and Michael's involuntary one is established in Roberta's gallows-humor joke to Jenny that "I had mine removed surgically under general anesthesia, but to have it bitten off.... It's a nightmare." The genital mutilation both hypermasculine men share renders them both literally and metaphorically impotent, "silencing" their dangerous alternatives to the kind of domesticated masculinity represented by Garp every bit as effectively as tongue removal (the female equivalent of castration in the symbolic superstructure of the story) silences the Ellen Jamesians. Michael, a conventionally heteronormative male right out of Jenny's worst assumptions about lust in his home-wrecker's obsessive drive to bed (repeatedly) his married teacher Helen, is horrifically punished by the narrative for the threat he poses to the Garp family. The instrument by which he violates the sanctity of the family literally gone, he is reduced to the object of a punch line by the narrative's favored castrated character and thus dismissed completely from the narrative as the Garps reconcile. For all of its radical depictions of alternative lifestyles, the film reinforces in no uncertain terms conventional morality through its gory resolution of the marital tension between Garp and Helen.

The parallel between the genital mutilation of Michael and Roberta is but one instance of the film's persistent portrayal of shocking mutilation—inflicted by the teeth of the Undertoad, so to speak—intruding into otherwise mundane settings: the crying young boy Jeffrey (Brett Littman) at Everett Steering Academy who has caught his penis in his zipper; Bonkers interrupting Garp and Cushie's childhood sexual exploration by biting off Garp's earlobe; the teenaged Garp biting off part of Bonkers's ear in an act of thematic symmetry; Garp's son Duncan losing an eye in the car accident; Garp breaking his jaw and biting through his tongue in the same car accident and, temporarily mute, able only to communicate through scribbled notes, just like the Ellen Jamesians; and, of course, the already mentioned tongue and penis removals. In the narrative, mutilation is a metaphor for the walking wounded of the modern age, the Fisher Kings alluded to in Eliot's "The Wasteland" who are unable to heal. Mutilation, either self-inflicted or imposed from without, as a trope haunts the story. Each instance is mirrored in other parts of the narrative and foreshadowing even greater bodily horrors to come. For example, Jeffrey's penis injury in the opening minutes of the film foreshadows the more drastic amputations of Roberta and Michael. The other mutilations, though not specifically genital or reproductive, nevertheless serve as symbolic castrations directed at those organs through which we make sense of the world in our negotiations with our fellow humans: eye (sight), ear (hearing), tongue (speech). Each instance of bodily mutilation afflicts the sufferer in ways that he or she can never fully heal from, leading to profound disaffiliation from the social world tantamount to a sentence of exile handed out to wrongdoers and other transgressors against the social order.

Of all the wounded "Fisher Kings" in the story, Garp is the one who most consistently finds enough regenerative powers to re-engage with life and community. Tellingly, he does not become either literally or symbolically castrated; his body and voice, however battered, remain relatively intact and in fact grow in power until the three bullets that end his world. Garp escapes the castration that Michael suffers, though some parallels are drawn between Michael and Garp. For instance, Cushie is fellating Garp when Bonkers attacks Garp the first time; though Garp loses part of an ear, he does not lose part of his penis. He is later injured in the car accident that costs Michael his penis, but though Garp's tongue is injured and he is unable to speak for a time, he recovers the power of speech (and his marriage). He thus avoids the permanent silence of the Ellen Jamesians, even while becoming more sympathetic to them because of sharing at least the external trappings of their condition. When Ellen rescues Garp, the narrative implies that through his Ellen Jamesian–like suffering, Garp's written voice earns the right to become that of Ellen James herself and, not incidentally, dethrone his mother's book and its fanatical following in the world of gender politics in favor of his own more tempered take upon feminism. Garp reclaims a suspect radical feminism (a world without men) and rebranding it for the more moderate hybrid of feminity/masculinity Garp represents, a world in which men and women who desire each other can somehow negotiate an existence (albeit a scarring one) with each other.

The dialectical tension throughout the narrative between Williams's exuberant portrayal of Garp and the darkness conspiring to kill him lends the film a quality composed of equal parts excruciating heartbreak and good-humored inspiration: heartbreak because of the pain Garp and his friends and family suffer but inspiration because Garp, even in his dying moments soaring off into the sky aboard the medical helicopter in a visual reprise of the film's happy opening sequence in which Jenny tosses her smiling baby boy into the blue sky, smiles as he tells Helen to "remember everything" (about their lives together) and that he is "flying." His ascendant death scene pulls together many of the film's earlier scenes and images involving Garp's foiled flights that connect his life throughout every stage. One of the most poignant yet whimsical of these scenes is the animated sequence during the segment of the film dealing with Garp's boyhood, when Garp draws himself as wingman to his heroic father who rescues Garp from the Grim Reaper and then flies off into the sun where Garp cannot follow. He later becomes a wrestler because the wresting helmet reminds him of a pilot's helmet, but the first time he tries it on the roof of his boarding school dorm, he nearly falls to his death. His adult substitute for flying, which involves turning off the lights of the family car at night and letting it coast at high speed to a last-second "landing" at the end of the driveway, results in the terrible accident that nearly destroys his family. As the adult Garp now ascends toward the heavens where his father, son, and mother have preceded him, Garp is content that at last he is finally flying. This serene acceptance of imminent death is not painful but transcendent. As this scene illustrates so well, Garp finds joy at even the worst times in his life.

The last fifth or so of the film, in which Garp finally finds peace while contemplating the adventure of his life thus far, mitigates against much of the bleakness of much of the film's middle segment. Garp's personal apoca-lypse, while terminal, is offset by the joy he takes in existence. According to Bruce Bawer, *Garp* as a film is more sentimental than the novel it is based on, but shares with its source novel the escalating sense of doom awaiting its likable protagonist. Garp "is an all-too-mortal Everyman, at war with the Undertoad, the symbolic embodiment of the omnipotent supernatural entity that lies in wait to crush us all."[25] While the Undertoad relentlessly stalks the characters throughout the film in as implacable a manner as any 1980s cel-luloid slasher,[26] the film also suggests how the Undertoad, even as it kills, may ultimately be transcended. For Hill, and reinforced by Williams's vibrant portrayal of Garp as man of both libido and letters, the act of creation through both sexual reproduction and writing defeats the Undertoad by giving the creator a kind of immortality. One may accuse Hill of sentimentality in reworking Irving's bleaker vision, focusing more on the affirmation of life than the finality of death.

Nowhere is this optimism seen more than in Garp's love for his family, a love that endures emotional estrangement, infidelity, and the death of one child and the maiming of another. In his interactions with his children, Garp is at his most optimistic and eloquent, seeing in his family a poetry he cannot capture in his own writing. He expresses this sentiment at three key moments in the story. Even as his marriage wobbles, he finds purity in the two lives they have created and nurtured. Watching their sons sleep, Garp tells Helen: "Being a husband and father, I really adore it. I will never write anything that lovely." After playing with his sons in the mock sword fight in their yard, he shares the following wisdom with Helen: "Sometimes you can have a whole lifetime in a day and never even notice this is as beautiful as life gets. I just feel happy that I noticed. I had a beautiful life today. I even died and lived to tell about it. What a day!" Finally, after Garp and Helen reconcile and look in at their children from outside the house on what turns out to be their last date before Garp dies, Garp expresses to her what could serve as the film's primary theme amidst all the violence: "You know what I really love, though? Thinking about everything. How we met.... I can live in the present, and think about the past.... It's really nice, you know? To look back and see the arc of your life. It's all connected. How you got from there to here. To see the line, you know? It really has been an adventure." Garp's last monologue echoes what his mother said to him as a boy: "Everybody dies. I'm going to die too. So will you. The thing is to have a life before we die. It can be a real adventure, having a life." Garp and Jenny both come to see their lives as connected and meaningful, which prevents them from surrendering to despair. While not denying the inevitability of death or the frailty of the physical body, they embrace an existentialism of joy.

In these narrative grace notes, one can clearly see Hill as the unseen mover urging the viewer to forgive Garp and Jenny all their foibles. Through all that they endure together, for all the mistakes they make, they achieve new levels of enlightenment, even wisdom. Life's joy and mystery is revealed to them through the paradox of hardship. As writers and thinkers, they communicate their insights to their audiences both within the film and outside the film watching it. So while the Undertoad may be the film's lurking apocalyptic monster whose teeth are ever ready to tear and rip, Garp and Jenny are the prophets emerging from their own personal apocalypses to share their revealed knowledge with the world. Preceded by his son and mother in death, Garp's world ends for him. The larger world continues. So too does the terrible, the ugly Undertoad, waiting beneath the waves.

NOTES

1. Janet Maslin, "Robin Williams Stars in 'Garp' Adaption," *The New York Times*, July 23, 1982, http://www.nytimes.com/movie/review?res=9C0DE6DB103BF930A15754C0A964 948260.

2. John Irving, *My Movie Business: A Memoir* (Toronto, Canada: Vintage Canada Edition, 2000). PDF e-book.

3. Wes D. Gehring, *Genre-Busting Dark Comedies of the 1970s: Twelve American Films* (Jefferson, NC: McFarland, 2016), 118.

4. Andrew Horton, *The Films of George Roy Hill*, rev. ed. (Jefferson, NC: McFarland, 2005), 160–61.

5. By extension, the Undertoad is a fitting symbol for the depression and paranoia, exacerbated by the degenerative disease Lewy Body Dementia, that contributed to Williams's death.

6. John J. Collins, *The Apocalyptic Tradition: An Introduction to Jewish Apocalyptic Literature*, 2nd ed. (Grand Rapids, MI: William B. Eerdmans Publishing Company, 1998), 2.

7. Klaus Koch, *The Rediscovery of the Apocalyptic: A Polemical Work on a Neglected Area of Biblical Studies and Its Damaging Effects on Theology and Philosophy* (S.C.M. Press, 1972), 28.

8. Stephen D. O'Leary, *Arguing the Apocalypse: A Theory of Millennial Rhetoric* (New York: Oxford University Press, 1994), 4.

9. *Ibid.*, 5.

10. *Ibid.*, 5–6.

11. John J. Collins, *The Apocalyptic Imagination: An Introduction to Jewish Apocalyptic Literature*, 3rd ed. (Grand Rapids, MI: William B. Eerdmans Publishing Company, 2016), 10.

12. Conrad Ostwalt, *Secular Steeples: Popular Culture and the Religious Imagination* (New York: Bloomsbury, 2012), 196.

13. Elizabeth K. Rosen, *Apocalyptic Transformation: Apocalypse and the Postmodern Imagination* (Lanham, MD: Lexington, 2008), xi–xii.

14. The number of times the film flips, conflates, or relocates traditional signifiers of masculinity or femininity are legion. The most significant, however, include the "swap" in traditional domestic roles in the Garp home, where Garp is "house husband" and Jenny is the career professional woman working outside the house. Roberta Muldoon is signified as both male and female, though she identifies as female and has sexual relationships with men. Though not truly an instance of "drag," Garp also dresses as a woman in order to "crash" his mother's women-only memorial service.

15. Andrew Hewitt, "Coitus Interruptus: Fascism and the Deaths of History," in *Postmodern Apocalypse: Theory and Cultural Practice at the End*, ed. Richard Dellamora (Philadelphia: University of Pennsylvania Press, 1995), 35.

16. Horton, 163.

17. *Ibid.*, 152.

18. Nazza, "The World According to Garp: A Review," *Feministing Community*, 2011, http://feministing.com/2010/09/22/the-world-according-to-garp-a-review/.

19. R.W.B. Lewis defines this figure in his *The American Adam: Innocence, Tragedy, and Tradition in the Nineteenth Century* (Chicago: The University of Chicago Press, 1955).

20. Giles Gunn, finding similarities between the American Adam story and the classic American "rags to riches" success story, may as well be referring to Garp when he writes that both kinds of stories "focus on the career of an isolated hero who must learn how to survive and succeed in an often unfriendly world. And both make much of the central figure's self-reliance, which encourages him to define the world in terms of himself rather than himself in terms of the world. But where the Horatio Algers always win, the American Adams frequently lose." So in Garp's world, which is definitively, even heroically defined in Garp's own terms, his ultimate loss places him more in the American Adamic tradition than the Algerian one. Giles Gunn, "The Myth of the American Adam," in *Handbook of American Folklore*, ed. Richard M. Dorson (Bloomington, IN: Indiana University Press, 1983), 82.

21. Horton, 160.

22. Sally Robinson, *Marked Men: White Masculinity in Crisis* (New York, Columbia University Press, 2000), 110.

23. Lithgow was nominated for an Academy Award for Best Supporting Actor.

24. Julia Serano, *Whipping Girl: A Transsexual Woman on Sexism and the Scapegoating of Femininity* (Berkeley, CA: Seal Press, 2016). PDF e-book.

25. Bruce Bawer, "*The World According to Garp*: Novel to Film," in *Take Two: Adapting the Contemporary American Novel to Film*, ed. Barbara Tepa Lupack (Bowling Green, OH: Bowling Green State University Popular Press. 1994), 77.

26. Perhaps a better analogue is the *Final Destination* horror film franchise (2000–2011), in which Death is an unseen but palpable entity manipulating elements of the physical environment to kill the main characters one by one in gruesomely spectacular ways.

BIBLIOGRAPHY

Bawer, Bruce, "*The World According to Garp*: Novel to Film," in *Take Two: Adapting the Contemporary American Novel to Film*, ed. Barbara Tepa Lupack. Bowling Green, OH: Bowling Green State University Popular Press. 1994, 77–90.

Collins, John J. *The Apocalyptic Imagination: An Introduction to Jewish Apocalyptic Literature*, 3rd ed. Grand Rapids, MI: William B. Eerdmans Publishing Company, 2016.

_____. *The Apocalyptic Tradition: An Introduction to Jewish Apocalyptic Literature*, 2nd ed. Grand Rapids, MI: William B. Eerdmans Publishing Company, 1998.

Croteau, Melissa. "Introduction: Beginning at the Ends," in *Apocalyptic Shakespeare: Essays on Visions of Chaos and Revelation in Recent Film Adaptations*, eds. Melissa Croteau and Carolyn Jess-Cooke. Jefferson, NC: McFarland, 2009, 1–28.

Gehring, Wes D., *Genre-Busting Dark Comedies of the 1970s: Twelve American Films*. Jefferson, NC: McFarland, 2016.

Hewitt, Andrew. "Coitus Interruptus: Fascism and the Deaths of History," in *Postmodern Apocalypse: Theory and Cultural Practice at the End*, ed. Richard Dellamora. Philadelphia: University of Pennsylvania Press, 1995, 17–40.

Horton, Andrew. *The Films of George Roy Hill*, rev. ed. Jefferson, NC: McFarland, 2005.

Irving, John. *My Movie Business: A Memoir*. Toronto, Canada: Vintage Canada Edition, 2000. PDF e-book.

Koch, Klaus. *The Rediscovery of the Apocalyptic: A Polemical Work on a Neglected Area of Biblical Studies and Its Damaging Effects on Theology and Philosophy*. S.C.M. Press, 1972.

Lewis, R.W. B. *The American Adam: Innocence, Tragedy, and Tradition in the Nineteenth Century*. Chicago: The University of Chicago Press, 1955.

Maslin, Janet., "Robin Williams Stars in 'Garp' Adaption," *The New York Times*, July 23, 1982, http://www.nytimes.com/movie/review?res=9C0DE6DB103BF930A15754C0A9649 48260.

Nazza, "*The World According to Garp*: A Review," *Feministing Community*, 2011, http://feministing.com/2010/09/22/the-world-according-to-garp-a-review/.

Ostwalt, Conrad. *Secular Steeples: Popular Culture and the Religious Imagination*. New York: Bloomsbury, 2012.

Robinson, Sally. *Marked Men: White Masculinity in Crisis*. New York, Columbia University Press, 2000.

Rosen, Elizabeth K. *Apocalyptic Transformation: Apocalypse and the Postmodern Imagination*. Lanham, MD: Lexington, 2008.

Serano, Julia. *Whipping Girl: A Transsexual Woman on Sexism and the Scapegoating of Femininity*. Berkeley, CA: Seal Press, 2016. PDF e-book.

Toying with War

Exploring the Connection Between Militarization and Education

KENYA WOLFF *and* LUDOVIC A. SOURDOT

> There was always a kindness to Robin. An inquisitive man
> trying to understand the madness of mankind. But when the
> comedy motors were off, you could sense the vulnerability
> of the man. There was always a sense that he could easily be
> hurt. And if he were hurt, how quickly could he heal? A
> bleeder in a world of sharp edges. There was an innocence
> to his thoughtful intelligence. If there were an endangered
> species list for mankind, he would have been first on that
> list. He was perhaps too delicate for this difficult world. We
> lost one of a kind. We all lost a friend.
> —Barry Levinson in *Variety Magazine*[1]

Director Barry Levinson and actor Robin Williams collaborated on three films together over the course of their careers. *Good Morning, Vietnam* (1987), *Toys* (1992) and *Man of the Year* (2006). Though each film is categorically unique, all explore issues related to militarism, greed, the limitations of democracy and the human condition. In these three films, the protagonist (Williams) faces a crisis that forces him to challenge the dominant power structures that are in place. Levinson's three films tackle serious messages and rely on Williams's trademark humor to soften the biting critique of the United States political and foreign policy. The first collaboration between Levinson and Williams resulted in movie magic with *Good Morning, Vietnam* (1987). It earned Williams an academy award nomination and became Levinson's first huge commercial success at the box office (the movie grossed 123 million dollars, making it the fourth movie in terms of domestic gross for movies released in 1987).[2] Unlike *Good Morning, Vietnam, Toys* and *Man of the Year* were not embraced by audiences or critics. Ironically, both box office flops, seemed to be eerily prophetic—from Toys' prediction a military force run by weaponized toys (aka-drones) to an out-of-nowhere loud mouthed, tell-it-like-it-is television star winning the presidency. This essay will explore the similarities in all three films, the issues addressed throughout (militarism, patriotism, the limitations of democracy) and how Williams's characters challenged the dominant power structures in place.

"I love the smell of napalm in the morning"

Good Morning, Vietnam is a fictionalized account of Adrian Cronauer stint in Vietnam as an Air Force disc jockey. In the movie, Adrian Cronauer (Robin Williams) is sent to Vietnam to entertain troops on the radio. His program is well received by the soldiers but he constantly runs into trouble with his superior officers because of his irreverent tone and commentary on the conflict. In his review of *Good Morning, Vietnam* legendary film critic Roger Ebert explained how Levinson helped Williams bring Air Force high octane Disc Jockey Adrian Cronauer to life "Levinson used Mitch Markowitz's script as a starting point for a lot of Williams' monologues, and then let the comedian improvise. Then he put together the best parts of many different takes to create sequences that are undeniably dazzling and funny. Williams is a virtuoso."[3] Cronauer's love interest in the film is a young Vietnamese woman and through interactions with her family members and friends, Cronauer discovers the atrocities of the Vietnamese conflict. *Good Morning, Vietnam* was a turning point for Robin Williams, he was nominated for an Academy Award, won a Golden Globe and was widely recognized as a brilliant comedian all over the world.

Producer Larry Brezner later explained that his intention was to make *Good Morning, Vietnam* as a metaphor for the war. The production team decided to focus on the year 1965, because it is universally viewed as a crucial year in the conflict. Brezner explained further "no one was taking the Vietnam situation very seriously, but by the end of the year, the number of troops had increased by the thousands. 1965 was the year that Jekyll became Hyde."[4] The real-life Cronauer indicated that the movie took many historical liberties when it came to portraying his experience in the South Pacific. While Cronauer was not necessarily pleased with all aspects of the film, he recognized that the movie helped to provide moviegoers with a better understanding of what life as a soldier was like in Vietnam. In an interview with *USA Today*'s Jeff Schogol, Cronauer expounded, "First of all, as far as I know, it's the first film that began to show Americans in Vietnam as they really were instead of a bunch of murderers and rapists and baby-killers and dope addicts and psychotics. That was sorely needed at the time."[5]

Williams's portrayal of wartime DJ Adrian Cronauer led to many prize roles including *Dead Poets Society* (1989), *Awakenings* (1990), *The Fisher King* (1991), *Hook* (1991), *Aladdin* (1992). By 1992, Barry Levinson had established himself as a successful writer/director. *Good Morning, Vietnam* was released in January 1988, in the four years that followed Levinson made three movies *Rain Man* (1988), starring Dustin Hoffman and Tom Cruise, *Avalon* (1990), and *Bugsy* (1991) starring Warren Beatty and Annette Bening. These movies earned a combined 22 academy awards nominations (8 for *Rain Man*, 10 for *Bugsy* and 4 for *Avalon*) and $237 million in U.S. box office receipts. Levinson's biggest box office success is *Rain Man* (1988) starring Tom Cruise and Dustin Hoffman earned Levinson an Academy Award for Best Picture and Best Director while Hoffman took home the Oscar for Best Actor.

Toying with War

By 1992, Robin Williams and Barry Levinson had showed the world their range of talents and were both mega Hollywood stars. It looked like they couldn't be stopped ... then came *Toys*. *Toys* marks the second collaboration between Barry Levinson and Robin Williams. The movie was released a few days before Christmas 1992. Coincidentally, Disney's *Aladdin* was released in early November. Williams reportedly asked Disney for his voice not be used to market toys as he wanted to make movies, not sell merchandise. Disney didn't adhere to these requests and instead heavily promoted Aladdin, using the Genie (Williams's voice) in the movie trailer. *Toys* was overshadowed by *Aladdin* upon its release in theaters.

Toys is a surrealist tale where idealist toy maker Leslie Zevo (Robin Williams) attempts to save his father's toy factory from his uncle, an army general obsessed with making war toys with the ultimate goal to sell his creations to the U.S. government. Upon its release, *Toys* received mixed reviews from movie critics and was rejected by audiences. Roger Ebert started his review with these words, "*Toys* is visually one of the most extraordinary films I've seen, a delight for the eyes, a bright new world. It takes place within the entirely imaginary world of a giant toy corporation, which springs from a limitless grain field as if there were no other buildings on earth." He ended his review writing "The production design deserves Academy recognition. But at the most fundamental level, *Toys* is a film not quite sure what it's about."[6] *Los Angeles Times* writer Elaine Dutka described Toys as "an absurdist fantasy about the attempted takeover of a family toy factory by a mean-spirited general-is nevertheless a greater departure than usual: a wacky, over-the-top film more representative of Terry Gilliam than of the reserved and low-key Barry Levinson."[7]

In an interview given to *The Seattle Times*, Levinson revealed that *Toys* was written in the late 1970s and that he thought of the script after reading a newspaper article "Whether the story was bogus or not, I don't know, but I'd read something about the Russians getting the plan for a submarine from a toy kit. It seemed totally preposterous, but Valerie (Valerie Curtin, co-writer) and I liked the idea of the video generation meeting up with military hardware, blurring the lines between video games and reality."[8] Levinson also explained that while *Toys* was 12 years in the making, his movie was very timely especially since television viewers around the world were able to follow the beginning of the Gulf War in real time thanks to the Cable News Network (CNN). For the first time, the 24-hour news network (the only one at that time) was also able to broadcast pictures of missiles hitting their targets as well as fighter jets fighters taking off from aircraft to complete missions in the Gulf. Levinson explained, "The title is ironic, big toys, little toys—it's all a game, watching that missile go down the chimney blowing up that factory in Iraq could have been in a video arcade. The timing of this movie actually couldn't be better. Communism had collapsed and it's hard getting money to raise the flag. Investing in a force of tiny, remote-controlled $5,000 planes instead of $450-million one is one way of beating the cutbacks."[9]

Toys was released following the United States–led international coalition campaign to remove Iraq president Saddam Hussein from Kuwait. General Norman Schwarzkopf commanded the coalition forces during the *Gulf War*, becoming a household name, conducting media briefings broadcast live on CNN where he informed the American public (and many viewers across the world) about the progress of operation *Desert Shield* and subsequently *Desert Storm*. Scholars and media observers criticized the media coverage of the *Gulf War* at the time. They disapproved of the unilateral pro–American coverage, the use of video feed depicting aerial attacks by CNN, making the war an exciting spectacle instead of also reporting the consequences of aerial bombing on civilian population. Overall, the news coverage of the first Gulf War can be equated to an orchestrated drumbeat of war promoting the conflict in print and on television without fully grasping the long-lasting consequences of such actions on civilian populations in the region. In the end, Levinson was right, a new era of modern warfare had emerged thanks to advances in technology. The Gulf War ended in late February 1991, *Toys* was released in theater 22 months later, by then American moviegoers were not ready to be lectured about the war; the movie flopped at the box office.

On November 3 1992, roughly one month prior to the movie release the American people decided not to give George H. Bush (the architect of the Gulf War) a second term in office. Bill Clinton was elected president with a large majority in the Electoral College. The Gulf War was barely 2 years old, George H. Bush was no longer president, Norman Schwarzkopf had retired, Saddam Hussein was still in power and despite *Toys* disappointing returns at the box office Barry Levinson and Robin Williams were still making movies.

Two Very Different Approaches to Exploring Issues of War

Both *Good Morning, Vietnam* and *Toys* explored issues of war. Yet one film was praised and one was panned. We believe that the audience rejection of *Toys* wasn't so much about the messages in the movie, but in the expectations from the moviegoers. Toys was marketed as a family movie, and while it used childhood as a metaphor, it was not meant for children. Moviegoers hadn't purchased tickets to a movie entitled *Toys* to be lectured to about the dehumanization of war at the expense of innocence. In contrast, moviegoers understood when they purchased tickets to see *Good Morning, Vietnam,* which was rated R, they were seeing a war movie (albeit one that was also billed as a comedy). And while, Toys was panned for its overtly "preachy-tone," Good Morning, Vietnam was subtle in its message. Williams's character, Cronauer never overtly questions the U.S. involvement in the war. He certainly pokes fun at some of the armed forces strict and regimented culture, rails against some of the stupidity and disobeys orders when asked to censor his broadcast. But at no time does Cronauer overtly criticize the U.S. decision to be in Vietnam or to escalate the war. Only after being sent home for insubordination and fraternizing with the enemy does he hint at his feelings about U.S. involvement in Vietnam. In his final broadcast, he states:

> That's right, I'm history, I'm out of here, I got the luck ticket home, baby, Rollin', rollin', rollin'. Keep them wagons rollin'. Rawhide. Yeah, that's right. The final Adrian Cronauer broadcast. And this one is brought to you by your friends at the Pentagon. Remember the people who brought you Korea? That's right, the US Army. If it's being done correctly, here or abroad, it's probably not being done by the Army.[10]

In the movie *Toys*, the villain is much more obvious. General Leland Zevo (Michael Gambon), the film's greedy, militaristic villain is over-the-top. He is never seen out of military uniform and is so devoted to his plan of recruiting children into his army in order to use their gaming skills to fight, that he is even willing to kill his own son. Interestingly, Zevo's son, Capt. Patrick Zevo, is played by a young LL Cool J. The script never introduces Patrick Zevo's mother or attempts to explain away the difference in race between father and son. While it wasn't explicitly addressed in the film, it may be that the casting was a recognition of the many sacrifices made by African-American soldiers who fought for freedom overseas while returning to discrimination at home. Since the release of *Toys* in 1992, several movies have addressed the tremendous contributions of African American soldiers (*The Tuskegee Airmen*, 1995 and *Red Tails*, 2012).

Toys provides us with a glimpse into the future of drone warfare. In 1992, Zevo's vision of children using their video gaming skills to drop bombs with robotic toys seemed rather far-fetched. However, looking back, this futuristic picture of warfare was more prophetic than science fiction, a little over 20 years after *Toys*, the United States launched the first drone strikes over Pakistan, for the past 12 years the U.S. military has used drones to attack specific targets in the Middle East, unfortunately too often the collateral victims of such attacks are children.

In 1992, audiences who went to see *Toys* and Williams, the man who they could count on for a good laugh let them down. Rather than a lighthearted, feel-good comedy, American movie goers looked into a mirror and what was staring back, wasn't a pretty picture. Levinson's surreal world was more real than fantasy. They saw an overzealous general, laughing about taking out the *United Nations* supply trucks, zombie-like children honing their battle-skills in the video-arcade, and toy companies making a profit off of war toys. Art was definitely mirroring life. General Leland Zero's vision of war in *Toys* was part of the new military. One in which was relatively safe and sanitized. Bombs dropped from planes operated remotely. And while the U.S. pilots may not be children, they are certainly removed from the action and the harsh realities that would face traditional soldiers.

In contrast, *Good Morning, Vietnam* does the opposite. It aims to show the messiness of war. The complexities and the absurdity of it. In 1965, military tactics had shifted from traditional warfare to the guerrilla-style tactics used by the Viet Cong. Cronauer laments after his Jeep is hit and he is forced to walk thru the jungle:

> How can you fight a war in this shit?
> I don't know where they are.
> I don't even know where I am.
> Can't see dick.
> Like hunting with Ray Charles.

Throughout the film, Cronauer struggles between his desire to support the troops and entertain them, while at the same time adhering to the strict protocols required of the Army. Prior to his arrival, the airwaves are filled with lighthearted fluff … soldiers are reminded to beat the Christmas mail rush, to use lather to shave and to label their duffle bags lest they be lost during travel. Hard news of the "conflict's" escalation is censored and Cronauer struggles to keep his show light and upbeat. After he witnesses the bombing of a local GI watering hole, he defies orders from the Army censors who want him to keep this news off the air. Ultimately, he is confronted by the often-contradictory nature of war when he discovers Tuan, his Vietnamese friend, is a Viet Cong bomber:

> CRONAUER: I fought to get you into that bar, and then you blow the fuckin' place up. Listen. I gave you my friendship and my trust ... and now they tell me that my best friend is the goddam enemy!
> TUAN: Enemy? What is enemy? You killing my own people so many miles from your home. We not the enemy. You the enemy!
> CRONAUER: You used me to kill two people. Two people died in that fuckin' bar.
> TUAN: Big fucking deal! My mother is dead. And my older brother, who be years old, he dead. Shot by Americans. My neighbor, dead. His wife, dead. Why? Because we're not human to them. We're only little Vietnamese. And I'm stupid enough to save your bullshit life at An Lac.
> CRONAUER: Wait. We're here to help this country. Where the fuck you goin'? It's unbelievable. Five months in Saigon ... and my best friend turns out to be a VC. This will not look good on a résumé!

What *Good Morning, Vietnam* does very well is to challenge the "Othering" of the Vietnamese people during wartime. It shows that there are good Americans and bad Americans, good Vietnamese and bad Vietnamese. It is not our nationality that defines us. Rather, we are all humans capable of the full range of human experience. This was one reason Williams reportedly took on the role. He told a reporter that he was initially attracted by the project because of the tone of the movie, "I thought the script made a great effort to show the Vietnamese as people rather than 'the enemy.' They have families and needs ... they laugh and play and are afraid, just like everyone else."[11] This was exemplified in his final request as he is being escorted to his plane to go home. He asks for time to play baseball on the street with some of the Vietnamese families he'd befriended. It is this scene in the street, made up of families enjoying America's beloved pastime that was a real departure from a traditional war movie with a clear enemy. Lines were blurred between "us" and "them."

Othering has been defined in this case as the separating or differentiation between one's self and another group or individual in order to hold the "Other" to a different set of morals or standards. It is about understanding difference as inferior[12] This is not surprising given that we have a long and sordid history of discrimination against non–Europeans in the U.S. Dominant representations of people of color in the media have helped to entrench hegemonic ideologies. As these ideologies become naturalized and internalized they fade into the hegemonic background and out of view. What is out of view is rarely questioned. Without critical questioning, "the Other" can easily be vilified and made into "the enemy" as we have witnessed all too recently. In 2016, anti-immigrant sentiments led to a wave of populism throughout world, first with Brexit and later with Trump's successful bid for the presidency.

Images of Children and War

While it may be easier to "Other" a foreign enemy and ignore their suffering, it is harder for adults to "Other" children. There is something about the image of war and children that captures our attention in ways that other images can't. Perhaps it is because we tend to be more protective of children and view them as innocent. While we can more easily vilify adults. For example, in 1972 a photographer captured the public's imagination when his photograph of a naked nine-year old girl was published on the cover of the *New York Times*. The photo captured her running from her village after it had been napalm bombed and she was forced to flee. This photo captured the hearts and imaginations of the American people in a way that no news report had been able to do. Similarly, Oran Daqneesh became a symbol of the Syrian refugee crisis as a video of him bloodied and covered with dust, sitting silently in an ambulance awaiting help went viral. These images of young children affected by war are powerful. They present images of stark contrast—childhood interrupted.[13]

Both *Good Morning, Vietnam* and *Toys* heavily utilized the film technique of juxtaposition. This technique, places opposing ideas next to each other for comparison. In *Toys*, Levinson's design team creates a fantastical, cartoon-like world inside the toy factory. The whimsical factory is made up of vibrant primary colors—the kind you'd find if you stumbled upon an expensive shiny new playground at Disney World. The factory is surrounded by untouched fields of grain underneath a canopy of cobalt sky. These bright colors (sky-blue, sunny yellow and fire-engine red) bring to mind childhood, just as effortlessly as the nostalgic toys take one back to a simpler more innocent time. Wind-up cars, pull-behind wooden ducks and slinkies are all a nod to an era before technology revolutionized the toy industry. These toys invoke a longing back to the days when children could entertain themselves. Their toys were props to be cast in the elaborate theater of life. Children didn't need toys to interact with them electronically, they could use their imaginations to bring them to life. These simple toys predate current parental concerns about things like attention deficit disorder and childhood obesity. It is this innocent and colorful world that Levinson juxtaposes beside weapons, tanks, military attire and camouflage. In one memorable scene, there is a baby doll in a stroller, holding a bottle and the bottom of the bottle opens up, exposing the barrel of a loaded gun. After the bottle attacks, you can hear Alsatia Zevo (Leland's eccentric sister) saying, "Now that's a bad baby!"

Similarly, in *Good Morning, Vietnam*, Levinson uses the cinematic effect of dissonance by pairing images of war with the Louis Armstrong's ballad "What a Wonderful World" (1967). Levinson felt the song worked so well in this scene, he decided to ignore the fact that it was an anachronism (the song came out in 1967 and the film was set in 1965). The lyrics, from Louis Armstrong's "What a Wonderful World" were paired with powerful images of women, children, soldiers, villagers, bombs and the devastation of war.

Recruitment—From the Couch to the Classroom

Because globalization sets up unequal power relations, it becomes necessary to have a powerful and ever-present military. In order to have an ever-present military, one must have not only public support, but also a large supply of fresh and ever-ready supply of young and talented recruits. *Toys* explores the topic of war and the marketing of war toys (and ultimately the training and use) of children for military purposes. Leland explains that "Four stores and many Christmases ago, my father brought forth a factory conceived in innocence and joy and squeezable fun for everyone." Prior to the factory being taken over by General Zevo, one can see visions of happy workers (and also listen to the Tori Amos song entitled "Happy Workers").

In reality, war toys, movies and video games are being sold by U.S. toy and entertainment companies who make large profits. The marketing war-related video games and toys are something that parents have cited as a concern for many years. Worldwide there is vigorous debate about whether marketing of anything to children should be legal.[14] Individual countries have taken various approaches to the regulating of advertisements aimed at children. For example, Greece has a ban on children's toy advertisements during a typical child's waking hours (from 7 AM until 10 PM). They also have a complete ban on the advertising of toys that encourage or glorify war.[15] In Iraq war toys have been banned because there have been too many accounts of children with toy guns being killed by soldiers because they were mistaken for real weapons.[16] In Afghanistan, they were banned with the intention to "curb the culture of violence."[17]

Gentile, a leading expert on video games and children, was quoted that he was "perplexed that the same parents who take pains to keep children from witnessing violence in the home and neighborhood, often do little to keep them from viewing large quantities of violence on television, in movies, and in video games"[18] He went on to explain that parents are left in the dark because the industry works so hard to neutralize their concerns. In *Toys'* arcade scene, the introduction to Tank Gunner is actually the intro to

Absolute Entertainment's Super Battletank. You'd think that a movie whose message seems to be anti-war video games, would be the last to put one out. Ironically, Absolute Entertainment released the video game adaptation for *Toys*.

Much like General Zevo's plan to recruit children from the video arcades into his remote-control toy army, recruiters for the U.S. Army have been using video games to recruit since 2002. The game, *America's Army*, is a realistic video game that was developed by the U.S. military as an answer to the declining number of young people entering the military. This was the brainchild of the director of the Army's office of economic and manpower analysis, Col. Casey Wardynski. He explains "We want kids to come into the Army and feel like they've already been there. A game is like a team effort, and the Army is very much a team effort. By playing an online, multiplayer game, you can get the feel of being in the Army."[19] Several interactions of that game have taken place since 2002. The program has been so successful that additional games were developed and the community currently boosts over 100 million players.

In a recent documentary, Tonje Hessen Schei[20] explores the ties between the video game industry and the military. She witnessed military representatives talking to children about careers as drone pilots as young as 12 years old. Schei also reports that the military often consults with companies like Xbox and PlayStation on how to design their own drone interfaces in manners that will be most comfortable and recognizable to soldiers who have grown up on their games.[21]

In addition to the military's predatory recruitment practice of targeting low income and inner-city youth, the military also has many programs within schools aimed at the promotion of the U.S. military of our schools. The law mandates that the armed forces be given unlimited access to our school systems (sec. 9528 of the Elementary and Secondary Education Act). Part of the No Child Left Behind Act mandates that schools give the military the phone numbers and addresses of military eligible students so that they can be contacted and recruited. Additionally, American high schools the military Junior ROTC offers "junior military-like" training that is aimed at recruitment. Students go to school in military uniforms and take classes on military history and weaponry. In San Diego, a principal recently cut back on college preparatory programing in exchange for a JROTC unit with a fully operational firing range.[22] These programs are effective. Studies have shown that over half of the students enrolled in Jr. ROTC enlist in military service.[23]

Similar programs, such as the *Young Marines,* are available in middle school and junior high school and introduce students to the military lifestyle. The official stance on the JROTC website states that the program has shifted over the years "from a source of enlisted recruits and officer candidates to a citizenship program devoted to the moral, physical, and educational uplift of the American youth." Interestingly, this is not what William Cohen, Former Defense Secretary said in 2000 while he was under oath before the House Armed Services Committee. In that testimony, he referred to the JROTC as "one of the best recruiting devices that we could have."[24]

Man of the Year

What neither *Good Morning, Vietnam* or *Toys* take on is that fact that it is impossible to tackle the issue of the ever-growing military industrial complex without tackling the topic of economics and the role special interests plays in perpetuating it. It is hardly news that war is big business. In 2015, the U.S. government spent 54% ($598.5 billion) of its discretionary budget on the military. Compare that to the 6% that is spent on education.[25] Yet, in the movie *Toys*, Lt. General Leland Zevo envisions a leaner Army, one that relies less on troops and more on technology. What Zevo fails to mention is that technology is expensive and military contractors fund political campaigns. It is this issue that is the topic of the third and final Levinson and Williams collaboration, *Man of the Year.*

The last collaboration between Barry Levinson and Robin Williams took place in 2006, by then Robin Williams had won an Academy Award for *Good Will Hunting* (1997) and starred in 15 movies since his Oscar win. Levinson had directed several more movies in various genres including *Disclosure* (1994), *Sleepers* (1996), *Wag the Dog* (1997), *Sphere* (1998), *Liberty Heights* (1999). In *Man of the Year* talk show host Tom Dobbs (Robin Williams) is a popular comedian with his own TV show. During a rant about the failure of democracy, an audience member asks him to run for president. Encouraged by his audience's reactions to the idea, he enters the race as an independent candidate. During the debate Dobbs explains his reasoning for entering the election:

> I decided to run because I'm fed up with party politics. I'm tired of the Republican Party and of the Democratic Party. There's no real difference. It's a Mr. Potato candidate. Basically, you have a thing here where, here's the operative word: Party. Behind closed doors, I think they just have a good time. When you read the transcripts, some of the things your Secretary of Defense says, I think there must be an open bar somewhere. The bottom line is, they've lost track of what they're responsible for. They're responsible to the people, not party loyalties and definitely not lobbyists. That's why I want to run for President.

Dobbs character rails against corporate interests during his campaign. Stating that Congress should wear patches on their suit, like NASCAR drivers, alerting the public to who they are actually voting for (i.e., the big banks, oil and drug companies). His candor, off the cuff style and irreverence wins over voters (very reminiscent of Trump's campaign—only on the opposite side of the political spectrum). Unexpectedly, Dobbs is elected president—not due to a Russian-hacking scandal, but rather a major malfunction of a new electronic voting system. Quickly individuals in charge of the company who built the system decide to keep the embarrassing glitch a secret, realizing that this revelation would mean the end of their company. Greed is at the center of the scandal and drives those in on the cover-up to produce "alternative facts." However, one programmer Eleanor Green (Laura Linney) decides to do all she can to contact Dobbs and inform him of the mistake. In the end, Dobbs and Green fall in love and he announces that the results of the election were based on a computer glitch.

What stands out in this political film is Dobbs's integrity, honesty and wiliness to stand up for what he believes. He is the opposite of the politicians who he confronts in the film. In an interview that Levinson gave *Vanity Fair* he compared the villains in film with politicians:

> I find them a lot more human than the big con guys like the president. Those are the big hustlers, those are the men who can truly kill you. Like, for example, George Bush. He talks about the sanctity of life, but he believes in the death penalty: "When they're [embryonic] cells, we protect them; if they grow up and go bad, we kill 'em. We care about a fetus, but not about three million homeless people." I listen to these guys, and I don't know what they're talking about. The ozone levels disappearing; they tell us to wear hats. "Liberal" now means what "Communist" used to. No one can talk, no one can say things. It's as if you were writing a screenplay now about an important social issue and your producer said, "No, let's get them excited about the Pledge of Allegiance." It's staggering what's taken place, what's become accepted. What logic got in here that became the norm?[26]

Is it un–American to critique one's own country? Wouldn't it actually take more courage to do something that could have serious repercussions? It takes love for one's country to work to make it better. It also demonstrates a commitment to the American ideals of equality. During several National Football League (NFL) preseason games in August 2016, San Francisco 49er Quarterback Colin Kaepernick made headline news by refusing to stand for the National Anthem. Kaepernick told reports that he could not stand for a country that oppresses people of color. He went on to explain that this was a personal choice and that he felt that it would be selfish to look away from injustice. The NFL star was quickly joined in his protest by another teammate, then was joined by another player for the Seattle Seahawks, eventually soccer star Megan Rapinoe chose not to stand during the national anthem before a game as a gesture of solidarity with San Francisco's Kaepernick. Like characters in all of the three films we've explored, Kaepernick took a stand against what he believed in and challenged oppressive structures that are in place in this country. NFL fans flocked to social media to criticize Kaepernick's actions as un–American.

Williams can be seen as someone with a strong commitment to his country. He took on roles that critiqued U.S. policy and questioned the role of the military while at the same time volunteering extensively for the United States Organization whose mission is to support the men and women in the armed forces. In 2014, *Time* magazine reported that Williams made six tours to Iraq, Afghanistan, Kuwait and 10 other countries, performing for 60,000 troops.[27]

"Never Use a Cannon to Kill a Fly"—Confucius

The Levinson and Williams partnership was a unique one. They chose to make movies that dealt with important social and political issues. Some of their movies were more successful than others and this could have something to do with the need to balance craft with message. No one wants to go to a film and leave feeling they have been hit over the head with a political commentary. In *Toys*, General Zevo gets annoyed with a fly and begins shooting frantically at it, destroying his office in the process. The film scene was a metaphor inspired by the Confucius quote, "never use a cannon to kill a fly."

With that in mind, now, more than ever we need people like Williams and Levinson who are willing to make movies that examine important issues. A recent headline read, "Next President Will Decide the Fate of Killer Robots and the Future of War." While this sounds like a line from the movie *Toys*, it is actually in reference to the Defense Directive 3000.09, which dictates how the Pentagon will move forward with any new technological advances regarding weapons and the use of artificial intelligence (i.e., killer robots). With over 21 projects that utilize this technology already in development, the future of war is upon us.[28,29] In February 2016, after barely a month into his presidency President Donald Trump indicated that he would ask Congress for a $54 billion increase in military spending.[30] It appears that, like Zevo, Donald Trump is ready to cut nonmilitary programs in order to get his own toy chest. To quote Williams's character Leland Zevo, "In the words of Mahatma Gumby— we are toys of tolerance, but there's only so much that a toy can tolerate."

NOTES

1. Jesse Kornbluth. "From Tin Men to Rain Man," *Vanity Fair* last modified December 1988, http://www.vanityfair.com/news/1988/12/hollywood-code-198812
2. http://www.boxofficemojo.com/movies/?id=goodmorningvietnam.htm
3. Roger Ebert, *Toys*. http://www.rogerebert.com/reviews/toys-1992
4. Larry Brezner, "Good Morning, Vietnam." Production Notes.
5. Schogol 2014.
6. Ebert 1992.

7. Dutka 1992.
8. John Hartl, *Seattle Times*.
9. Dutka, 1992.
10. Schogol, 2014.
11. Williams Robin. *Good Morning, Vietnam*. Production Notes. http://www.levinson.com/index_bl.htm
12. Pickering, 2001
13. Euan McKirdy and Mohammed Tawfeeq. "Omran Daqneesh, Young Face of Aleppo Suffering, Seen on Syrian TV." *CNN*. June 7, 2017. https://www.cnn.com/2017/06/07/middle east/omran-daqneesh-syrian-tv–interview/index.html
14. Gunter, Oats, & Blades, 2005
15. Kenya Wolff. "Globalized Childhood," *Encyclopedia of Educational Philosophy and Theory* Springer: Singapore, 2015.
16. Dan Pearson. "War Games: The Link Between Gaming and Military Recruitment," *Gamesindustry.biz* last modified February 2, 2015, http://www.gamesindustry.biz/articles/ 2015-02-02-the-military-recruitment-of-gamers
17. Ann Jones. "America's Child Soldiers: JROTC and the Militarizing of America," *Truthout* last modified December 16, 2013, http://www.truth-out.org/news/item/20657- americas-child-soldiers-jrotc-and-the-militarizing-of-america
18. Joel Bakan. *Childhood Under Siege: How Big Business Targets Your Children*. New York: Free Press, 2011. p. 43
19. Josh White. "It's a Video Game, and an Army Recruiter," *The Washington Post* May 27, 2005. http://www.washingtonpost.com/wpdyn/content/article/2005/05/26/AR200505260 1505.html.
20. *Drone*. Directed by Tonje Hessen Schei. 2015. http://www.dronethedocumentary. com/#top
21. Dan Pearson. "War Games: The Link Between Gaming and Military Recruitment." *Gamesindustry.biz*, last modified February 2, 2015, http://www.gamesindustry.biz/articles/ 2015-02-02-the-military-recruitment-of-gamers
22. Giroux, 2013.
23. Saltman & Gabbard, 2010.
24. Ann Jones. "America's Child Soldiers: JROTC and the Militarizing of America," *Truthout* last modified December 16, 2013, http://www.truth-out.org/news/item/20657- americas-child-soldiers-jrotc-and-the-militarizing-of-america
25. National Priorities Project. "Fighting for a U.S. Federal Budget That Works for All Americans," *National Priorities Project* last modified 2015. https://www.nationalpriorities. org/campaigns/military-spending-united-states/
26. Jesse Kornbluth. "From Tin Men to Rain Man," *Vanity Fair* last modified December 1988, http://www.vanityfair.com/news/1988/12/hollywood-code-198812
27. Mark Thompson. "The Military Absolutely Loved Robin Williams," *Time*, August 12, 2014.
28. Heather M. Roff and P.W. Singer. "The Next President Will Decide the Fate of Killer Robots—and the Future of War." *Wired Magazine* last modified September 6, 2016. https:// www.wired.com/2016/09/next-president-will-decide-fate-killer-robots-future-war/
29. Michael D. Shear and Jennifer Steinhauer. "Trump to Seek $54 Billion Increase in Military Spending," *The New York Times* last modified February 27, 2017. https://www. nytimes.com/2017/02/27/us/politics/trump-budget-military.html?_r=0
30. *Ibid.*

BIBLIOGRAPHY

Anderson, Nick. & Michael D. Shear. "A $4 Billion Push For Better Schools." *The Washington Post*. July 24, 2009. http://www.washingtonpost.com/wp-dyn/content/article/2009/07/ 23
Bakan, Joel. *Childhood Under Siege: How Big Business Targets Your Children*. New York: Free Press, 2011.

Box Office Mojo. "Good Morning, Vietnam." http://www.boxofficemojo.com/movies/?id=goodmorningvietnam.htm. Accessed June, 25, 2018.

Brezner, Larry. *Good Morning, Vietnam,* Production Notes. http://www.levinson.com/index_bl.htm

Dutka, Elaine. "The Toys in His Attic: Barry Levinson Intended *Toys* to be His Directorial Outing, But Somehow: *Diner, Good Morning, Vietnam, Rain Man* and *Bugsy* Got in the Way." *Los Angeles Times.* December 13, 1992. http://articles.latimes.com/1992–12-13/entertainment/ca-3759_1_barry-levinson

Ebert, Roger. *Good Morning, Vietnam.* http://www.rogerebert.com/reviews/good-morning-vietnam-1988

Ebert, Roger. *Toys.* http://www.rogerebert.com/reviews/toys-1992

Euan, McKirdy and Mohammed Tawfeeq. "Omran Daqneesh, Young Face of Aleppo Suffering, Seen on Syrian TV." *CNN.* June 7, 2017. https://www.cnn.com/2017/06/07/middleeast/omran-daqneesh-syrian-tv-interview/index.html

Giroux, Henry, A. "Henry Giroux on the Militarization of Public Pedagogy," 2013. http://www.counterpunch.org/2013/09/27/teaching-and-learning-with-henry-giroux/

Gunter, Barrie, Caroline Oates, and Mark Blades. *Advertising to Children on TV: Content, Impact, and Regulation.* Mahwah, NJ: Lawrence Erlbaum Associates, 2005.

Hartl, John. "For *Toys,* Director Barry Levinson Invented His Own World." *The Seattle Times.* December 13, 1992. http://community.seattletimes.nwsource.com/archive/?date=19921213&slug=1529832

Linn, Susan. *Consuming Kids: Protecting Our Children from the Onslaught of Marketing & Advertising.* New York: Anchor Books, 2005.

Pickering, Sharon. "Undermining the Sanitized Account: Violence and Emotionality in the Field in Northern Ireland." *British Journal of Criminology.* 41, no 3, 2001: 485–501.

Saltman, Kenneth J. & David Gabbard. *Education as Enforcement: The Militarization and Corporatization of Our Schools.* New York: Routledge, 2010.

Schogol, Jeff. "Real-Life 'Vietnam' DJ Recalls Williams' Portrayal." *USA Today,* August 12, 2014.

Thompson, Mark. "The Military Absolutely Loved Robin Williams." *Time.* August 12, 2014.

White, Josh. "It's a Video Game, and an Army Recruiter." *The Washington Post.* May 27, 2005. http://www.washingtonpost.com/wpdyn/content/article/2005/05/26/AR2005052601505.html

Williams Robin. *Good Morning, Vietnam,* Production Notes. http://www.levinson.com/index_bl.htm

Wolff, Kenya. "Globalized Childhood." *Encyclopedia of Educational Philosophy and Theory.* Springer: Singapore, 2015.

The Face of Robin Williams and the Enigma of Stardom

REBECCA A. UMLAND *and* SAMUEL J. UMLAND

The face of Robin Williams displayed "an infinite complexity of mor-phological functions."[1] His stardom coincided with the modern audience's desire for idiosyncrasy, and its taste for actors who possess what Robert B. Ray calls "the eccentric detail."[2] In fact, had Williams's career begun in the Classic Hollywood Era, his idiosyncrasies might well have limited him to supporting rather than leading roles. As he began his career in television, Williams enjoyed immediate popularity, because of his spontaneity, extraor-dinary ability to *ad lib* and his charm but, as David Thomson observes, he also possessed a "a nervousness ... that supplied the energy for his improv-isations."[3] As he transitioned to Hollywood films, his career eerily mirrored the creation of a character to which he is popularly associated, Mrs. Doubtfire: that is, he "invented a personality into which he grew."[4] In so doing, Williams acquired a star quality similar to that which Sir Ralph Richardson associated with John Wayne, that the latter "projected the mystery required of a great actor."[5] Robin Williams created an image that grew into a unique, elusive per-sona.

Yet what Robert B. Ray asserts regarding the overpowering screen pres-ence of the fabled Greta Garbo, that she was "a supernova always on the verge of becoming a black hole,"[6] might also be said of Robin Williams. The flam-boyant histrionics of his comic performances and impersonations from which he initially derived his stardom only partially obfuscated its antithesis: a brooding introspection, insecurity, and anxiety. His stardom was therefore vaguely threatening, and it is this instability in his onscreen persona that allowed Williams to portray such characters as the corrupt celebrity host of a children's TV program in *Death to Smoochy*, the disturbed villain in *Insom-nia*, and the alienated anti-hero in *One Hour Photo*, all released in 2002.

131

Williams's duplicitous star personality is apparent in his first real success in a dramatic film role as John Keating, an English teacher who returns to his own former prep school, in *Dead Poets Society* (1989). An idealist, Keating tries to infuse in his young male students a passion for life and the importance of independent thought. Reclusive outside of the classroom, in it, Keating comes alive, using extraordinary methods to engage the passive boys he wants to electrify, and the film chronicles the manner in which several of the boys respond. He repeatedly reminds his students of life's brevity and the shadow of death under which they all exist, in order to urge them to live life to its fullest. Keating challenges authority and privilege, and attempts to teach the courage of conviction to his students, but he is also the catalyst that precipitates the film's tragic end—not so much for him but for one of his students, Neil (Robert Sean Leonard). Two years later, in *The Fisher King* (1991), Williams reprises his role as an idealistic English teacher (this time, a professor at Hunter College) who, having been traumatized by his wife's murder, must be healed by the popular radio shock jock, Jack Lucas (Jeff Bridges) who has inadvertently brought tragedy into both of their lives.

In both films, Williams's character is a static one that represents what Robert B. Ray in his study, *A Certain Tendency in the Hollywood Cinema: 1930–1980*, would identify as its "moral center"[7] in that he espouses the values the audience is inclined to applaud, but his screen presence is so compelling that it threatens to impinge on the "center of interest"[8] that Ray identifies as the character(s) who is the true protagonist(s)—the story of the boys who undergo a *rite of passage* in *Dead Poets Society* and the transformative quest of Jack Lucas from shallow radio personality to a fully realized human being. *Dead Poets Society* and *The Fisher King* thus introduce that which became vaguely threatening about Robin Williams's stardom, an instability fully exploited in the series of films mentioned above that, serendipitously, were all released in 2002, all of which feature child exploitation. These three films, we contend, demonstrate how Williams created an onscreen persona that helps to account for his stardom, employing his "nervous energy," not to a comic but to a menacingly serious end, exploring the depths of his acting abilities, and providing an opportunity for Williams to tap into his own hidden demons.

In *Death to Smoochy*, directed by Danny DeVito, Williams plays Randolph Smiley, a clown who hosts a popular children's program, "The Rainbow Randolph Show." Enthusiastic and in his element in front of the camera, surrounded by an *entourage* of midgets and children, Rainbow Randolph's dark underside is soon revealed when he is arrested by the FBI for accepting bribes from parents whose children wish to be featured on the show. Rainbow is subsequently fired and his program cancelled. He loses all of his perks and his credibility, which leaves him homeless, desperate, and vengeful, after the network hires a Pollyanna, Sheldon Mopes (Edward Norton), who has created a clown persona named "Smoochy the Rhino," to replace him. In this dark world of children's entertainment, the studio and its sponsors are as corrupt as Rainbow and the parents who bribe him. At first Rainbow contrives to ruin Smoochy's career and even plots his murder, but in the end, the two clowns and the producer, Nora Wells (Catherine Keener) team up to defeat the corrupt forces that exploit children, and the film concludes happily with Rainbow and Smoochy launching a new program together.

A box office bomb, *Death to Smoochy* was released on March 29, 2002. Its $50 million budget was not offset by the $8.4 it earned, and it generally received unfavorable critical reviews as well. Roger Ebert gave it one-half star, largely because it "violates a cardinal rule of modern mass entertainment, which is that everyone hates clowns almost as much as they hate mimes."[9] Worse yet, Ebert avers, *Smoochy* includes two types of clowns: the "secretly vile" and the "guileless and good."[10] Ebert argues that Robin Williams should "never ever play a clown of any description, because the role writes a license for him to indulge in those very mannerisms he should be striving to purge from his repertory,"[11] a penchant for excess, which is to say "bad taste." Ebert was not alone in this assessment; Robin Williams was nominated for a Golden Raspberry Award for Worst Supporting Actor for this role. Ebert seems not to grasp, however, that the character of Rainbow Randolph embodies the very quality that distinguishes Williams and defines his stardom—the public persona of the comic actor whose need for audience approval expressed by an appreciative audience also generates an awareness of his anxious, nervous, and self-destructive tendencies. This complex and duplicitous nature of his character in the film reflects the brilliantly funny but introverted, conflicted actor who plays him.

Death to Smoochy failed not because of its subject, but because of its plot and execution. For instance, critic Kevin Thomas asserts that "DeVito and Resnick, a TV veteran, blow their terrific setup by piling on the excesses and bringing in an awkward and unpersuasive subplot involving a punch-drunk prizefighter (Michael Rispoli), with whom Smoochy forms a mutual admiration society, and who is associated with a fierce but good-hearted Irish restaurateur (Pam Ferris) and her tough guys," which makes the film "overly complicated and overly long."[12]

Maitland McDonagh labels *Smoochy* "a garish train wreck of a dark comedy," noting that the film fails as a satire because: "It's hardly news that commercial television is a venal business or that children's programming is primarily a delivery system for advertising."[13] For McDonagh, the film's "look veers between primary-colored compositions shot in the flat, over-lit style of youth-oriented TV and a grotesquely exaggerated gloss on *film noir* conventions—all vertiginous angles and ominous shadows," which are intended to work as "ironic contrast, but since both aesthetics are equally cartoon-like, it's hard to discern the point."[14] We concur that *Smoochy* probably did poorly at the box office because the plot becomes too convoluted, the object of satire too well worn to be refreshing.

What the film does manage is to utilize Williams's capacity to show the dark underside of TV and the jaded entertainment industry, which discards its stars the minute they become a detriment to commercial success. The onscreen character of Rainbow Randolph at the film's opening is beloved, but Randolph Smiley, the actor who plays him, is shown to be corrupt, taking bribes from parents eager to see their children on his show; thus, we are initially forced to acknowledge that Rainbow is simply an illusion, a false construction whose artifice is exposed. However, as the convoluted plot unfolds, the audience sees that Smiley really *does* care about the young audience that had once adored him; despite his corruption, one that mirrors the entire artifice of the commercial world of television, Smiley's fierce loyalty to the goodness of his character, Rainbow, is shown to be genuine. This revelation that he has a sincere belief in his mission, allows for a reversal—Rainbow is eventually redeemed from true villainy, reserved for the individuals actually responsible for exploiting the programming, and reverts to the image of himself that he enjoyed before he succumbed to bribery. Rainbow Randolph is both a fiction, and a real part of Randolph Smiley, and the exploration of the relationship between an actor and the persona he portrays is a feature of these films that tie them together. It is important to note that even in 2002 when Williams was in his early fifties, he was still called upon in *Smoochy* to approximate "child impersonations," as we see from his Rainbow character (an adult acting as and relating to a child's sensibilities) just as Ginger Rogers, at thirty-one, was cast as a teenager in *The Major and the Minor*.[15]

Actress Mercedes Ruehl, who co-starred with Williams in *The Fisher King*, remembers how Williams was painfully shy around another cast member when the cast was waiting between takes, but when a make-up artist or other crew member arrived, he would become instantly animated, galvanized by an audience.[16] Ruehl's observation identifies the two sides of Robin Williams, the energetic, quick-witted comedian who elicits instant applause from an audience, and the introspective, brooding star that resides behind the mask of humor. *Death to Smoochy* shows also that Williams drew upon his inner resources to transition instantly from Rainbow, a jovial children's show personality, to his vindictive, self-destructive side, that of his off-screen character, Randolph Smiley, a part presaging his performance in the other two films released in 2002.

Released on May 24, 2002, *Insomnia*, directed by Christopher Nolan, is a remake of a 1997 Norwegian psychological thriller directed and co-written by Erik Skjoldbjærg, starring Stellan Skarsgård as a police detective investigating a murder in a small town that lies above the Arctic Circle. The remake is set in Nightmute, Alaska (the town's name a humorous reminder of the insomnia caused by the constant daylight of the frozen north) and features Al Pacino as the Los Angeles police detective, Will Dormer who, with his partner, Hap Eckhart (Martin Donovan) is called in to help solve the murder of a teenage girl. As in the original film, the detective contrives a trap for the killer, but he fatally shoots his partner when the plan goes wrong. In Nolan's remake, though not in the original film, there had been tension created between Dormer and Eckhart because of an ongoing internal investigation about a previous homicide case in Los Angeles. This fuels Dormer's guilt when he accidentally kills Eckhart in the foggy Alaskan stakeout, but he tells his fellow law officers that the murderer whom they failed to catch shot Eckhart. Ellie Burr (Hillary Swank) is a young officer assigned to investigate Eckhart's death, even as Dormer continues to lead the homicide investigation of the teenage girl, Kay Connell (Crystal Lowe).

Dormer soon finds himself in a deadly cat-and-mouse game with the murderer (at first just a voice), a crime novelist named Walter Finch (Robin Williams), who taunts and attempts to control Dormer by insisting that they are doubles who share a secret. Finch saw Dormer shoot his partner when they were trying to lure Finch to the scene of the murder; he asserts that his killing of the girl, Kay, was likewise an "accident"—he lost control and beat her to death when she rejected his sexual advances. Dormer breaks into Finch's apartment and plants there the gun that had killed Eckhart (his own .38 pistol) to frame him for Eckhart's death. Finch, however, discovers the gun and frames Kay's abusive boyfriend, Randy Stetz (Jonathan Jackson). Eventually, Ellie Burr discovers Dormer's culpability in Eckhart's death. The sleep-deprived detective (whose guilt about Eckhart and the 24-hour daylight make slumber impossible) also confides in the hotel manager he has befriended that he had earlier planted evidence in the Los Angeles apartment of a pedophile that he was sure had murdered a child, but who would not have been otherwise convicted. Dormer's character thus enjoys a complexity and ambivalence that makes him vulnerable to Finch's psychological taunts.

In the end, Finch and Dormer have a showdown at the former's lake house, where he has lured Ellie Burr, with the intent of killing her as well. During this final sequence, Burr confronts Dormer with knowledge that it was his bullet that killed Eckhart; Dormer confesses that, angered because Eckhart was going to turn state's evidence against him, his shooting of Eckhart may not have been an accident. Dormer kills Finch but is himself fatally wounded. Burr, who idolizes Dormer as a detective, believes still that Dormer's shooting of Eckhart was accidental, and prepares to destroy the bullet; Dormer, however, urges her not "to lose her way," but to report her findings, suggesting that, at the moment of his death, he regrets some of the instances in which he tampered with the justice system, having "lost" the idealism that Ellie, a figuration of his younger self, possesses.

This is a different outcome than that of the original, which hinges mostly on the accidental shooting of the partner (no animosity exists between the detective, Jonas Engström, and his slain partner, Erik Vik, and the shooting is unambiguously an accident) and the withholding of evidence. In both cases the truth is eventually uncovered by a female police officer, Swank's counterpart in the original, who reveals to the detective what she knows only when he is preparing to depart after the crime has been solved. He is not killed, and there will be no official accusation of his guilt. Nolan's remake, however, introduces the larger context of the internal police investigation in order to explore the ethical issues that plague Dormer, who fears justice won't be served in the murder cases and who transgresses the law by planting evidence to convict the guilty.

Williams, like Pacino, turned in a star performance, meaning, as Robert B. Ray observes, "an actor has reached stardom when the audience can accept discrepancies between performer and actor,"[17] and the film's emphasis on the characters as doubles provided the opportunity for each to develop his role in extraordinary ways. Pacino's character, Will Dormer—the surname serving as a wry commentary on his inability to sleep in the relentless daylight of the north—possesses a passionate desire to see justice done, acting on his own when the law would not guarantee a just end. The investigation into the case in which he had planted evidence to convict a pedophile comes back to haunt him when his partner, Hap Eckhart (whose first name implies "mishap") tells Will he is going to cooperate with internal affairs and reveal Dormer's actions. Dormer finds himself in that instance caught between his individual sense of justice and an inept legal system, and with Eckhart's imminent betrayal, he has to wonder also whether his shooting of Hap was subconsciously an act of angry retaliation. And once again, in the current murder case, he tampers with evidence to keep himself above suspicion in Eckhart's death, but also to implicate the true killer, Walter Finch. Yet, Dormer has a conscience that will lead to a final self-reckoning, which redeems his integrity.

Finch is a novelist who is obviously fascinated with crime. His bestsellers attract the admiration of a seventeen-year-old girl who is at first flattered by Finch's attention and lavish gifts. The introverted, intelligent writer tries to rationalize his brutal murder by stating that Kay's rejection sent him into a momentary, uncontrollable rage, and was thus an "accident." Dormer counters that the marks on the body suggest she suffered a sustained, deliberate beating. In the game of psychological chess between Finch and Dormer, Finch manages to keep one step ahead of the seasoned detective; he holds Eckhart's death over Dormer's head. When Dormer tries to frame Finch for Eckhart's murder, Finch coolly telephones him while Dormer is in the apartment, inviting him to make himself at home. He discovers the plant and uses the gun to frame Kay's boyfriend and arranges a meeting with Dormer on a ferry—the most chilling scene in the film.

Williams is flawless in his performance during this confrontation, trying to convince Dormer that they are both transgressors and that they need to work together to convict Randy Stetz, the scapegoat. It is a kind of lucid madness—a clear and rational, but ultimately wrong appeal. Dormer's motive in the two cases in which he tampers with evidence is to convict the guilty—the child pedophile and Finch, also a child predator—and it is difficult to believe that Eckhart's death was caused by anything other than fog, tension, and a rash error in judgment when Dormer pulls the trigger, even though Eckhart seems to blame him at his dying moment. Finch not only enticed and murdered a teenage girl, but did so because she rejected his sexual advances; moreover, at the end, he intends to kill Burr, fulfilling Dormer's initial prediction that Kay's murderer was a serial killer in the making, that he would strike again. Finch becomes for Dormer what Dostoevsky's Svidrigailov is to Raskolnikov in *Crime and Punishment* (1868),[18] the devil that taunts him with shared knowledge of a hidden crime. Both Raskolnikov and Dormer are good men who commit a crime that they rationalize will serve real justice; both are haunted by "doubles" who assert their affinity with them, but who are motivated by self-serving interests.

Director Christopher Nolan considered Williams's to be a "flawless performance" as the villain in this psychological thriller, identifying a quality of stardom: "I wound up watching the film hundreds of times as we cut it, and I never hit that point with the performance where you start to see the acting. Most performances, at a point, bits start to peel off and away, but with Robin's he was very much in that character. Not that he's a very dark person to work with—he's very lively and friendly and amusing to work with. He really found something within himself. I think it's a very underrated bit of work on his part."[19]

Unlike *Death to Smoochy*, *Insomnia* enjoyed considerable box office success, raking in $113 million dollars. In *Smoochy*, Williams was required to make dramatic swings in the character he portrayed, and showed that he could play a dark figure, his anger erupting several times, his aborted public suicide attempt representing but a few of many punctuations in the otherwise comic "clown" he depicts, and to which he returns in the film's resolution. Walter Finch in *Insomnia*, released a few months later, provided Williams the opportunity to play a chilling villain, an unredeemed murderer and master manipulator, thus "upping the ante" in the demands it made on his acting talents.

The final film of 2002 that starred Robin Williams, *One Hour Photo* (released on August 21), features the lonely, introverted Seymour (Sy) Parrish, an employee of a large discount chain, SavMart, where he develops photos for its customers. This represents one of Williams's finest performances, and the film itself has achieved cult status. If we are correct in our observation that Williams's face, like John Wayne's, projects the mystery required of a great actor, *One Hour Photo* provides Williams the opportunity to demonstrate fully this intangible, mysterious dimension that contributed so heavily to his acting success. One the one hand, Sy Parrish is ingratiating and accommodating to his customers, even as he begins to reveal a deep pathology and seething disdain for both bourgeois hypocrisy and its disregard for his own sense of moral decency. From the opening moments of the film, Williams's Sy keeps us uncomfortably off-balance as we wish to believe in the benign, shy persona of the employee who genuinely cares for his customers, but who is also from the start on the verge of invading their privacy, thereby conveying a vaguely threatening air. This duplicitous character that Williams so convincingly creates becomes the enigma that unfolds as the film arrives at its disturbing revelation at the end.

Sy Parrish knows his customers well. A lonely, middle-aged man, he has taken a special interest in one particular family, the Yorkins, whose photos he has developed during his eleven years at SavMart: Will (Michael Vartan), his wife Nina (Connie Nielsen), and their nine-year-old son, Jake (Dylan Smith). Sy imagines them to be the "perfect family" he has never had, and imaginatively inserts himself into their lives as their "Uncle Sy." He secretly makes duplicate prints of their photos, living vicariously through them, and erecting a colossal montage consisting of them in his otherwise sparsely furnished apartment. The film begins with a voiceover—Sy's—in which he avers that "No one takes a photo of something they want to forget," but rather to serve as a record of the happy moments in a family's life. Sy takes the job of photo developers very seriously, as a result, seeing it as fulfilling a sacred trust and expressing a "reverence for the service they're providing people." Sy insists on this view of his profession, even though he later asserts that on the busiest day of the week, Monday, the customers who line up to have their film developed include those of eccentric cat owners, banal insurance adjusters, and amateur porn artists. None of this seems to affect Sy's dream of the Yorkins as an ideal family, an image he attempts to keep inviolate. However, events unfold that threaten this image, and as it crumbles, so does Sy's fragile hold on reality.

Minutes into the film, the viewer sees that for the Yorkins, there is trouble in paradise. Shortly after perusing the recently-developed photos of Jake's ninth birthday party, Nina and Will argue, their sensitive young son listening in. Nina accuses Will of being "emotionally neglectful" as a father and husband; he counters by quipping that his frequent absence is a result of his need to work in order to pay for the Mercedes and the "Jill Sanders blouse" she wears. We know that Nina is not the contented wife and mother she would appear to be; Sy notices that she has purchased a copy of Deepak Chopra's 1998 self-help book, *The Path to Love: Spiritual Strategies for Healing*. In a ruse to insinuate himself into her confidence, Sy stages a "chance encounter" with Nina in a shopping mall restaurant, making a point of reading the same book. He quotes from it: "The things we fear the most have already happened to us," which, as it turns out, is true for Sy, the secret of his hidden trauma having occurred in his childhood. Sy's dark side occasionally emerges, not only in staging this encounter with Nina, but in other ways. He fantasizes entering the Yorkin home; a voyeur, he visits the bedrooms of the couple and their son, watches television on their sofa, and is shown using their toilet— a more sinister act, known to occur when intruders enter a home. Sy also begins to stalk Jake, watching him at soccer practice, after which he takes him to his car to offer him a coveted toy his father had refused to buy him days before (which Jake politely refuses) and probing him about his father's absence at his sporting events. He confides in Jake that as a boy he himself was "fat and sick" and once suffered a broken collar-bone, our first clear sense that Sy was victimized as a child. Jake makes excuses for his father; Sy backs off, and keeps a respectful distance.

Sy soon learns, however, that Nina has reason to be uneasy in her marriage. A woman who looks familiar to him (it turns out, she has been featured in some of the Yorkin family photos of a neighborhood softball tournament) brings in a roll of film. When he develops the prints, Sy sees Maya Burson (Erin Daniels) in compromising positions with Will Yorkin, and realizes they are having an affair. This shatters his faith in the ideal family that has helped him keep his life together; coupled with this, Sy's manager, Bill Owens (Gary Cole) having noticed his occasional losses of temper and a discrepancy in the photo count—the result of Sy making years of duplicate photos of the Yorkin family photos—fires Sy, an act that pushes him over the emotional edge. With no future photos of the Yorkins, coupled with the shattering of their holy family image he has formed, Sy becomes vengeful, vindictive, and dangerous.

Naturally, he sympathizes with the wronged wife and her son, so to expose Will's affair, he places Maya's developed photos in with those that Jake has dropped off the day before. He then follows Nina and Jake, witnessing her obvious distress when she discovers these incriminating pictures among her son's photos. Sy spies on the family, expecting to see a major upheaval when Nina confronts and rejects her husband. Instead, watching from a safe distance in his car, he zooms in on a scenario that belies this—Nina serving dinner to her family in a seemingly tranquil fashion, a hypocrisy that enrages Sy: "What the hell's wrong with these people?" he asks himself, as he speeds off. Sy also engages in altercations with his ex-manager, threatening him by planting photos to suggest he has been stalking Owens's young daughter. This, then, brings in the authorities, even as Sy prepares to take the matter of Will's infidelity into his own hands.

He stalks Maya and Will, following them on "Hunter Valley Road" to the Edgerton Hotel. Clearly unhinged (we see that he has scraped Will's face from every image of his family photo montage), Sy had stolen a hunting knife from SavMart when he was terminated, and now contrives to exact revenge for the betrayal he feels. When he breaks into their hotel room, he "directs" the naked couple to "pretend" they are having "fun," forcing them into various obscene positions and inventing scenarios for them to "perform." He insists that they should only "act" and not actually perform these deeds, as he pretends also to be photographing them. The viewer suspects, and this is soon confirmed, that this is a psychotic episode, a compulsive re-enactment of the defining traumatic experience of Sy's early life, only this time he is the perpetrator rather than the victim. He flees without harming the two but is soon caught by the police. Director Mark Romanek says of Sy's arrest scene on the canted exit ramp of this large hotel, surrounded by menacing authorities, faces obscured in shadow, that to Sy they must seem "terrible father figures, all."[20]

In the film's conclusion, we see the safe return of Will to his wife and son, by a disgusted Detective, James Van Der Zee (Eriq La Salle) who clearly disapproves of Will's affair, the detective's name a sly nod to the famous photographer of the Harlem Renaissance. (Minutes earlier, fleeing police in the hotel, Sy had run through a conference room in which a doctor was discussing "retinal implants," another nod to the film's focus on images.) The final scene, which takes place in a spare white room without décor, a claustrophobic, sterile enclosure except for an observation window, features Detective Van Der Zee at the police station, awaiting the arrival of Sy's attorney. Sy asserts that if he is a family man, he knows Van Der Zee would "never neglect, abuse, or make horrible demands" of his children. *He* would never have his children do "things that children should not do, and take pictures of them doing these things"; *he* would never "treat them like animals." The detective, who earlier disapproved of the tawdry hotel scene between Maya and Will, understands that Sy's motive is rooted in his own exploited childhood: "I think I understand, sir. Thank you for answering my questions so candidly." Sadly, Sy imagines himself—depicted in a split screen—as "Uncle Sy" once again in a Yorkin family photo. He then asks the Detective for the developed prints they found in his possession when he was arrested. It turns out these are not staged pornographic hotel room shots, but consist of quotidian objects, amateurishly out of perspective and context. In the final shot, Sy is seen puzzling over them, trying in vain to arrange them in an "order" that will once again make sense of the world for him.

Written and directed by Mark Romanek, *One Hour Photo* benefits not only from Williams's stellar performance and its inherently interesting take on the themes of voyeurism and the manipulation of images in the contemporary world, but also from Romanek's own phenomenal success as a director of music videos—notably for Johnny Cash ("Hurt"), Nine-Inch Nails ("Closer" and "The Perfect Drug"), and Michael and Janet Jackson ("Scream"). Critic Elvis Mitchell, in his *New York Times* review of *One Hour Photo*, noting Romanek's success in the music video industry, comments: "The depth of feeling in the videos Mr. Romanek directed comes through his deployment of color and the suggestion of violence. He does much the same thing in 'Photo.'"[21] Romanek's visual sense lends a decided aesthetic dimension to certain scenes in the film: the revelatory montage that covers a whole wall of Sy's apartment, the lurid red used in the scene in which Sy discovers photos that incriminate the father of the family he has "adopted," the sterile white room (save for the blood oozing from his eyes) of Sy's nightmare when he realizes his own violent potential, prompted by having discovered Will's infidelity. Some shots show a keen awareness of spatial manipulation, as well, as when Sy is filmed, sitting cross-legged on the floor, looking with delight at the childish photographs Jake took with the disposable camera Sy gave him as a birthday present. This underscores Sy's own vulnerability and his genuine affection for the boy, perhaps serving as an embodiment of the childhood Sy himself was never allowed.

The audio commentary for the 2003 DVD features Mark Romanek and Robin Williams. At that time, this was Williams's first commentary. Williams remarked that watching himself in this role drove home the point that Sy was "someone so unlike myself,"[22] in that the character had been abused as a child. Yet, Williams talks also of being lonely as a child. He had two half-siblings, but all were raised separately. With his much older half-brother, Todd, born in 1938, he shares the same father; with his other half-brother, McLaurin Smith-Williams, born in 1947, he shares the same mother. In a 1991 interview McLaurin remarked: "All three of us grew up as only children—Todd, myself, and Robin" because of the age gaps and different parents.[23] Williams recalls that he learned to "Fixate on other things to find a way around it (loneliness)."[24] Drawing on the feeling of isolation and sadness, despite the economic privileges he knew from being the son of a Ford Motor Company executive and an old, established Mississippi family on his mother's side, Williams was able to find that place in his own past that helped him create such a convincing psychological portrait of a disturbed individual who managed to exist under the radar for so many years before confronting his own childhood trauma. Sy Parrish is a convincing but compelling almost-villain, a scourge on a hypocritical component of society too worried about its material well-being to foster a decent environment for its children. Jake is a victim of this—sometimes benignly ignored by his unfaithful father, he saw the photos of this same parent cheating on his mother. He, too, is an only child, one who is so sensitive as to worry about Sy who, at the opening of the film, he intuits to be a lonely adult, and confides this to his mother, who tries in turn to assuage Jake's sadness by instructing him to send good thoughts to Sy.

Details in the film corroborate Jake's insight: we see Williams purchasing photos of strangers; in one scene, he shows Nina a wallet photo of a young woman and tells her it is an image of his mother, clearly a fabrication. Sy's mother was absent or totally ineffective in protecting him from an abusive father; Romanek refers to the "dark father figures" and the "ultimate repressed memory"[25] at the end of Sy's own abuse, one that redeems him from one-dimensional villainy. Coupled with this childhood horror, we must feel some affinity with Sy's disgust at the facile manner with which Will betrays his family, but also with the minimal consequences when this is exposed. Nina is willing to live with the man she knows is having an affair; Will returns to the arms of his forgiving son, and probably also to his wife. The vacuous nature of a relationship that closes ranks to protect its own class and material interests, is surely intended to enlist our affinity with Sy, who feels disgust at this hypocrisy. This behavior, and the critique of it, has deep roots in American culture. Witness F. Scott Fitzgerald's Nick Carraway in *The Great Gatsby*, a nocturnal voyeur watching Tom and Daisy Buchanan through the window of their home, conspiring about what to do just after Daisy has run over Myrtle Wilson, her husband's mistress, and killed her: "They weren't happy together, and neither of them had touched the chicken or the ale—and yet they weren't unhappy either … anyone would have said they were conspiring together."[26] Later, Nick moralizes: "They were careless people, Tom and Daisy—they smashed up things and people and then retreated back into their money, or their vast carelessness, or whatever it was that kept them going, and let other people clean up the mess they had made…."[27]

This conspiratorial relationship seems an equally apt description of Nina and Will in the final scene. Interestingly, earlier in 2002, Adrian Lyne directed Diane Ladd and Richard Gere in *Unfaithful*, about a husband who, upon discovering his wife's affair, murders her lover. When she learns her husband is the murderer, and he is ready to turn himself in, she refuses to let him, and proposes they move away, assuming new identities, with which he concurs. Once again, we see an affluent couple conspire together to cover their criminal activity, burning evidence and lying to authorities. Like Will and Nina, they have one young son (eight years old); in the end, they close ranks to avoid the consequences of her reckless affair and his violent murder, a cynical commentary on affluent suburban hypocrisy. Reaching back further in cinematic time, critics have noticed its similarity as social criticism of suburban life to *American Beauty* (1999) and the influential *Taxi Driver* (1976), the latter a film that features "God's lonely man," Travis Bickle (Robert De Niro), a term that might be aptly applied to Sy Parrish.

Why did Williams enjoy this role in *One Hour Photo*: "Number one, not having to look a certain way, number two not being bound by the same rules of likeability which Anthony Hopkins says is the kind of the joy that comes from playing disturbed or villainous characters"[28] is his answer. Even more than the earlier experimental *Death to Smoochy* and the masterful remake, *Insomnia*, *One Hour Photo* afforded Williams the opportunity to alternate between extreme character traits: that of the sensitive, introverted photo-developer and the dark, mercurial scourge who stalks others and harbors an explosive anger, the crippling effect of repressed childhood trauma. This, he does masterfully. As Roger Ebert observes: "Robin Williams plays Sy, another of his open-faced, smiling madmen, like the killer in *Insomnia*."[29] But Ebert is not quite correct: Sy Parrish is not a madman, but is instead filled with moral outrage—some of it understandable. Moreover, in *One Hour Photo*, Williams is given more to do; his role in *Insomnia* is a supporting one, with the focus on Pacino's detective and his own moral ambiguity. In *One Hour Photo* the entire center of interest is watching the enigma of Sy Parrish unfold.

These three films of 2002 represent what is perhaps unique about Robin Williams's stardom, a comedian who expresses joy at playing unpredictable, even villainous characters. In *Insomnia* and *One Hour Photo*, he moves out of the "child impersonation" phase entirely, playing the role of villain and child murderer in the former, and a ticking time-bomb of an adult who was exploited as a child in the latter. These films also activate that mystery that often envelops major stars—the ability to make an audience wonder whether what they are seeing is artifice or something deeply personal. The source of the idiosyncrasies of the actor and the characters he plays remains an enigma, but one that adds to, rather than detracting from, his stardom.

NOTES

1. Roland Barthes, *Mythologies*, trans. Annette Lavers (New York: Hill and Wang, 1972). 75.
2. Robert B. Ray, *The ABCs of Classic Hollywood*. (New York: Oxford University Press, 2008). 30.
3. David Thomson. *The New Biographical Dictionary of Film*. (New York: Alfred A. Knopf, 2004). 963.
4. Andrew Sarris, *"You Ain't Heard Nothin' Yet": The American Talking Film: History and Memory, 1927–1949*. (New York: Oxford University Press, 1998). 384.
5. Sarris, *"You Ain't Heard Nothin' Yet."* 410.
6. Ray, *The ABCs*, 38.
7. Robert B. Ray, *A Certain Tendency of the Hollywood Cinema, 1930–1980*. (Princeton: Princeton University Press, 1985), 73.
8. Ray, *A Certain Tendency*, 73.
9. Roger Ebert, *"Death to Smoochy."* *Chicago Sun-Times*. March 29, 2002. http://www.rogerebert.com/reviews/death-to-smoochy-2002
10. *Ibid.*
11. *Ibid.*
12. Kevin Thomas, "Satirical Overkill in 'Death to Smoochy.'" *Los Angeles Times*, March 29, 2002. http://articles.latimes.com/2002/mar/29/entertainment/et-thomas29

13. Maitland McDonagh, "*Death to Smoochy*: Movie Reviews and Movie Ratings." 38: 2002. http://www.tvguide.com/movies/death-to-smoochy/review/135728/
14. *Ibid.*
15. Thomson, *The New Biographical Dictionary*, 769.
16. *Robin Williams: Behind Closed Doors.* Documentary Interviews. REELZ 2015.
17. Ray, *The ABCs,* 162.
18. Feodor Dostoevsky, *Crime and Punishment.* trans. Jessie Coulson. (New York: W.W. Norton 1975).
19. Mike Eisenberg, "Chris Nolan Speaks at the Hero Complex Film Festival. Screen-Rant, June 16, 2010. http://screenrant.com/christopher-nolan-interview-hero-complex-film-festival-mikee-64419/.
20. Mark Romanek, *One Hour Photo,* DVD Audio Commentary.
21. Elvis Mitchell, "Film Review: That Orderly World of Appearances He Lives In? It's About to Explode." *New York Times*, August 21, 2002. http://www.nytimes.com/movie/review?res=9f0ce4db1e3df932a1575bc0a9649c8b63.
22. Mark Romanek, *One Hour Photo* Audio Commentary.
23. Michael Donahue, "Robin Williams' Half-Brother Is an All-Out Fan: Interview with McLaurin Smith-Williams." *Chicago Tribune*, December 25, 1991. http://articles.chicagotribune.com/1991-12-25/features/9104250678_1_robin-williams-peter-pan-todd-williams.
24. Robin Williams, *One Hour Photo,* DVD Audio Commentary.
25. Mark Romanek, *One Hour Photo,* DVD Audio Commentary.
26. F. Scott Fitzgerald, *The Great Gatsby.* (New York: Charles Scribner's Sons, 1925) 146.
27. *Ibid.,* 180–181.
28. Robin Williams, *One Hour Photo,* DVD Audio Commentary.
29. Roger Ebert, "One Hour Photo." *Chicago Sun-Times*, August 23, 2002. http://www.rogerebert.com/reviews/one-hour-photo-2002.

BIBLIOGRAPHY

Barthes, Roland. *Mythologies,* trans. Annette Lavers. New York: Hill and Wang, 1972.
Donahue, Michael. "Robin Williams' Half-Brother is an All-Out Fan: Interview with McLaurin Smith-Williams." In *Chicago Tribune*, December 25, 1991. http://articles.chicagotribune.com/1991–12-25/features/9104250678_1_robin-williams-peter-pan-todd-williams.
Dostoevsky, Feodor. *Crime and Punishment,* trans. Jessie Coulson. New York: W.W. Norton, 1975.
Ebert, Roger. "*Death to Smoochy.*" *Chicago Sun-Times*. March 29, 2002. http://www.rogerebert.com/reviews/death-to-smoochy-2002.
_____. "One Hour Photo. *Chicago Sun-Times*, August 23, 2002. http://www.rogerebert.com/reviews/one-hour-photo-2002.
Eisenberg, Mike. "Chris Nolan Speaks at the Hero Complex Film Festival. ScreenRant, June 16, 2010. http://screenrant.com/christopher-nolan-interview-hero-complex-film-festival-mikee-64419/.
Fitzgerald, F. Scott. *The Great Gatsby.* New York: Charles Scribner's Sons, 1925.
McDonagh, Maitland. "*Death to Smoochy*: Movie Reviews and Movie Ratings." *TV Guide* 38: 2002. http://www.tvguide.com/movies/death-to-smoochy/review/135728/.
Mitchell, Elvis. "Film Review: That Orderly World of Appearances He Lives In? It's About to Explode." *New York Times*, August 21, 2002. http://www.nytimes.com/movie/review?res=9f0ce4db1e3df932a1575bc0a9649c8b63.
Ray, Robert B. *The ABCs of Classic Hollywood.* New York: Oxford University Press, 2008.
Robin Williams: Behind Closed Doors. Documentary Interviews. REELZ 2015.
Romanek, Mark, *One Hour Photo,* DVD Audio Commentary.
Sarris, Andrew. *"You Ain't Heard Nothin' Yet": The American Talking Film: History and Memory, 1927–1949.* New York: Oxford University Press, 1998.
Thomas, Kevin. "Satirical Overkill in 'Death to Smoochy.'" Los Angeles Times, March 29, 2002. http://articles.latimes.com/2002/mar/29/entertainment/et-thomas29.
Thomson, David. *The New Biographical Dictionary of Film.* New York: Alfred A. Knopf, 2004.

"I like New York in June"?

Terrors of the City in The Fisher King

CYNTHIA J. MILLER *and* A. BOWDOIN VAN RIPER

The Fisher King, Terry Gilliam's 1991 comedy-drama featuring Robin Williams, has been variously discussed as a "quest" film, a religious narrative, an update of Arthurian legends, a fairytale, and an exploration of traumatic mental illness. Williams plays a homeless man whose belief that he is a knight errant brings comic nobility to life on the streets, but whose inner world is chaotic and menaced by visions of the evil Red Knight, who seeks to bring about his destruction.

It is possible, however, to read *The Fisher King* as neither latter-day Arthurian fantasy nor poignant drama, but as a horror narrative that—straddling the boundary between the real and the surreal—excavates the multiple layers of fear and monstrosity embedded in urban New York. The disabled and destitute inhabit alleys, condemned buildings, and empty lots; a caustic, self-serving radio host berates callers to his late-night show; a disturbed loner walks into an upscale restaurant with a shotgun and opens fire, exacting vengeance on diners he barely knows; a pair of vicious teens defend "their" neighborhood by prowling its shadowy margins, seeking defenseless prey to beat and set on fire; a flaming supernatural horseman appears unpredictably on tree-lined streets and in trash-strewn wastelands, a portent of chaos and destruction for all in his path.

Gilliam's vision depicts a city unraveling into disease, decay, and mass murder, and presents its inhabitants—through fear-evoking urban stereotypes—at their worst and most dangerous, but veils the horrors in bittersweet comedy, allowing audiences to indulge in comfortable fantasy. Williams's character Parry, whose life and mind have been shattered by the city's horrors, is the gatekeeper. Armed with gentle humor, he shields audiences (and his fellow

145

characters) from the terrors that fight to define urban life, failing only when he, himself, is overcome. In an extreme act of foolhardy optimism, he lies naked on the grass in Central Park, attempting to break apart the clouds covering the moon with his mind ("cloud-busting"), and leads a crowd of battered and broken homeless people, gathered around a fire in a trash can, in a rousing chorus of Sinatra's "How About You." Squatting in a filthy, junk-filled basement, Parry smiles and beckons: "Come back! We'll rummage!"

Because the film's portrayals of the monstrous are almost immediately redeemed by Williams's comedy, they pass largely unnoticed; overlooked in favor of the film's ultimate heartwarming message of redemption. This essay, then, is a drawing-back of the veil that Gilliam drapes over the urban horrors in *The Fisher King,* and an exploration of Williams's role in enabling the characters—and the audience—to carry on in spite of them.

Two Men and a Grail

The Fisher King begins at a New York radio station where DJ Jack Lucas (Jeff Bridges) is delighting his engineers (and presumably his listeners) with his cynical wit, mocking and belittling callers to his show. Returning to his starkly modern high-rise apartment, he is jolted out of his fog of self-regard by a breaking news report. A regular caller—hearing Jack's tossed-off comment that Yuppies are "evil" and "must be stopped before it's too late" as a call to action—has opened fire with a shotgun in a crowded Manhattan restaurant, killing seven patrons before taking his own life. Three years pass in the space of a title card. Jack—still haunted by the mass murder, for which he blames himself—has left broadcasting for a part-time job as a clerk in the video store owned by his endlessly patient lover Anne (Mercedes Ruehl), with whom he lives in her apartment above the store. His misanthropy deepened by depression and his lacerating tongue loosened by alcohol, Jack is only intermittently (and then only barely) capable of civil interactions with anyone else.

One night, having hit rock bottom, Jack wanders aimlessly through the city until he reaches the Manhattan Bridge, where he prepares to commit suicide. He is interrupted by two young thugs who, believing him to be homeless, are preparing to burn him alive when they, in turn, are interrupted by a strangely dressed man (Robin Williams) who speaks in vaguely medieval cadences and wields a non-lethal bow and arrow. The stranger, aided by several homeless-looking allies, drives off one thug and subdues the other, leaving him hogtied and at the mercy of passersby. He then brings Jack first to a homeless encampment under the bridge, and then to his own makeshift "home" in the basement-level machinery spaces of an apartment building. The stranger introduces himself as "Parry" and explains that he is a knight, on a quest to find the Holy Grail and return it from its hiding place in the castle-like mansion of a noted New York City architect. Parry is advised by cherubic "little people" and opposed by the terrifying Red Knight (both delusions, but utterly real to him); Jack, he insists, has been sent to aid him on his quest. The building superintendent explains to Jack that Parry—once a professor at Hunter College—suffered a mental break three years before, when his wife was gunned down before his eyes in the restaurant shooting committed by Jack's disturbed caller. Deinstitutionalized, he returned to his old building, where the superintendent took him in.

Jack reluctantly agrees to help Parry, seeing it as a way to atone for his perceived sins. Parry leads him on a quixotic tour of Midtown Manhattan, during which they rescue a suicidal, homeless ex-cabaret performer (Michael Jeter) in Central Park, and "meet" the young woman that Parry loves from afar: a sweet, shy accountant named Lydia (Amanda Plummer). Late that night, as they lay on the grass in Central Park, staring at the moon, Parry tells Jack the medieval legend of the Fisher King, who once had the Holy Grail within his grasp, but lost it because he chose to pursue wealth and power rather than use the relic to heal wounded souls. Despondent and suffering after a lifetime of searching for the Grail, he asks a passing Fool for a drink of water, only to realize that the cup the Fool holds out to him is the Grail itself. Asked how he came find it when the King and all his knights could not, the Fool replies: "I don't know. I only knew that you were thirsty."

Jack, determined to help Parry meet Lydia, enlists Anne and the cabaret singer in an elaborate ruse that brings Lydia to the video store, where Parry is posing as a clerk and Jack "casually" suggests the foursome have dinner together at a local Chinese restaurant. The evening is a success, and Parry walks Lydia home, soothing her fears of abandonment by pledging his unwavering love for her. They part happily, but Parry's newfound self-confidence triggers an attack by the Red Knight. Fleeing in terror, he finds himself beneath the same bridge where he saved Jack on the night they met, and is attacked by the same thugs, leaving him catatonic.

Jack, freed from his burden of guilt by his success as a matchmaker, has just begun the process of reclaiming his old life when the police alert him to Parry's condition. He visits the hospital, but—distracted by his comeback in broadcasting and the offer of a possible television series—slips back toward his old, self-centered ways: breaking up with Anne for reasons he can barely articulate, snubbing the cabaret singer during a chance encounter on the sidewalk, and declining to carry out Parry's wish that he complete the quest to find and retrieve the Grail. As he listens to an unctuous TV producer (John DeLancie) describe Jack's proposed new series as a situation comedy about the carefree lives of three "wacky but wise" homeless people, however, Jack experiences an epiphany. He bolts from the producer's opulent office without a word, and (using Parry's notes) begins making plans to storm the "castle" where the "Grail" is kept.

The plan, as makeshift and complicated as the one that brought Parry and Lydia together, works with improbable smoothness, allowing Jack to scale the building's walls, enter the architect's study, and retrieve the Grail. It is an unremarkable silver trophy cup, but when he brings it to the hospital and lays it on his friend's chest, Parry is miraculously revived. Having fallen fast asleep beside the hospital bed, exhausted by his night's exertions, Jack awakens to find a newly confident, clear-headed Parry leading the ward's other patients in a chorus of "How About You?" as Lydia looks on, tearful and beaming. Jack returns to the apartment above the video store and reconciles with Anne—his inner demons, like Parry's, now vanquished at last.

New York City as Horrorscape

The gritty realities of life on the streets of New York were documented in the still photography of Jacob Riis and Lewis Hine well before Hollywood entered the sound era, but the Production Code and the pressure to produce commercial entertainment kept such images off movie screens.[1] Well into the early 1960s, the slums, tenements, and industrial wastelands of cinematic New York had—even in "message pictures" like *Dead End* (1937), *On the Waterfront* (1954), and *West Side Story* (1964)—a tidy, well-scrubbed ambience. Only in the late 1960s, with the collapse of the Code and the rise of a new realist aesthetic, did films begin to depict New York as a nightmare-world where decades of violence, poverty, and hopelessness had left the social fabric in tatters. *Midnight Cowboy* (1969), an early example, won an Oscar for its portrayal of two desperate hustlers slowly dying on the sidewalks of a city indifferent to their existence. Crime dramas like *The French Connection* (1971), *Mean Streets* (1973) and *Death Wish* (1974) brought to life Raymond Chandler's famous vision of a city where "no man can walk down a dark street in safety because law and order are things we talk about but refrain from practicing."[2] The films resonated with contemporary headlines about rising crime rates, crumbling infrastructure, and looming fiscal collapse.[3] Even Neil Simon's *The Out-of-Towners* (1970)—a farce about a hapless Ohio couple whose best-laid travel plans unravel in the face of transit strikes, muggings, and street protests—evoked a city teetering on the verge of chaos.

Depictions of New York as a grim urban battleground riven by crime and steeped in alienation grew steadily more surreal as the 1970s gave way to the 1980s. Robert DeNiro's performance in the title role lent *Taxi Driver* (1976) the ambience of a fever dream, and the poster for Walter Hill's *The Warriors* (1979) depicted garishly clad street gangs as "the armies of the night

... 100,000 strong" who "outnumber the cops five to one" and could "run New York City." Two years later, John Carpenter's dystopian science-fiction adventure *Escape from New York* (1981) imagined Manhattan as a walled maximum-security prison, teeming with free-range murderers, rapists, and thieves. The image of New York as hell on earth—the city of Riis and Hine reimagined by Dante and Hieronymus Bosch—thus became a familiar, though not exclusive, cinematic image of the city in the 1980s and beyond.[4]

The New York that Gilliam brings to the screen in *The Fisher King* is less overtly broken than Carpenter's and less uniformly grim than Scorcese's, but no less horrific. Its horrors bubble and seethe beneath the city's veil of normality, and lurk on darkened street corners. Agents of chaos roam the streets, waiting to fall upon the weak, vulnerable, and unwary.

Jack is only a few stumbling steps beyond the door of Anne's apartment when he first enters Gilliam's nightmare-world, falling over a curb lined with cans and sacks of uncollected garbage and into a gutter filled with pooled, filthy water. Garishly lit signs illuminate a steady rain—film *noir* grace notes in a world defined by wet pavement, rusting fire escapes, and grimy brick walls. The steel shutters and iron bars that cover every ground-floor window testify to the ubiquity of crime. The chaos and squalor becomes more extreme, and the danger more immediate, when Jack reaches the river. The world beneath the bridge and its approach ramps is a chaotic jumble of dumped trash, crumbled building materials, and junked cars inhabited by men (Parry and his latter-day "knights") whose scavenged clothes and improvised weapons suggest a post-apocalyptic wasteland. The thugs who nearly kill Jack come equipped for violence—emerging from their jeep with a baseball bat and cans of gasoline already in their hands—determined (they declare) to protect the sanctity of "their" neighborhood. That Parry and his friends are equally prepared, and similarly motivated, reinforces the post-apocalyptic quality of the scene.

Gilliam's camera makes the world through which Jack drunkenly rambles—from the time he stumbles out of Anne's apartment to the time he wakes up in Parry's workshop-turned-bedroom—even more nightmarishly distorted. Tilted shots, low-angle shots, forced perspectives, and shifting points of view follow each other in rapid succession, suggesting Jack's own sense of disorientation and turning the city around him literally topsy-turvy. His torments in the homeless encampment—accidentally lighting his gasoline-soaked coat sleeve on fire, vomiting after a bite of a proffered convenience-store cherry pie, and having liquor poured down his throat—are framed so that the towering, blue-lit walls and arches of the bridge loom above and behind him like a cathedral. His conversations with Parry in the latter's makeshift home are staged with the walls—so laden with chains, tools, and improvised weapons that they suggest a dungeon or torture chamber—are always visible at the edges and in the background.

The horrorscape that lurks beneath the surface of Gilliam's version of New York also outcrops in more genteel surroundings. Ragged, desperate people line Grand Central Terminal's marble-clad walls and slump on its varnished benches—walking-wounded casualties of a never-ending battle for survival. The cabaret singer, draped across Jack's lap in a pose than evokes Michelangelo's *Pietà*, laments that he "watched all my friends die," a line that reinforces the wartime atmosphere while subtly evoking the AIDS epidemic. Strolling through Central Park late at night, Parry is serene—delighted by the beauty of the moonlit world—but Jack is visibly anxious. "Walking around here during the day is one thing, but at night we could be killed by a wide variety of people." Parry acknowledges the danger, even though he refuses to be cowed by it, declaring that "this park is mine as much as it is theirs." Gilliam's sympathies are clearly with Parry, but he punctuates the scene with a cutaway shot of three figures scuttling along the tree-line, silhouetted in the moonlight. Their bent-kneed, loose-limbed gait gives them a vaguely atavistic quality, and allows them to stand for all the dark things that lurk in the shadows of Gilliam's nightmarish New York.

Parry as Gatekeeper

Robin Williams's Parry is at once a pivotal and liminal figure in the film. He is the source of action and the catalyst for change, but is, at the same time, physically, psychologically, and socially vulnerable and marginalized. His mind acknowledges none of the limitations placed on his status, endowing him with an agency that other characters, both homeless and mainstream, lack.

Formerly a successful professor, Parry had been a member of society's privileged class, enjoying opportunities and resources that, as a homeless and mentally ill individual, he is now denied. But the character shaped by the influence of his past remains—he is literate, outgoing, and clever—and is augmented by the childlike qualities engendered by the fantasy world he now inhabits. He possesses an ethical clarity unencumbered by economics or social hierarchies, and a buoyant humor that is key to the narrative strategy.

For Parry, the terrors of the unconscious invade everyday life and are made manifest, reconfiguring the city into a horrorscape in which he regularly fights (or flees) for his life. He exists on multiple borders—between fantasy and reality; being and becoming; sanity and the loss of self—simultaneously functioning as victim, guardian, and vanquisher. While in the eyes of those around him, he is the victim of multiple social ills, his self-ascribed role is to beat back the monsters, keeping those around him safe, and in fact, unaware of the peril he battles on their behalf.

With one foot in that fantasy world, and the other in harsh reality, Parry retains an awareness of their overlapping existences that no other characters possess. This is his burden and his responsibility—to bear the weight of both. Parry may thus be seen as a guardian or gatekeeper—both within the world of the film and generically—as he traverses the frontier between mainstream and margin, safety and danger, fantasy and reality. Much as the scientists or journalists who encounter, filter, and disseminate the unknown, Parry's status is the result of social and political environments that create the conditions for his role. He resides on the jagged edges of society, yet is intricately interwoven with it.

This is a complex role, one that requires tenacity, as well as an acceptance of inconsistency and failure. Williams plays Parry as flawed, fallible, and broken, yet inflected with bravery and honor as well as fear. He, like the classic gatekeepers of science, defends the sameness of the world around him against disaster—guarding and controlling knowledge and access—while at the same time venturing after the unknown, flirting with possibility, and forging the path of change.[5] He alone understands the fantasy world beyond the frontier, which he adapts and interprets for Jack and others around him. And when the unknown becomes too vast and overwhelming to be comprehensible, he falters and fails. His visions of the Red Knight terrify him, as the horror of one world bleeds into the other, reminding him that, even in his role as gatekeeper, he is limited and vulnerable.

The knight, as Jeffrey Cohen observes of the monstrous, represents "a double narrative, two living stories: one which describes how the monster came to be, and another, its testimony, detailing what cultural use the monster serves."[6] As a product of Parry's psychic break over the death of his wife, the manifest function of the Red Knight is to punish Parry for a crime that was not his; the latent function, however, is to provide him with a role and an identity through which he can reestablish himself as guardian and protector. Parry's monster lies, as Cohen suggests, at the edge of possibility—of becoming—beating back his social, emotional, and psychological advances toward change: "The monster prevents mobility (intellectual, geographical, or sexual), delimiting the social spaces through which private bodies [or minds] may move. To step outside this official geography is to risk attack by monstrous Border Patrol, or (worse) become monstrous oneself."[7] Still, Parry presses on in his multiple roles, even as the monstrous knight seeks to limit his emotional, psychological, and social terrain.

Parry's first encounter with Jack blends these roles of fantasy and reality, as Parry, the noble defender—a ragged knight errant—and his band of homeless warriors come to Jack's aid. Severely beaten, Jack is nearly set on fire by a brutal pair of street thugs until Parry intervenes, vanquishes the foe, and ushers Jack to safety. The next morning, Parry confides in Jack about his status as "the janitor of God," his quest for a symbol of grace, and the fairies and monsters of a fantasy world that bleeds, unbidden, into his reality. Jack, he believes, is "the one"—heralded by the fairies—chosen to help him. Jack rejects the notion, and Parry, and makes a hasty retreat, but later returns, thinking that it is he who must battle Parry's monsters. It is unclear at this point who is intended to save whom, but while Jack attempts to address the social and economic monsters that afflict his homeless new friend, Parry retains his role as guardian and gatekeeper. He places himself between Jack and the city's horrors, both real and imagined, and bestows upon Jack the knowledge he needs to battle his own monsters. Ultimately, as Jack (albeit temporarily) succeeds Parry in his role as guardian, he is able to aid his friend in merging worlds and roles and emerge from his battles whole.

While it is true that, as the narrative progresses, Parry very nearly loses the battle for change against the monsters that dwell along the frontiers of his mind, he succeeds not only in protecting his new friend from the fantastic incursions of the Red Knight, but also in reviving Jack's humanity. By the film's end, the horrors of the city are, for both of them, effectively held at bay.

Mitigating the Horror

"Come back! We'll rummage!"

The success that Williams's Parry finds as gatekeeper and guardian is due to one significant factor: the gentle, unassuming humor that animates his role. His social, economic, and psychological vulnerability become, throughout the film, assets for heartwarming comedic moments, rather than stark reminders of the horrors of life on the city's streets.

From his entrance into the film's action, as a bold, but bedraggled, knight errant, leading his band of merry men in a rousing chorus of "How About You?" to the mirroring scene in the film's closing segment in the mental hospital, where he leads a new band—of fellow patients—in the same buoyant tune, Parry softens the jagged edges of the world he inhabits with a humor that ranges from affectionate to bawdy, but bears no trace of malice. It is this humor that highlights Parry's humanity and saves him from succumbing to either agonizing melodrama or tortured insanity.

When Parry and his friends come to Jack's aid, the comedy is surreal. Jack is lying on the ground, drunk and beaten, his clothes soaked with gasoline. The homeless man appears, seemingly from out of the darkness. When Jack's assailants refuse his order to release their prey, Parry shoots one in the crotch with a suction-cupped arrow from atop the hood of an SUV. The pair of thugs turn on him, asking:

"Are you a faggot, too?"

"Faggot? No. But I *do* believe in fairies!"

As the nearest of the two swings a baseball bat at Parry, he deflects the blow with a trash can lid shield, pulls the youth close, playfully quips "Ah! Not without dinner!," and kisses him, immediately turning a grim urban nightmare into theater of the absurd. After serenading the thugs by flashlight, Parry moves in for the finale, swinging homemade bolos:

"You know, boys, there's three things in this world that you need: Respect for all kinds of life; a nice bowel movement on a regular basis; and a navy blazer. Oh, one more thing: Never take your eye off the ball." And lets his weapons fly.

Later, as Parry guides Jack through his world, audiences immediately connect with his childlike innocence. Diegetic onlookers, like the diners in a restaurant where Parry plasters himself to gaze at Lydia fumbling with her dumplings, see the monstrosity, filth, and danger of the city in his character, but the film's viewers see innocence, devotion, and a gentleness that bathes her clumsiness in a kind, adoring light.

"Ah... She loves dumplings. That's her Wednesday ritual."

She drops a dumpling into her lap, and he presses closer to the glass, and smiles:

"That's so sweet... She does that every time."

When Jack lashes out at a pair of diners gazing scornfully at them from their table by the window, Parry stops him, carefully rubs his own nose prints off the window with the folds of his coat, smiles again, and takes his leave of the couple, bridging the gap—for a fleeting moment—between his world and theirs. And when Jack attempts to buy his way out of his guilt over Parry's condition, handing him $70, Parry, now holding more cash than he has likely seen in a while, offers to take him to lunch. Jack declines and begins his retreat back to the safety of his own world when he sees Parry give the money away to another homeless man. Furious, Jack attempts to stop him, and when he asks why Parry would do such a thing, Parry's whimsical response is simply "What am I going to do with it?"

Later in the film, amidst the dangers of Central Park at night, Parry introduces Jack to "cloud busting." Disrobing, he explains:

"You ever done it? You lie on your back, and you concentrate on the clouds, and you break 'em apart with your mind. It's wild. But you have to be nude, though, Jack, 'cause You can't diffuse the psychic energy."

Jack responds: "You can't do this! This is New York—no one's allowed to be naked in a field in New York. It's too Midwestern," but Parry, now fully naked and dancing with joy, begs him: "Aw, come on, Jack! It's fun!! It's really freeing—the air on your body, your nipples are hard, your little guy's dangling in the wind." He gyrates, rubs along the grass, and howls at the moon, all the while urging his friend to join him. "I'm not doing this. I'm leaving." Jack strides away, loudly lamenting the insanity of the situation, and shouts "You're out of your fuckin' mind!" at Parry, who responds "BINGO!!!" and begins to dance again, chanting "Free up the little guy; let him flap in the breeze!"

Moments like these are seamlessly interwoven with some of the darkest nightmares of urban life, shifting the narrative focus from the horrific to the heartwarming, and illustrating the ways in which humor may be used to mitigate horror. Comedy seizes elements of everyday life—from the socially awkward to the politically charged—and uses them, as *New Yorker* columnist Robert Mankoff observes, "as material within the larger context of dramatic form."[8] Parody, satire, burlesque, irony, black humor, absurdity, and farce all shine a spotlight on the human condition, yet break the tension in life's darkest moments by infusing them with laughter. As irrational as it may seem, humor can do very serious social work, and Williams takes full advantage of that ability in his performance of Parry, commenting on urban horrors and the plights of those trapped within them, while softening their impact with the sad smiles of a clown. Additionally, Noël Carroll reminds us that horror is only as effective as its monsters, which are "designed to arouse emotions of fear in the audience in virtue of [their] harmfulness, and that of revulsion in virtue of [their] impurity."[9] The worlds Parry straddles are brimming over with such monsters, both human-made and fantastic, yet Williams's incongruous antics in the city's most horrific spaces evoke laughter from audiences that mitigates any such fear or revulsion.[10]

Darkness-Busting

The story of *The Fisher King* unfolds in dark places, from Jack's cavelike studio and Parry's windowless basement room to the fire-lit netherworld beneath the Manhattan Bridge and the cloud-shrouded lawns of Central Park. Even the interior spaces that are meant to be welcoming—Anne's apartment and shop, or the Chinese restaurant—are notably under-lit, as if the burning-out of even a single lamp would cloak them in twilight, and the loss of more than one would plunge them into night. Deep in the soul of Terry Gilliam's New York, it is always 3:00 AM.

The darkness surrounding the characters mirrors the darkness within them, but it also underscores a central, albeit overlooked, truth about *The Fisher King*: That it is a horror story. The heroes of traditional quest narratives may travel to dark places, facing down their fears in order to defeat the monsters that lurk there, but the monsters are (in the end) always defeatable. There can be, for the questing hero, no goal but victory. The protagonists of horror stories enter *their* dark places on very different terms. Outright victory is not required; enduring—surviving the darkness and emerging, even if exhausted and bloodied, on the other side—is triumph enough. The monsters that lurk around the corner in horror stories need not (necessarily) be slain; they can be evaded or outflanked instead, their power to terrorize muted or neutralized.

So it is, in *The Fisher King*, with Jack and Parry. They enact—first separately and then, haltingly and uncertainly, together—the character arc of all horror-story heroes: plunging into the darkness before them and surviving, strengthened by the experience, to walk into the light. Both men survive, their psychic traumas apparently healed (Parry regains love and sanity, both lost to him in the restaurant massacre, while Jack sheds the armor of sour cynicism that he has worn since his first moments on screen) but horror-story rules are still at work. No monsters, save the Red Knight born of Parry's trauma, have been vanquished. New York City is still riddled with decay, despair, and danger. Jack has learned, however, what Parry has seemingly always known: that love and laughter can break apart the darkness, just as surely as focused thoughts can bust the clouds blocking the moon.

NOTES

1. Overviews of Hine's work include Lewis Hine, et. al. *America and Lewis Hine: Photographs, 1904–1940* (New York: Aperture Monographs, 1997) and Allison Nordström and Elizabeth McCausland, *Lewis Hine* (New York: Distributed Art Publishers, 2012). The definitive work on Riis is Bonnie Yochelson, *Jacob A. Riis: Revealing New York's Other Half: A Complete Catalogue of His Photographs* (New Haven: Yale University Press, 2015). On the impact of the Code, see Thomas Doherty, *Joseph I. Breen & the Production Code Administration* (New York: Columbia University Press, 2007).

2. Raymond Chandler, "The Simple Art of Murder," in *The Simple Art of Murder* (1950. New York: Vintage, 1988); also at http://www.en.utexas.edu/amlit/amlitprivate/scans /chandlerart.html (accessed October 9, 2016). The title of Scorsese's film about small-time hoods in Little Italy is an ironic nod to a later sentence, by far the best-known, in Chandler's essay: "But down those mean streets a man must go who is not himself mean, who is neither tarnished nor afraid."

3. Ken Auletta, *The Streets Were Paved with Gold: The Decline of New York, an American Tragedy* (New York: Random House, 1975); Martin Shefter, *Political Crisis/Fiscal Crisis* (New York: Basic Books, 1985).

4. Miriam Greenberg, *Branding New York: How a City in Crisis was Sold to the World* (New York: Routledge, 2008), 133–159.

5. Wesley M. Cohen and Daniel A. Levinthal. "Absorptive Capacity: A New Perspective on Learning and Innovation." *Administrative Science Quarterly* (1990): 128–152; Karine Barzilai-Nahon, "Toward a Theory of Network Gatekeeping: A Framework for Exploring Information Control," *Journal of the American Society for Information Science and Technology* 59, no. 9 (2008): 1493–1512.

6. Jeffrey Jerome Cohen, "Monster Culture (Seven Theses)," in *Monster Theory: Reading Culture* (Minneapolis: University of Minnesota Press, 2007): 7.

7. *Ibid.* While a significant amount of critical work has been carried out regarding issues surrounding the monstrous, our analysis here traces its roots, in part, to Cohen's early formulations, exploring the monstrous in the context of being and becoming.

8. Robert Mankoff, "Untitled," *The New Yorker*, January 27, 2014. http://www.new yorker.com/cartoons/bob-mankoff/untitled. Accessed October 13, 2016.

9. Jeffrey S. Miller, *The Horror Spoofs of Abbott and Costello: A Critical Assessment of the Comedy Team's Monster Films* (Jefferson, NC: McFarland, 2004), 152.

10. *Ibid.*, 157.

BIBLIOGRAPHY

Auletta, Ken. *The Streets Were Paved with Gold: The Decline of New York, an American Tragedy.* New York: Random House, 1975.

Barzilai-Nahon, Karine. "Toward a Theory of Network Gatekeeping: A Framework for Exploring Information Control." *Journal of the American Society for Information Science and Technology* 59, no. 9, 2008: 1493–1512.

Chandler, Raymond. "The Simple Art of Murder," in *The Simple Art of Murder.* 1950. New York: Vintage, 1988.

Cohen, Jeffrey Jerome. "Monster Culture (Seven Theses)." In *Monster Theory: Reading Culture,* 3–25. Minneapolis: University of Minnesota Press, 2007.

Cohen, Wesley M. and Daniel A. Levinthal. "Absorptive Capacity: A New Perspective on Learning and Innovation." *Administrative Science Quarterly,* 1990: 128–152.

Doherty, Thomas. *Joseph I. Breen & the Production Code Administration.* New York: Columbia University Press, 2007.

Gilliam, Terry. *The Fisher King.* Culver City, CA: TriStar Pictures, 1991.

Greenberg, Miriam. *Branding New York: How a City in Crisis was Sold to the World.* New York: Routledge, 2008.

Hine, Lewis, et. al. *America and Lewis Hine: Photographs, 1904–1940.* New York: Aperture Monographs, 1997.

Mankoff, Robert. "Untitled," *The New Yorker,* January 27, 2014. http://www.newyorker.com/cartoons/bob-mankoff/untitled. Accessed October 13, 2016.

Miller, Jeffrey S. *The Horror Spoofs of Abbott and Costello: A Critical Assessment of the Comedy Team's Monster Films.* Jefferson, NC: McFarland, 2004.

Nordström, Allison, and Elizabeth McCausland. *Lewis Hine.* New York: Distributed Art Publishers, 2012.

Shefter, Martin. *Political Crisis/Fiscal Crisis.* New York: Basic Books, 1985.

Yochelson, Bonnie. *Jacob A. Riis: Revealing New York's Other Half: A Complete Catalogue of His Photographs.* New Haven: Yale University Press, 2015.

Psychological Trauma and the Quest for the Grail

Supposed Redemption in The Fisher King, Good Will Hunting and What Dreams May Come

STACY C. PARENTEAU *and* ERIC J. STERLING

The Fisher King (1991), *Good Will Hunting* (1997), and *What Dreams May Come* (1998) are critical and commercial film successes starring Robin Williams. These popular films deal with traumatic psychosis, love, death, the quest for the Holy Grail, and redemption. This essay differs from others on redemption in Robin Williams's movies in regard to our focus on trauma theory—a perspective rarely discussed in relation to these films. The trauma involves Jack Lucas's horror after discerning the ramifications of his provocative remarks as a disc jockey; Parry's trauma upon the murder of his wife; the effects of child abuse in *Good Will Hunting*; and unbearable guilt following the death of family members in *What Dreams May Come*. The relationship between the films in regard to trauma theory, redemption, and forgiveness has not been explored and yields a unique interpretation, such as an investigation of how the Robin Williams characters deal differently with the traumatic loss of their wives. These films contain plots with the potential for tragedy but conclude hopefully because the protagonists are purportedly redeemed through love, friendship, sacrifice, and the acquisition of the Grail—a symbol, not a real object. Parry (Robin Williams) in *Fisher King*, Will Hunting (Matt Damon) in *Good Will Hunting*, and Annie Collins-Nielsen (Annabella Sciorra) in *What Dreams May Come* seem to be redeemed as they reclaim the other main protagonist with whom they're paired: Jack Lucas (Jeff Bridges), Sean Maguire (Robin Williams), and Chris Nielsen (Robin Williams), respectively.

157

In the process of redeeming (or restoring) the wounded hero, the redeemer, who is wounded to a lesser extent, matures and consequently also becomes healed. In these films, the quest for the Grail involves self-sacrifice, self-acceptance, and self-forgiveness. The death of a loved one incites the noble quest that leads to the alleged healing in these three poignant, feel-good, mainstream films. However, the redemption that scholars and critics have accepted in *Fisher King* and *Good Will Hunting* as complete isn't genuine or fully realized, but full redemption is achieved in *What Dreams May Come*, whose ending demarcates realistic movies and fantasy film.

Remorse and Atonement in The Fisher King

Jack Lucas's quest is to make amends for his glib and insensitive comment to a mentally disturbed radio show listener that inadvertently leads to the murder of the wife of Henry Sagan (Parry, before his psychological dissociation from his former self). Lucas is all arrogance, all talk. When the movie opens, the camera zooms in exclusively on his mouth, as if it is disembodied.[1] Lucas mocks radio listener Edwin Malnick, insisting he has no chance of dating a beautiful upper-class woman who parties at exclusive clubs:

> They only mate with their own kind. It's yuppie inbreeding.... They don't feel love.... They're evil, Edwin. They're repulsed by imperfection, horrified by the banal ... everything that America stands for! They must be stopped before it's too late. It's us or them.[2]

After Lucas tells him that he will never date a rich, beautiful woman, that yuppies "must be stopped," Malnick murders seven people, including Sagan's wife. Scholars blame Jack for the murders because he incites Malnick's hopelessness. Susan Aronstein claims, "*For Jack*, Edwin's actions—and the despair that drove him to them—are not his responsibility."[3] Aronstein's statement signifies that Jack is responsible for the deaths of the people Malnick murdered but is too selfish to feel remorse or blame himself. This statement seems misguided because Lucas does feel responsible and expresses remorse. Aronstein confuses responsibility with atonement: Jack admits responsibility but lacks the desire to atone for his mistake. Yet the music in the disc jockey's room on that fateful morning plays "Hit the Road, Jack," apropos because Jack hits the road on his quest for the Grail to restore Parry to romantic fulfilment and happiness.

After the murders, Jack relinquishes his penthouse and good job, becoming a traumatized, emotionally disturbed man living above a video store.[4] Jack's incessant guilt renders him mired in an emotional abyss, making him decide to drown himself. Lucas asks the Pinocchio doll rhetorically, "You ever get the feeling sometimes … you're being punished for your sins?"[5] Even though he isn't directly culpable for the nightclub shooting, he considers Edwin's actions his responsibility. In this film, as in the other two, responsibility is specious. Lucas feels guilty and loses self-confidence, no longer thinking, "Thank God I'm me."[6] His promising life disintegrates into one of failure and remorse—leading to his suicide attempt. Parry's rescue begins Jack's quest and the introduction to the Fisher King myth.

The popularity of *Fisher King* derives partly from the quest for the Grail and the Fisher King myth. The success of *Monty Python and the Holy Grail* (1975; directed by *Fisher King's* Terry Gilliam) inspired public interest in quests for the Grail. The story of an Everyman-figure (Lucas), who wishes to make amends and seeks the ideal object of hope, appealed to a wide audience, particularly males. Screenwriter Richard LaGravenese believed that "the Fisher King, or Grail, myth—when paralleled with the male psyche—becomes the story of every man's psychological and spiritual growth."[7] The film's popularity derived partly from the universal, accessible story of two males who bond when one hurts the other and seeks redemption to make amends and heal himself. Everyone has regrets and has wished to make amends to family and friends, so the plot of someone engaging in a quest to achieve redemption possesses a universal appeal.

The Medieval Fisher King myth involves a knight who seeks the Grail, the chalice from which Jesus drank during The Last Supper, to heal his wounded king. Jack represents the knight, with Parry as the wounded king. After his wife is murdered in the nightclub, Sagan falls into a catatonic trance. When he awakens, he suffers from dissociation, shedding his identity as Sagan and becoming a new person, Parry, with no knowledge of his past. The wound consists of psychological trauma derived from witnessing the tragic murder of his beloved wife—a loss represented by the haunting and foreboding Red Knight. The Red Knight, a threatening visual manifestation of his trauma, hurtles toward Parry with ferocious, threatening strides, cloaked behind a nondescript mask, wildly sprouting streams of fire. The blistering streaks of red fire emanating from the Red Knight represents Parry's unresolved past horror and terror at seeing his wife murdered, and the searing sense of helplessness and despair that follows him in his present everyday life.

Whenever Parry has a chance at happiness—like after his successful date with Lydia—the Red Knight vision chases him and reactivates his traumatic flashback of his wife's murder and death in his arms. After Parry kisses Lydia, he looks at her apartment door. Gilliam changes the camera shot so that viewers see the building from Parry's perspective. In the glass door, Parry sees the nightclub where his wife died. Parry stands outside while the camera is inside, so "his image is caught in the splitting effect of the glass door's bevelled edge. We see two Parrys, side by side. The camera pans in from the long shot to a close up of Parry's face, split into two overlapping images, clearly literalising his psychotic mind-state."[8] The diplopic visual image reflects his madness and trauma of dating another woman after his wife's murder.[9] Because of his catatonic state and subsequent dissociation, Sagan/Parry never accepts the murder of his wife and endures these nightmarish visions until he acknowledges the death. Parry believes that Jack possesses the courage and friendship to bring him the Grail, which will heal him.

Lucas feels obligated to help Parry because he considers himself responsible for his wife's murder and because Parry saved his life when ruffians attempted to murder him.[10] Jack embarks on the quest to heal the wounded king (Parry) to ease his guilt and make himself whole again. A deeply flawed man, Jack must experience life from the perspective of Parry and other homeless, suffering people to empathize with their pain—hopelessness he ignored in Malnick. When knights begin their quests for the Grail, they are flawed yet redeem themselves while healing the wounded king. Before Lucas embarks on his quest, he must understand the pain he caused Parry and empathize with him, not try to rid himself of his guilt or change his luck. Although Jack feels responsible for Parry's tragedy and traumatic psychosis, he wants to do the bare minimum to help Parry and helps him for selfish reasons. It isn't Jack's nature to be contrite, which is evident in his inability to say "forgive me" sincerely.[11] Initially, Jack considers helping Parry to be a chore: "I wish there was some way I could … just pay the fine and go home."[12] Jack gives Parry money to ease his conscience, but Parry is selfless, the opposite of Lucas, and gives away the money to a homeless man. Lucas responds by lifting his eyes toward God and saying, "I just want You to know I did give him the money, okay?,"[13] as if he has paid his fine and God should forgive him. He becomes enraged when Parry gives away the money, as if Parry's selfless act voids Jack's good deed. As Lucas confesses to Anne, "I feel indebted to the guy. … I thought that if I could help him in some way … get him this girl that he loves … that maybe, you know … things would change for me."[14] Clearly, Lucas initially has selfish motives for helping Parry, thinking his karma will change by performing a good deed.

Although some might consider the Grail a literal cup, Jack's empathy, friendship, and emotional maturation lead him to embark on the quest that leads to healing; it's not the cup itself but the altruistic willingness of a friend to secure it (and the change in Lucas's behavior) that heals Parry. Gilliam notes that when the Red Knight appears, "Jack holds him to try to shake him out of his terrified fit; this is the first real human touch he's had since his slide into madness. … Perry is being embraced for the first time, and Jack is making the first breakthrough in his own life by holding this smelly, awful creature that he's been trying to escape from."[15] Lucas's journey is a learning experience and maturation. Helping Parry makes Jack respect and empathize with the poor and mentally ill; bringing Parry and Lydia together enables him to realize that he loves Anne.

Scholars write about the successful quest and redemption, but that interpretation seems like a facile reading. Although Michael Herzog considers the redemption complete because Lucas performs a "sacrifice on behalf of another..., an act Jack carries out in blind faith,"[16] Lucas admits to Anne that he aids Parry only to help himself and assuage his guilt, and labels the Grail cup a worthless trophy that he retrieves out of obligation, not blind faith. Because Lucas retrieves the cup to make himself feel good, the altruistic nature of Jack's gesture is problematic. Previous reviews and interpretations of *Fisher King* discuss the restoration of Parry after he receives the cup and finds Lydia yet overlook the fact that his beloved wife is still dead; their relationship must have been profound because he is traumatized by her death. Although anyone witnessing a horrific event can be traumatized, the catatonia and dissociation—his inability to recover—suggest that a strong love for his wife exacerbated the trauma. The fake Grail doesn't restore her to life, and it's highly debatable whether Lydia is an adequate substitute, given the shallow beginning of their relationship. Parry claims to have fallen deeply in love with her before he even meets her or knows her name, casting doubt on the depth and permanence of their relationship, just as the ancient Holy Grail chalice that Lucas appropriates is actually a cheap silver memento.

Merely an hour before his date with Lydia, Parry expresses his fascination with Anne's breasts and tries to copulate with her: "Parry focuses on her robust breasts bouncing beneath the sweater. Parry, getting overly heated. ... He starts to unzip his pants."[17] If Parry truly loves Lydia and she replaces his deceased wife, why would LaGravenese include a scene in which Parry obsesses over Anne's breasts and tries to have sex with her as she prepares him for his date with Lydia? LaGravenese subverts the sincerity of Parry's feelings for Lydia.

Parry thinks he loves Lydia but has never heard her speak nor spoken to her. She literally does not know he exists, so how could he love her? Parry feels his purpose in life is to make others happy. He says, "Heaven be praised for an opportunity to fulfill my profession."[18] Noticing that Lydia is lonely and no one loves her, he helps her. Does he care for her or simply fulfil his profession by courting her? When telling Lydia he loves her, the reasons he gives suggest pity, not love: "I know you hate your job and you don't have many friends. Sometimes you feel uncoordinated ... and you don't feel as wonderful as everybody else. Feeling as alone and separate as you feel you are.... I love you."[19] Given Parry's nurturing and empathetic nature, his feelings for Lydia are pity masquerading as love. And she thinks she has met the perfect man after only one date, making filmgoers question whether she is an adequate substitute for his deceased wife and whether redemption takes place. In his first scene, when saving Jack from the ruffians and conversing with imaginary floating fat people, Parry is clearly psychotic and sings Sinatra's "How about You?" Toward the end, he sings the same song after regaining consciousness in the hospital, suggesting that he remains psychotic. The repetition of the song and cyclical nature of the film don't bode well for him having a redemptive experience, symbolizing that his supposed journey seems circular, not linear or progressive. Cory James Rushton agrees that redemption doesn't occur in the film because Parry is still traumatized, has "lost a kind of personal power" by the end of the movie, and won't be able "to get a job and hold down a mortgage just because he drank from a cup."[20] The happiness and redemption are illusions in a film replete with illusions.

Furthermore, Parry never comprehends Jack's role in his tragedy. This point relates to both Jack and Parry's redemption, for Jack never tells Parry that he inspired Malnick's shooting spree. If Parry would recognize Lucas's part in his tragedy and still accept his help acquiring the Grail, rather than being saved by an act of kindness from a stranger, it would signify redemption in regard to learning to forgive and receiving forgiveness.

Redemption is "the action of saving or being saved from sin, error, or evil."[21] In a narrower sense, forgiveness is a process in which an individual lets go of negative emotions, cognitions, and motivations towards an offender and renounces any desire to retaliate or seek revenge,[22] with some theorists further opining that forgiveness involves replacing the relinquished negative responses with positive emotions and attitudes.[23] Thus, if Parry recognized who Jack really is and the harm his actions cause, but still accepted his help, instead of seeking revenge, forgiving would be an important aspect in Parry's redemptive journey. Jack cannot achieve full redemption because Parry cannot truly forgive him, given that Lucas never confesses his role in the murder of Parry's wife.

Abuse and Abandonment Issues in
Good Will Hunting

Good Will Hunting is a successful film because audiences enjoy heartwarming stories involving suffering characters who try to help each other endure and recover from their pain. Everyone likes success stories in which people strive to reach their potential and happiness. Audiences identify and empathize with Sean Maguire as he attempts to redeem the wayward Will Hunting. Will represents the wounded king, traumatized by years of abandonment and physical abuse from foster parents. His trauma leads to his self-destructive and violent behavior. Despite his genius, Will works as a custodian, and he quits after Lambeau catches him solving a complex math problem. Will sabotages promising job prospects and is content, despite his academic gifts, to work construction with Chuckie. Being tossed around from foster home to another, where he endured horrific physical abuse, makes him truncate romantic relationships and jobs. His knight is Sean Maguire, whose quest is to make Will realize that he isn't responsible for his trauma. Maguire stresses repeatedly, "It's not your fault."[24] The therapy sessions in his office and on the park bench represent a knight's journey. The trauma they both endured—child abuse—creates a bond that allows Will to trust Sean and work toward healing.

Will has been repeatedly abandoned, betrayed, and physically abused, leading him to have trouble maintaining relationships and to be self-destructive. When Will meets Skylar (Minnie Driver), their blossoming bond seems destined to be another truncated and failed relationship for Will until psychologist Maguire gets through to him, enabling Hunting to confront his past. Maguire's quest is to get Hunting to trust him and make peace with the inner demons in Will's past, so the Grail is not a physical object but rather within. As the psychologist helps Will realize that his troubled past isn't his fault, his patient enables Maguire to come to terms with his wife's death and start living again as both men work toward redemption and a better future, which is dramatized by Hunting's decision to leave his construction job and move to California to join Skylar. Scholars discuss the successful redemption in *Good Will Hunting* while oversimplifying the complex relationships between the characters, as they do in *Fisher King*.

In the bar scene in *Good Will Hunting*, Chuckie (Ben Affleck) expresses interest in Skylar, who then becomes fascinated with Will after he embarrasses pretentious Harvard student Clark (Scott William Winters) for plagiarizing a historian. When Will challenges Clark about the latter's historical analysis, the camera focuses on Skylar for reaction shots. She beams with pleasure as Will quotes from the historian whose ideas Clark is borrowing. When Will cuts in between Chuckie and Clark as a buffer and starts to talk about history, the camera switches to Clark as he takes a step back and, realizing he is in for a battle, puts down his beer (which he ultimately abandons in his embarrassment) and swallows hard. As Will schools Clark, the camera maintains Skylar in the background on the left, beaming with admiration. She smiles with wonder at Will as the bar lights shine bright on him, virtually giving him a halo. Her concerned look (that Clark is humiliating Chuckie) is replaced first with shock and then a large smile as she stares at Will, with the blurred yellow lights of the bar creating a luminescent glow, almost a halo, reflecting her feelings for this stranger. When Will mentions the historian Vickers and reveals that Clark is merely plagiarizing the scholar, he turns to Skylar as if to show that she sides with him, with the camera subsequently providing a reaction shot as Clark turns around in vain to his acquaintances for support. It's intriguing that the camera includes Will and Skylar in the shots together, even though they have never met before, with Clark being isolated, never included with Skylar in the reaction shots. After Will embarrasses Clark for plagiarizing American history scholarship, Clark walks away in shame, with the camera showing a huge American flag prominently displayed in the background.

Skylar is impressed even though Will merely memorizes historical sources as well. She admires him for his memory and his ability to humiliate Clark. Will impresses Skylar not because he cares for her but rather to defend Chuckie, whom Clark is mocking. Will considers Skylar a trophy he wins for besting Clark, not as a soulmate. Those scholars who disagree with this statement should consider Will's action after he receives Skylar's number (the spoils of his contest with Clark). He finds Clark and mocks him, showing him her phone number and bragging, "Do you like apples? ... I got 'er number. How do you like dem apples?" In the bar, Skylar is clearly an object of contention, a coveted trophy between three males. His inclination to challenge Clark and view Skylar as a trophy reflects his tendency to intellectualize rather than invest in emotions. Their relationship begins with this scene, calling into question whether their bond contains a solid foundation. When they eat out, Skylar quizzes Will about his intellect and is so impressed that she kisses him. The kiss suggests admiration for his intellect, not genuine affection. She continues to pursue him romantically even after she realizes that he lies to her repeatedly about his house and pretend-family. Viewers see nothing, aside from his genius, that attracts Skylar to Will: he is dishonest, indifferent (ignores her rather than calling her), and not romantic, tender, or caring, yet she claims to love him and wants him to move to California with her. Filmgoers should wonder why such an intelligent woman should fall in love with a man who seems indifferent to her, moody, and dishonest. Perhaps she senses that Will has emotional problems that preclude him from trusting people and making an emotional commitment. Mario Falsetto questions the worth of their relationship: "The relationship between Will and Minnie Driver's character is so idealized that it feels phony. ... [T]here is such a sense of manipulation in the film that the onscreen emotions seem more manufactured than earned."[25] Because of the inevitable compression of film, not all of their dates can be shown, but viewers might wonder what attracts her to him and makes her claim to love him. The relationship lacks substance, romance, and potential for sustainability. Filmgoers might wonder how this relationship between two people who have yet to establish trust or a strong personal bond can lead to redemption and permanent emotional fulfillment for Will.[26]

When following Skylar, Will copies Maguire by relinquishing his new job opportunity with McNeill and his Southey friendships. Falsetto says confidently that "when Will gives up an excellent work opportunity to pursue his relationship with Driver's character, ... there is never any doubt that Will has only temporarily delayed his ambitions by following Driver's character to the other coast."[27] How can Falsetto be sure? Will has quit every job he has had and sabotaged all his relationships with women. When Will pursues Skylar, viewers must contemplate whether Hunting loves her or merely copies Maguire, now that the psychiatrist has just shared that he was also physically abused. The film leaves it ambiguous regarding whether the emotional bond is strong or if Will copies a mentor with whom he has built a rapport. The question about what Will might do when he gets to California (if he continues his journey to the end) is muddled because of Will's lifelong fear of abandonment and rejection, his separation anxiety, and his truncated relationships. Some might assume that Will is cured of his psychological problems because the sessions are over and Sean hands Hunting his file, but the termination of court-ordered treatment sessions does not constitute proof of a cure from trauma and mental illness or redemption. Falsetto admits that Hunting's emotional recovery is artificial, and "[t]he overly pat psychology, and too-easy emotional breakthrough of both Will and Sean's characters, is true to formula. ... [B]y idealizing (and condensing) the reality of years of therapy work into a few office-session scenes, and in particular one tremendous breakthrough scene between Williams's and Damon's characters, the film feels phony."[28] Audiences cannot assume that Maguire has redeemed him. The trauma has not been "worked through," so Will probably still experiences PTSD symptoms, especially the emotional numbing and detachment. PTSD is treated with a technique called prolonged imaginal exposure[29] in which the patient recounts the traumatic event (in this case, abuse) in vivid detail. However, Will doesn't mention his abuse in Sean's therapy until his last appointment.

Will tells Skylar that he doesn't love her, but that is debatable because he still is bothered by the demons in his mind because of the abuse he suffered. As Maguire points out, Will doesn't understand love because he intellectualizes the feeling, resorting to books, not genuine feeling. Thus, redemption at the end is questionable because although he drives toward California and says that the physical and emotional abuse he suffered isn't his fault, the trauma he endured still affects him, undermining his ability to commit to a relationship with Skylar. Leaving for California doesn't signify redemption (inner peace), happiness, or recovery from his trauma because he still sabotages important relationships. Because Will achieves greater insight and seems willing to take risks, he is on the road to redemption but far from redeemed, given the severity of the abuse and the lack of appropriate therapeutic techniques to treat PTSD. Maguire's desire to travel seems pleasant, but when he returns home, his beloved wife will still be dead, so his trip represents a temporary escape, not true redemption.

Traumatizing Guilt and Redemption in What Dreams May Come

Annie Collins-Nielsen is an emotionally wounded queen whose husband Chris embarks on a dangerous quest to save her. He is so devoted to her that he literally journeys to Hell and back to rescue her. Annie goes to Hell after she commits suicide upon the accidental deaths of her two children and her husband, all of whom die in car accidents before coming to Heaven. Her suicidal thoughts echo those of Hamlet from his famous "To be, or not to be" soliloquy that bears the title of the film. As with Hamlet's dilemma, the concern is not her suicide but the lingering effects of it. Given the rich and imagistic scenery, such as the Impressionistic canvas-like imagery in Heaven, viewers might question whether Heaven and Hell are real or simply dreams the characters experience. Nate Yapp notes, "Shot on Fuji Velvia film for enhanced color saturation, the visions of the Great Beyond's brighter points are truly Elysian. Rolling hills, majestic mountains, fields of wonder—if there is an afterlife, please let it be this. Hell, on the other hand, gives Dante a run for his money. Screaming lost souls, begging for relief to the pain they themselves caused."[30]

Director Vincent Ward considered the visual aspects of Heaven and Hell to be a vital part of the film. The rich and intense colors create a dream-like, fantastic, other worldly feeling, indicating that Chris and Annie are no longer on Earth. The rich, saturated colors boldly attempt to create the illusion that Chris and Annie are truly in Heaven and in Hell, attempting to endow a fantastic illusion with the sense of verisimilitude. Heaven seems like a dream because there is no fear of death; for instance, Chris travels everywhere quickly through the use of his mind; there is no need for cars—machines that have destroyed every member of his family but his wife.

Annie becomes psychologically wounded because she cannot handle the deaths of her two children and the subsequent loss of her husband, for the trauma is unbearable and she seems weak. Annie blames herself for the death of her loved ones. However, she, like Jack and Will, is too hard on herself, blaming and tormenting herself unfairly. She needs Chris and her children to tell her that their deaths aren't her fault so she can be at peace in the afterlife. Once she realizes that it's not her fault, she can forgive herself. Rather than driving her two teenagers one day, Annie allows one of her teenagers to drive. When the teenager is involved in a fatal car accident, which is not her fault, Annie still blames herself for the deaths of her children, claiming she would have been a more protective driver and would have avoided the accident. She also blames herself for Chris's death because he dies retrieving some paintings for her art gallery. It doesn't matter that she isn't at fault; the problem is that she blames herself, so she must forgive herself to be redeemed and escape from Hell. Although the two wounded kings and the wounded queen in this essay suffer trauma, some of their pain is self-inflicted because they are excessively harsh with themselves. This self-blame derives in part from mental illness and psychopathology—Jack Lucas's excessive narcissism, Hunting's trauma from years of emotional abandonment and physical abuse, and Annie's trauma from her tremendous grief over the deaths of her two children. She almost divorces Chris because she cannot understand why he handles his grief stoically while her inner turmoil upon their children's deaths becomes so potent that she is committed to a mental institution.[31]

Despite the conclusions of previous scholars that these three movies end happily, with the wounded being redeemed, the only one with a truly happy ending and a sustained, satisfying redemption is *What Dreams May Come*. Although Chris and Annie cannot redeem themselves in life, they redeem themselves in the afterlife. Chris fails to adequately support Annie emotionally in life, but he is able to express his support and admiration for her in Hell, where he apologizes to her, thereby redeeming both of them. We often leave our feelings unspoken; we wait until it's too late to tell people how much we love and need them and to express forgiveness. Chris has an opportunity that no filmgoer has—to have a conversation with, and express regret to, a deceased love one. That is the beauty of this surrealfantastic (as in unrealistic) movie about the afterlife and one reason for its box office success. We enjoy watching movies that allow us to fulfill our dreams vicariously for a second chance. After Chris finally gets through mentally to Annie in Hell (manifesting their strong bond and symbiosis) and redeems her, he starts to lose his mind, so his recovered wife, in turn, saves him and brings him to Heaven. They redeem each other as their marriage is repaired. Chris's words of love and compassion release Annie from the chains of guilt that bind her, healing her. He assures her that she has been a good mother and wife, that the trauma isn't her fault—as Sean Maguire attempts to stress to Will. Chris evidently gets through to her because her memory is restored and she takes Chris with her to Heaven. In *Good Will Hunting*, contrariwise, Maguire tells Will repeatedly, "It's not your fault," and he responds, "Don't fuck with me"[32] before breaking down and crying. Therapy ends not because Hunting is healed but rather because the court order has been fulfilled. As Sean says, "Time's up!"[33] Unlike the other two films, which have a linear narrative, the narrative in *What Dreams May Come* is circular and time becomes limitless. It ends where it began, if not before it began, for after they are reincarnated, Chris and Annie meet as children.

The broad appeal of *What Dreams May Come* derives from its fantastic elements, with audiences wishing they too could experience Heaven and have a second chance to redeem themselves and change the past. This wish fulfillment and quest for redemption are demonstrated visually in the movie. The film uses visual imagery, with intense colors that affect the hues, saturation, and value, and creates a "Thomas Kincade Glow" to affect audiences' emotions and make them feel emotionally attached to Chris and Annie and their surroundings. The colors used to portray Chris's view of Heaven are also employed by Anne in her paintings upon Chris's death, thus merging Heaven and Earth, husband and wife. Dan Fleming agrees, noting, "By decomposing the digital into 'paint' that acts like paint, not just looks like paint never mind light, the film pushes the intensity of its effects-driven spectacle beyond a point of extremity in a way that is unavailable to the perfect digital simulations of possible worlds."[34] Audiences see the paint that acts like paint in Heaven and in Annie's art work as she mourns Chris's death.

A primary distinction between the movies involves genre. Although Chris loses his wife when she commits suicide, unlike in the other two films, this character played by Robin Williams fights to get her back. All three films stress redemption at the end, but the restorations and happy endings in the relationships seem facile and unsatisfying in *Fisher King* and *Good Will Hunting* because they are unrealistic conclusions in realistic movies; however, the redemption in *What Dreams May Come* is more satisfying and believable because it is a fantasy film. The more fantastical and unrealistic the film, the more believable the redemption becomes. Although scholars call *Fisher King* and *Good Will Hunting* fantasy films and Jacqueline Furby labels the former "a fairy tale of redemption,"[35] they are realistic. *Fisher King* concerns mental illness, homelessness, poverty, mourning, and death—common themes in American culture. The insensitive television show title "Home Free" indicates the film's disdain for humorous and unrealistic portrayals of the homeless or mentally ill. When Sagan's wife dies, she, unlike Annie in *What Dreams May Come*, is dead forever and cannot be restored to life. Even the Red Knight and the Grail are realistic, the former being a genuine figment of the imagination of a realistic psychotic man suffering from dissociation and the latter being an actual cup in a man's house. *Good Will Hunting* is realistic because prodigies do exist in real life, particularly in math and music, so conceivably a man who never attended college could be a math genius. And child abuse and excessively mourning the death of a wife (who can never return to life) are realistic themes. Therefore, it's logical to assume that Sagan's/Parry's wound can never be fully healed; he can never get his wife (or job as a college professor) back, and he has tricked himself into considering Lydia a suitable substitute for his deceased wife. He cannot support her financially because he is still psychotic and homeless and cannot hold a job. Lydia has no knowledge of Parry's psychosis and doesn't know he is homeless and unemployed,[36] so after only one date, there is no reason to assume they will become a couple or that Lucas successfully redeems Parry by uniting him with Lydia.

Hunting's trauma is severe and thus not easily healed. He informs Sean that one foster father who physically and emotionally abused, and then abandoned him, placed "a wrench, a stick, and a belt on the table, and just say choose…. I used to go with the wrench."[37] Will chose the wrench to be perverse, although he obviously knew it would hurt more than the stick or belt. Such hurtful abuse, and his willingness to be hurt in the most painful way, suggests his traumatic psychological problems will not heal quickly. The open-ended conclusion with him driving out West all alone doesn't bode well for his redemption. And Maguire's wife cannot come back from the dead, and he seems defiant about getting over her demise; his decision to travel seems an escape from pain, not a resolution. Jack, Parry, Will, and Sean exist in a world constrained by the laws of nature, physics, time, gravity, and reality. However, in a fantasy flick, anything can happen. For instance, the "imagined childhood world" of Chris's daughter Marie (Jessica Brooks Grant)—"in the form of an enchanting toy theatre—is projected by the film into a strikingly realized afterlife through which her (also dead) father passes."[38] Her world becomes what she wants it to be. Similarly, Chris's supportive and hyperbolic comment to his son, "I believe in you. If I was going through fucking hell, I'd only want one person in the goddamn world with me"[39] becomes actualized and literal as Chris guides him through Hell to find Annie. Words, thoughts, and dreams become reality. Thus, Chris and Annie Nielsen do come back from the dead, and they both travel from Hell to Heaven and then back to Earth. In such a fantasy, redemption isn't merely possible but inevitable. Thus, redemption from the Grail is inconclusive and difficult to accept in a realistic film, but quite conceivable in a fantasy movie because anything can happen and all can be redeemed if that is what the characters desire.

Notes

1. Commenting on the opening shots showing Lucas only from the back, in silhouette, Peter Marks says that the camera creates the image of Jack "as a fractured or incomplete character … malicious, superior and emotionally vacuous." Peter Marks, *Terry Gilliam* (Manchester: Manchester University Press, 2010), 140.

2. Richard LaGravenese, *Fisher King Script: Dialogue Transcript*. http://www.script-o-rama.com/movie_scripts/f/fisher-king-script-transcript-gilliam.html. Accessed 11 July 2016.

3. Susan Aronstein, *Hollywood Knights: Arthurian Cinema and the Politics of Nostalgia*. (New York: Palgrave Macmillan, 2005), 161, emphasis added.

4. The once-confident Jack now fears people. Anne (Mercedes Ruehl) assures him that video store customers aren't dangerous: "They're not terrorists, Jack. They're just ordinary people like you and me." When a customer requests a comedy, the camera zooms in abruptly on the woman's face in a disturbing, close-up frame that makes her seem frightening. Director Terry Gilliam wants audiences to see the close-up from Lucas's perspective to comprehend how an ordinary person appears traumatizing to him because of his mental illness. She reaches out to Jack for help, but he responds callously, foreshadowing Lucas's initial indifference to Parry and his homeless, mentally disturbed friends. Nonplussed by Jack's fear of people, Anne asks, "Are you in an 'emotional abyss'?" (LaGravenese, *Fisher King Script*).

5. *Ibid.*

6. *Ibid.*

7. Richard LaGravenese, *The Fisher King: The Book of the Film* (New York: Applause Theatre Book Publishers, 1991), 124. Even the source for the myth is accessible to a varied and eclectic audience: "the source for the grail story in *The Fisher King* [Robert Johnson's *He: Understanding Masculine Psychology*] is a popular psychology book that applies a Jungian analysis to the medieval legend. The mode of transmission is a 'popular' and not an academic one, even though Johnson is a practicing psychologist."; Rebecca A. Umland, and Samuel J. Umland. *The Use of Arthurian Legend in Hollywood Film: From Connecticut Yankees to Fisher Kings* (Westport, CT: Greenwood, 1996), 176.

8. Jacqueline Furby, "The Fissure King: Terry Gilliam's Psychotic Fantasy Worlds," in *The Cinema of Terry Gilliam: It's a Mad World*, ed. Jeff Birkenstein, Anna Froula, and Karen Randell (London: Wallflower Press, 2013), 84–85.

9. Cathy Caruth, *Unclaimed Experience: Trauma, Narrative, and History* (Baltimore: Johns Hopkins University Press, 1996), 62.

10. As with Lucas, the first image of Parry is "visually occluded" and shows him in silhouette, Marks, 141.

11. LaGravenese, *Fisher King Script.*

12. *Ibid.*

13. *Ibid.*

14. *Ibid.*

15. Terry Gilliam, "Knights Errant and Distressed Damsels in Manhattan: *The Fisher King*," in *Gilliam on Gilliam*, ed. Ian Christie (London: Faber and Faber, 1999), 195.

16. Michael B. Herzog, "Attunement and Healing: *The Fisher King*," in *The Gift of Story: Narrating Hope in a Postmodern World*, ed. Emily Griesinger and Mark Eaton (Waco: Baylor University Press, 2006), 269.

17. LaGravenese, *Fisher King Script.*

18. *Ibid.*

19. *Ibid.*

20. Cory James Rushton, "Terry Gilliam's *The Fisher King*, in *The Holy Grail on Film: Essays on the Cinematic Quest*, ed. Kevin J. Harty (Jefferson, NC: McFarland, 2015), 152, 154.

21. "Redemption," *English Oxford Living Dictionaries*, https://en.oxforddictionaries.com/definition/redemption, Accessed 21 Jan. 2017.

22. Frank D. Fincham, "The Kiss of the Porcupines: From Attributing Responsibility to Forgiving. *Personal Relationships*," 7 (2000): 1–23; Margaret R. Holmgren, "Forgiveness and the Intrinsic Value of Persons" *American Philosophical Quarterly* 30 (4):341–352 (1993); Everett L. Worthington, Jr., "More Questions about Forgiveness: Research Agenda for 2005–2015." In *Handbook of Forgiveness*, ed. Everett L. Worthington, Jr. (New York: Routledge, 2005), 557–575.

23. Frank D. Fincham, "The Kiss of the Porcupines: From Attributing Responsibility to Forgiving. *Personal Relationships*," 7 (2000): 1–23; Frank D. Fincham, Julie H. Hall, Steven R. H. Beach, "'Til Lack of Forgiveness Doth Us Part: Forgiveness and Marriage," 207–225. In *Handbook of Forgiveness*, ed. Everett L. Worthington, Jr. (New York: Routledge, 2005); Margaret R. Holmgren, "Forgiveness and the Intrinsic Value of Persons" *American Philosophical Quarterly* 30 (4): 341–352 (1993); Joanna North, "Wrongdoing and Forgiveness," *Philosophy* 62.242 (Oct. 1987), 499–508; Everett L. Worthington, Jr. (2005); "More Questions about Forgiveness: Research Agenda for 2005–2015." In *Handbook of Forgiveness*, ed. Everett L. Worthington, Jr. (New York: Routledge, 2005), 557–575.

24. Matt Damon and Ben Affleck, *Good Will Hunting*, Accessed 11 July 2016. http://www.moviescriptsandscreenplays.com/BenandMatt/goodwilltrans.html.

25. Mario Falsetto, *Conversations with Gus Van Sant* (Lanham, MD: Rowman & Littlefield, 2015), 39.

26. The lack of an emotional bond between them appears symbolically when they travel separately to California; she flies, and he drives after her. The separate trips suggest a lack of emotional connection between them. And Will's decision to follow Skylar to California is not his own and is unoriginal; like his verbal attack on Clark, it is derivative. Hunting claims he is "going to see about a girl"—the same phrase that Maguire used in 1975 when he chose a woman over the World Series and his friends. Will mimics Sean, which undermines

the authenticity of their rapport. For instance, when Will is afraid to ask out Skylar again, Sean says, "I think that's a super philosophy, Will, that way you can go through your entire life without ever having to really know anybody" ; a minute later, Hunting parrots Maguire's words back to him, mocking Sean for not dating after his wife's death. Will's copying of Sean's words and actions undermines the sincerity and motives of Hunting's behavior.

27. Falsetto, 39.
28. *Ibid.*, 40.
29. Edna B. Foa, Barbara O. Rothbaum, David S. Riggs and Tamera B. Murdock, "Treatment of Posttraumatic Stress Disorder in Rape Victims: A Comparison Between Cognitive-behavioral Procedures and Counseling," *Journal of Consulting and Clinical Psychology*, 59, no. 5 (1991): 715–723.
30. Nate Yapp, "What Dreams May Come: Movie Review." CINEMABLEND. http://www.cinemablend.com/reviews/What-Dreams-May-Come-461.html. Accessed 16 Jan. 2017.
31. In this movie, the wounded monarch is female, not male, because of the sexist nature of the script. Dan Fleming claims that the portrayals of Annie and Chris are gender biased: "Stereotypical emotionality is often a principal characteristic.... We see Annie (Annabella Sciorra) once in her workplace—an art gallery—but only when phoning her doctor-husband Chris for his advice in the middle of an emotional crisis about paintings that have not turned up for an exhibition (he cures a girl with one hand and solves Annie's problem with the phone in the other.... Placing an 'emotional woman as a sympathy-eliciting fulcrum of a film in this way is an old gender-stereotyping Hollywood trick.'" The gender-biased portrayal of Annie is relevant to this essay because Bass characterizes her as emotionally weak and thus in need of rescue and healing by her husband. Chris must embark on a quest into Hell to rescue her because she cannot handle trauma well like her husband and succumbs to suicide. Fleming, 55.
32. Damon and Affleck.
33. *Ibid.*
34. Dan Fleming, *Making the Transformational Moment in Film: Unleashing the Power of the Image (with the Films of Vincent Ward)*. (Studio City, CA: Michael Wiese Productions, 2011), 152, 155.
35. Furby, 82.
36. Parry pretends to work in a video store.
37. Damon and Affleck.
38. Fleming, 26.
39. Ron Bass, *What Dreams May Come (1998): Movie Script*, Accessed 15 August 2016. http://www.springfieldspringfield.co.uk/movie_script.php?movie=what-dreams-may-come.

BIBLIOGRAPHY

American Psychiatric Association and DSM-5 Task Force. *Diagnostic and Statistical Manual of Mental Disorders: DSM-5*. 5th ed. Washington, D.C.: American Psychiatric Association (Author), 2013.
Aronstein, Susan. *Hollywood Knights: Arthurian Cinema and the Politics of Nostalgia*. New York: Palgrave Macmillan, 2005.
Bass, Ron. *What Dreams May Come (1998): Movie Script*. Accessed 5 August 2016.http://www.springfieldspringfield.co.uk/movie_script.php?movie=what-dreams-may-come.
Caruth, Cathy. *Unclaimed Experience: Trauma, Narrative, and History*. Baltimore: Johns Hopkins University Press, 1996.
Damon, Matt and Ben Affleck. *Good Will Hunting*. Accessed 11 July 2016. http://www.moviescriptsandscreenplays.com/BenandMatt/goodwilltrans.html.
Falsetto, Mario. *Conversations with Gus Van Sant*. Lanham, MD: Rowman & Littlefield,
Fincham, Frank D. "The Kiss of the Porcupines: From Attributing Responsibility to Forgiving. *Personal Relationships*, 7, 2000: 1–23.
Fincham, Frank D., Julie H. Hall, and Steven R. H. Beach. "'Til Lack of Forgiveness Doth Us Part: Forgiveness and Marriage." In *Handbook of Forgiveness*, 207–226. Edited by Everett L. Worthington, Jr. New York: Routledge, 2005.
Fleming, Dan. *Making the Transformational Moment in Film: Unleashing the Power of the*

Image (with the Films of Vincent Ward). Studio City, CA: Michael Wiese Productions, 2011.

Foa, Edna B., Barbara O. Rothbaum, David S. Riggs, and Tamera B. Murdock. "Treatment of Posttraumatic Stress Disorder in Rape Victims: A Comparison between Cognitive-behavioral Procedures and Counseling." *Journal of Consulting and Clinical Psychology,* 59, no. 5, Oct. 1991: 715–723.

Furby, Jacqueline. "The Fissure King: Terry Gilliam's Psychotic Fantasy Worlds." In *The Cinema of Terry Gilliam: It's a Mad World,* 79–91. Edited by Jeff Birkenstein, Anna Froula, and Karen Randell, London: Wallflower Press, 2013.

Gilliam, Terry. "Knights Errant and Distressed Damsels in Manhattan: *The Fisher King*." In *Gilliam on Gilliam,* 190–215. Edited by Ian Christie. London: Faber & Faber, 1999.

Herzog, Michael B. "Attunement and Healing: *The Fisher King*." In *The Gift of Story: Narrating Hope in a Postmodern World,* 263–277. Edited by Emily Griesinger and Mark Eaton, Waco: Baylor University Press, 2006.

Holmgren, Margaret R. "Forgiveness and the Intrinsic Value of Persons," *American Philosophical Quarterly,* 30 (4):341–352, 1993.

Johnson, Robert A. *He: Understanding Masculine Psychology.* New York: Harper & Row, 1989.

LaGravenese, Richard. *The Fisher King: The Book of the Film.* New York: Applause Theatre Book Publishers, 1991.

_____. *Fisher King Script: Dialogue Transcript.* Accessed 11 July 2016. http://www.script-o-rama.com/movie_scripts/f/fisher-king-script-transcript-gilliam.html.

Marks, Peter. *Terry Gilliam.* Manchester: Manchester University Press, 2010,

North, Joanna. "Wrongdoing and Forgiveness." *Philosophy* 62.242, Oct. 1987, 499–508.

"Redemption. *Oxford English Living Dictionaries.* https://en.oxforddictionaries.com/definition/redemption. Accessed 21. Jan. 2017.

Rushton, Cory James. "Terry Gilliam's *The Fisher King.* In *The Holy Grail on Film: Essays on the Cinematic Quest.* Edited by Kevin J. Harty. Jefferson, NC: McFarland, 2015. 143–157.

Umland, Rebecca A., and Samuel J. Umland. *The Use of Arthurian Legend in Hollywood Film: From Connecticut Yankees to Fisher Kings.* Westport, CT: Greenwood, 1996.

Worthington, Everett L, Jr. "More Questions about Forgiveness: Research Agenda for 2005–2015," In *Handbook of Forgiveness,* 557–575. Edited by Everett L. Worthington, Jr. New York: Routledge, 2005.

Yapp, Nate. "What Dreams May Come: Movie Review." CINEMABLEND. http://www.cinemablend.com/reviews/What-Dreams-May-Come-461.html. Accessed 16 Jan. 2017.

The Final Cut
Death, Memory and
the Past as a Contested Zone

LORI L. PARKS

> In this last of meeting places
> We grope together
> And avoid speech
> Gathered on this beach of the tumid river
> —T. S. Eliot, *The Hollow Men*, 1925

Known and loved for his humor and warmth Robin Williams became a household name through his comedy and a variety of film genres. As news of Williams's suicide broke, social media began an outpouring of Tweets, "RIP's" and various shared and repeated anecdotes and clips. Rosamund Urwin opined in the *Evening Standard*, "and yet these online outpourings often make me feel uncomfortable, as though I'm at a memorial service that I shouldn't have been invited to." In "Saint Robin: How Social Media Turns Every Celebrity Death into a Public Grieving Competition," Will Leitch calls out the hypocrisy:

> Americans, as a culture, have always been terrible at mourning. And it turns out we're worse at doing it in public, in real time. This is always an issue on social media when a celebrity passes away, and the person is transformed from a figure of ridicule (or at least grist for the relentless conversational/monologue mill) to some sort of angel who influenced us all in profound, eternal ways.[1]

Death and concepts of memory have been themes in a number of Williams's films. In *What Dreams May Come* (1998), he plays loving patriarch Chris Nielsen beset upon by tragedy. Nielsen must help his wife (Annabella Sciorra) reclaim her sanity after they lose their young children in a car acci-

173

dent only to later (and ironically) die himself in a car accident. The film uses flashback techniques to reveal his family life as he navigates heaven and then hell to reach his wife. Death, memory and immortality are again explored in *The Final Cut* (2008) and *World's Greatest Dad* (2009).[2] Both films revolve around themes of identity and memory as a site of psychological and social conflict.

This essay explores the entwined themes of death, memory and embodiment as a commodity that can be captured, disseminated and consumed. The film *The Final Cut* (2008), written and directed by Omar Naïm makes for an intriguing case study. Williams plays a man named Alan Hakman who works as a "cutter" for a company called EYE Tech. Set in the near future, where nanotechnologies and their applications in biomedicine have made it possible to record all human audiovisual perception with the "Zoe implant," an entirely organic biochip that is implanted in the brain before birth and becomes fully integrated in the brain tissue. Thus the "Zoe chip" cannot be removed while the person is alive without risking severe brain damage. According to the story, this is a wonderful gift that parents (if they can afford it), can bestow upon their children. Those who have the Zoe will not be aware of its presence, and the company EYE Tech advises parents to reveal this information to the child by the time they turn twenty-one. The Zoe records until the end of their lives, only to be surgically removed and "read" by a special computer that can retrieve the footage and categorize the memories in a variety of ways so the "cutter" can edit and compile it into a film of the deceased's life to be presented at the rememory ceremony.

The film begins with a scene that sets the narrative structure for the viewer. As a young boy on a day trip with his parents, he meets another boy named Louis and they proceed to run around an abandoned warehouse. The viewer watches as Alan walks across a precariously placed plank and then turns to coax his new friend across it. Louis is reluctant and ends up falling down through the opening, because Alan froze in fear and was unable to grab his hand. When Alan goes down to Louis, he cannot rouse him and the viewer is presented with a dramatic image of the young boy lying in the midst of a growing pool of blood.

Flash forward to the present: Alan Hakman is now a professional cutter, employed by EYE Tech to take the retrieved footage from the Zoe chip and edit and craft the rememory for the bereaved families. Hakman is considered the best. He presents as a well-groomed, quiet, unobtrusive, if not, at times, a tightly wound, socially alienated man. His work shows a penchant for splicing together the ordinary, nostalgic and upbeat in the rememories he creates. There are rules that must be followed. The Cutter's Code specifies three important guidelines: I. A Cutter cannot sell or give away Zoe footage, II. A Cutter cannot have a Zoe implant and III. A Cutter cannot mix Zoe footage from different lives for a Rememory. Alan's latest project is passed to him by a fellow cutter who does not want it because the "guy is human garbage." The wealthy businessman, Bannister is indeed horrible, as we learn that he sexually molested his young daughter and collaborated in crooked business schemes. Meanwhile, Fletcher (Jim Caviezel) a former Cutter and colleague of Alan's has become a leader within the anti–Zoe movement. He approaches Alan in hopes of purchasing Bannister's Zoe footage as a way of exposing his corporate crimes and attacking EYE Tech. *The Final Cut* becomes a complex web of guilt, sin, and power enacted through the commodification of the visual representation of human experience.

Saying Goodbye, the Body in Death and in Memory

The representation of death in the film is interesting to consider as there are a number of historical references that inform the Zoe chipped funerary process. Hakman has grown up convinced of his responsibility in Louis's death. This directly translates into his official position as a "Cutter" and personal obligation as a "sin-eater." Historically the funeral rite is a public and communal way for a family and community to acknowledge and honor the death of a person. Because of his childhood sin and the consuming guilt that has followed him; he sees his occupation as a way to atone for his sins through the sins of others. By "cutting" the lives of the sordid, he maintains his sinful and thus unclean position in society and seeks to redeem them by removing their sins. The sin-eater has early folkloric traditions and connects to contemporary ideas of the wake. Eating and drinking in the presence of the corpse was a way to bare the sins of the deceased and take on the burden for them. In some cases there was a designated "scape-goat" that "involved the ritual consumption of food and drink which had been in direct contact with the corpse or coffin, by a person who undertook to take upon him or herself the sins of the deceased."[3]

Yet Hakman is not dealing with the physical body, but rather the encompassing and abstract person as told through the deceased's eyes and ears and as further translated through his interpretive editing. In *Body Work: Objects of Desire in Modern Narrative* (1993), Peter Brooks comments on the changing boundaries and experiences of intimacy and privacy as it relates to the larger public. He argues that: "privacy and intimacy more and more appear to exist only by way of the violations and exploitations that define them as special spaces. Our consciousness of a reserved space of intimacy strangely, perhaps pathetically, depends on relentless intrusion into it."[4] Contemporary examples of mourning via social media can certainly test the limits of intimacy and privacy, for both the celebrity and ordinary person. Social media, Facebook and any number of other apps offer numerous ways for a person to curate and present their lives for public consumption.

Death in *The Final Cut* is presented as a fleshless one. The entire focus is on the two-dimensional imagery. Prior to film, and with the advent of photography, nineteenth-century post-mortem photographs gave people the means to capture an image for posterity. Photography allowed people to record the world around them in what seemed the most direct and real way. Typical post-mortem photographs took a tool that people attributed as a "truth" teller and used it as a means to create an illusion that the deceased was in fact, not dead. As Eye Tech advertises in the film:

> Is Zoe right for your family? Deciding whether to give the gift of a Zoe implant is an important decision, a decision that will affect your lineage for generations to come. What does it mean to purchase a Zoe chip for your unborn child? It means that his or her life will never really end and that long after you're gone, people will be learning about your child and the life that he or she led. No longer do our most cherished memories have to fade and disappear over time.

When Hakman's girlfriend Delila (Mira Sorvino) sees his editing equipment, or "guillotine," as those in the biz call it, she remarks, "You're a mortician—or a priest—or a taxidermist. All of them." What happens when memory which is multifaceted and interconnected with all of our senses is recorded as only visual and aural? Does the distinction between short term and long term memory matter any longer? What happens to the recording when someone experiences a cognitive loss? Social media and the internet have led to a saturation of death imagery in popular culture. The twenty-four hour news cycle and impact of popular culture in the reporting of a death, whether of a celebrity or a dramatic and violent act can easily become banal. Death is now disembodied and immortalized on the Internet.

Reality is built and transformed through memory. The promise of Eye Tech is that one can intervene upon memory. The cutter can reach into the past and create a different version. That the pain, despair and unfairness of life can be sanitized and re-envisioned into a version that one might like better. It is a fantasy that plays upon the idea of transcending the body as well as an indictment of a society that deploys and relies on the technology of visual representation to render and confirm the self, as if the process of objectification ultimately proves one's existence.

When Fletcher questions Hakman about how he can stand to delete so much evil from a person's life and create the illusion that bad people are decent, Hakman appeals to the tradition of "sin-eaters" and defensively retorts that he can "forgive" people for their sins, even if others cannot.

A continual and ongoing corporeal and symbolic negotiation is somewhat alluded to within the context of this film. Death as presented in *The*

Final Cut gives a nod to early cyber fantasies of the 1990s where freedom is found through disembodiment or leaving ones "meat" behind in favor of the endless possibilities of cyberspace. EYE Tech's promise of immortality plays on this notion as a prospect found only through the Zoe implant. Yet, in cyber fantasies one does not become a collection of sounds and observations but a cognizant being faced with endless possibilities that are beyond the corporeal world. Immortality through a Zoe implant is an edited and static collection of one's past life.

There is a pervasive sense of anxiety that informs the general attitude towards death in American society. In the text *Embalming History, Theory, and Practice* (2000), the authors Robert G. Mayer and Daniel E. Buchanan acknowledge the attitude of denial and defiance in Western culture.

> American culture in particular places tremendous value on things that are new, shiny, and healthy while devaluing things that are old, dull, and dead. Consequently, the value of a human corpse is often morally downgraded, because the dead human body symbolizes that which is abhorrent to our materialistically shallow culture— death—precisely what the culture is trying to avoid.[5]

Death is increasingly sanitized or removed from modern life. The corpse as object occupies the role of being present as part of the ceremonial encounter before it is disposed, *The Final Cut* bypasses this as memory displayed as image attempts to function as a valid description of existence, although still situated in the past, it defies decay and decomposition.

In *Natural Symbols: Explorations in Cosmology* (1970), Mary Douglas highlights the body as a symbolic site: "The social body constrains the way in which the physical body is perceived, and the physical experience of the body, which itself is always mediated and modified through the social categories with which it is known, sustains a particular view of society. There is a continual exchange of meanings between the two kinds of bodily experience so that each reinforces the other." Douglas's work is instrumental in establishing the body as a social metaphor and system that reflects cultural constructs. The routines and activities one establishes and attends acts as an "image of society."[6] Thus, a society that perceives itself under external attack will maintain strict rules that govern the body both internally and externally. This builds upon her earlier work in *Purity and Danger* (1966) where she argued that ideas of purity and pollution are based upon a culturally established system and "dirt is matter out of place" or a "by-product of a systematic ordering and classification of matter."[7] For Douglas "The focus of all pollution symbolism is the body; the final problem to which the perspective leads is bodily disintegration."[8] Yet, in *The Final Cut* the dead body is absent, as memory circumvents the flesh. Memories are collected through the flesh and the Cutter must still impose order upon them just as the social and cultural systems demand order upon the body and the way it interacts within the world.

Corporeal Absence, Prosthetic Memory

The first rule of the code is "A Cutter cannot sell or give away Zoe footage." Eye Tech is providing an important post mortem service for those who can afford it and as such must be above reproach. The irony, not lost on the viewers, is that memory is a commodity. The film reveals that the life footage from the Zoe implant belongs to Eye Tech and not the family and as such they only have access to the final product as edited for the ceremony. The memory is thus easily consumed by the family and friends of the deceased. It is flat and two-dimensional. John O'Neill explores the body and contemplates what he describes as the "abstraction of modern experience [as] based upon the removal of the human shape in favor of the measured— number, line, sign, code, index."[9] Memories have been systematized for organization and the focus is on the preservation of information rather than the flesh or some other tangible object. Hakman's "guillotine," translates a lifetime of thoughts, experiences, ideas and observations into more easily digestible categories allowing for one to quickly sweep through the mundane.

Visibility is often used as a guarantor of the physical body. *The Final Cut* pokes at this seemingly fundamental notion by presenting embodiment as a series of images or film clips. Technology is deployed in order to render the body as a system of visual tropes. The technology behind the Zoe chips is not without controversy. A group of vocal and at times violent protestors attempt to counter the extremely persuasive narrative presented by EYE Tech. Technology serves as a kind of visual armor for those who add electrosynth tattoos to their faces as a way to inhibit the implants within their bodies. "Remember for yourself" and "Live for today," become the chanted mantras of the group. EYE Tech exploits the limits of corporeality and fear of death by offering a way to archive our life. As EYE Tech reminds: "Memory fades. Even the most important moments in your life slip away over time. Colors change, participants are erased, added, and erased again. Even your most vivid memories are not quite how things actually happened. And when you pass away, those memories will disappear altogether." The ephemeral becomes measurable while EYE Tech embodies its name as an omnipresent surveillance system activated by the implant carriers themselves. Fletcher, former cutter and now enemy of EYE Tech comments on Hakman's seemingly unshakeable devotion to his guillotine. He responds to Fletcher's criticism by stating, "I didn't invent the technology, if people didn't want it, they wouldn't buy it, Fletcher. If fulfills a human need." Hakman's commitment to his profession is based on the enduring impact of his own childhood trauma. His memory is the unyielding wound of his lost self. Hakman spends most of the film clutching the guillotine to his body, its physical presence a prosthetic reassurance. The notion of "human need" is an interesting rebuttal to Fletcher's critique of EYE Tech. The term "need" has broad physical implications. The body "needs" food, water, shelter, air and protection from the elements in the form of clothing. O'Neill points to the myriad complications that have come with civilization and bodily need. "Intellectual, artistic, scientific, culinary, medical, legal, political, and even military culture expands beyond any level that can be contained by the simple standard of bodily need."[10]

Manipulated and edited memories are something that can occur naturally over the passage of time. People, places and events can ebb and flow in their potency and presence. Memories are not simplistic nor are they primarily visual, but can be activated through sound, scent, touch, taste and any combination thereof. Time and the measurement of time are another aspect of the final product as presented at the rememory ceremonies. The notion of recalling ones memories at will is not a new concept. Virtual Reality (VR) pioneer Jaron Lanier, imagined VR's potential on memory in the 1980s. "You can play back your memory through time and classify your memories in various ways. You'd be able to run back through the experiential places you've been in order to be able to find people, tools."[11] In this scenario memory is something that is accessible to the living. It is envisioned as something that can be recalled, and interacted with at will. The Zoe chip in contrast is presented as information to be organized and arranged after death. It takes the internal, the seemingly inaccessible and abstract experiences and turns them into external, technologically generated, publically curated and presented forms of representation. Technology has become the contemporary prosthetic god. It intercedes on ones behalf by allowing for instantaneous connections, real time imagery that become signs of personal and collective experiences and the Orwellian All Seeing Eye.

Roland Barthes argued that the image or photograph is a "witness to layers of meaning."[12] The complexity of the image and the historically problematic nature of depicting reality or recording the truth through photographs and film is now manifest in countless ways in which human life is recorded and distributed. Cameras capture daily life in many public areas where this kind of surveillance is meant to bring comfort against potential criminal deeds. Businesses often warn of telephone conversations being recorded as a way to assure quality. Black boxes record the flight patterns and communications of pilots and airplanes with the same concept soon to be applied to the surgical theater.

Susan Sontag has contemplated the power of the photograph in a number of essays. In *Regarding the Pain of Others* (2003), Sontag posits that modern life provides countless opportunities to bear witness to the horrors taking place throughout the world through television, the computer and the photograph. For Sontag, the photograph is integral to the act of remembering. "Memory freeze-frames; its basic unit is the single image. In an era of information overload, the photograph provides a quick way of apprehending something and a compact form of memorizing it."[13] The difficulties in representing reality or misconstruing the "real" are perhaps a byproduct of the increasing culture of spectatorship. The imagined technology of the Zoe chip and rememory ceremonies reflects the collective obsession to capture, collect and arrange images for public consumption. How sacred is personal experience anymore? Is it only made "real" by the clicks of others who gaze upon the images from a safe distance?

"Now I Remember..."

In *Embodying the Monster* (2002), Margrit Shildrick discusses the idea of identity as it pertains to the Western imagination. "To be a self is above all to be distinguished from the other, to be ordered and discrete, secure within the well-defined boundaries of the body rather than actually being the body."[14] *The Final Cut* makes its circuitous way back to the opening scene and lethal accident. Hakman's past has never been able to be fully in the past, but rather an omnipotent presence that informs everything he is and does. Throughout the film the viewer is offered clues that remind us of the unreliability and construction of memory. Hakman's personal and poignant collection of memories from various clients are revealed through a montage sequence of reverse aging as a man stares at himself in the bathroom mirror and clips of dream slippage involving surreal sequences of cars filled with fish while dogs surround a hotel. Not only is Hakman not above breaking the rules, nor do memories function in a coherent and linear path. Hakman initially presents as a mild mannered but decent and kind man, this is reinforced in part by his refusal to sell Bannister's Zoe footage to Fletcher. Yet his relationship to Delila (Sorvino) is based on manipulation. Delila lost a man she loved deeply and Hakman cut his rememory. Delila discovers that he has violated her trust on a number of levels as he used the footage of her dead lover to learn about her private feelings and desires and insinuate himself within her life. The revelatory moment comes when Hakman is working on Bannister's Zoe implant. While sifting through memories he is caught by what seems to be an adult double of the young boy Louis. Later, as he tries to track down adult Louis he discovers that he also has a Zoe implant. The Cutter's Code specifies that cutters are prohibited from having the implant. The shocking realization causes Hakman to contemplate himself in a manner in which he has previously been unable to. His carefully constructed boundaries and aloof professionalism collapse, he is not the autonomous observer but one of the many EYE Tech products.

The discovery of his Zoe implant and the questionable reliability of his memory set a number of things in motion. Hakman gets an electrosynth tattoo as a way of blocking the ever recording implant. His lack of knowledge of its existence was triggered by the loss of his parents at a young age. Thus, they were unable to share with him the so called wonderful gift of the Zoe implant. The discovery of the implant also offers Hakman the opportunity to access his own memory archive and revisit the incident that has had such a profound impact in his life. To attempt to access Zoe footage while alive is dangerous and can easily lead to brain damage. Nonetheless, Hakman is determined to try and with the help of his colleagues, the Zoe implant is connected so it transmits directly to his guillotine with the editing software running. He has only five minutes to access his memory or else he risks death. Hakman navigates back in time trying to reach the fateful day at age ten. The viewer experiences the growing urgency to find the truth and to prevent death while coupled with the bittersweet images of Hakman as a young boy staring in the mirror, revisiting his parent's funeral, and his first kiss.

When he finally arrives at the warehouse, the viewer is already primed from the opening scene of the film. Young boys running, play-acting, sword fighting, Louis shouting "come and get me." Hakman crosses over the board and tells Louis to meet him on the ground level. Louis insists on crossing. Panic, as young Hakman tries to stop him and implores "No. Wait. Wait. It isn't steady anymore." Louis does not listen and standing in the middle of the shaking board, cries out "I can't move." "Okay Louis, you can make it. Just a few more steps. Grab my hand" Hakman shouts. But it is too late, Louis falls through the hole, Hakman only managed to grab the necklace that Louis had been wearing around his neck. Hakman has kept the necklace with him as a talisman of this fateful day. A day he can never forget, but we soon realize, nor can he fully remember. Hakman is thrown off his chair by the force of an electric shock. This too seems to be attributed as much to his revelation as the time sensitive and dangerous method of accessing it. "I saw him. I tried to help. I told him to turn around. But he wouldn't listen. He fell but, he was breathing…! It wasn't blood. It was paint. Now I remember."

Hakman's whole sense of identity and purpose is the result of a mistaken memory, and the viewer understands that this is both a profound loss as well as potentially a new beginning for him. Hakman is an interesting representation of Freud's work on *Mourning and Melancholia* (1963). Freud's distinction between the two sees mourning as a normal process of grief that enables a person to move beyond the loss of a loved one. Melancholia on the other hand, is an inability to respond to and overcome loss and often results in some form of self-punishment. In melancholia the subject suffers an intense loss but "cannot clearly see what has been lost."[15] Hakman was unable to deal with the childhood trauma and loss, thus his role as a sin-eater and lifetime of self-punishment. As Delila points out "You've seen so much life and somehow you've missed the point of it." Thus, Hakman occupies what Eve Kosofsky Sedgwick terms as the "ontological crack between the living and the dead."[16] How does one bridge the gap between the self as one sees and as seen by others? The film plays with *mise en abyme* through the point of view of some of the characters recording Zoe footage, and through the intersections of his calm interactions with clients spliced with editing memories of the deceased beating a wife or having an affair. Cathy Caruth examines trauma and suggests that it is an "oscillation between a *crisis of death* and the correlative *crisis of life*: between the story of the unbearable nature of an event and the story of the unbearable nature of its survival."[17] Hakman's early childhood trauma sets in motion a narrative that is played out both psychically and bodily. He is unable to neither assimilate this experience nor forget it. Rememory ceremonies attempt to bypass the body and maintain the distance of memory and "reality" for the living. Yet, the site of the body is a spectral character throughout the film, as beatings, affairs and other kinds of assaults are edited out of the lives. Hakman's own body becomes an important commodity pursued by the Anti-Zoe forces determined to access and expose Bannister's Zoe footage even if it means killing. Hakman lost the footage when Delila realized he had been manipulating her and damaged his guillotine. Ironically, Hakman is chased and killed in a cemetery for his own Zoe chip which was recording as he reviewed the footage of Bannister's life. The end is left open, as we see Fletcher reviewing Hakman's Zoe chip on a large guillotine.

Hakman dies at the point of his revelation, are we to believe redemption comes in the form of his memory? *The Final Cut* does not feel final. Rather, there is an unsatisfactory resolution. Memory and identity is still reduced and repeated in the form of two-dimensional imagery to be recorded, edited and re-presented for public consumption. Images of Fletcher working with Hakman's Zoe footage at the guillotine mimic Hakman's own lifetime of vicarious moments there. The viewer is left with images of Hakman/Williams looking at his reflection in the mirror. Cultural and literary historian Sander Gilman astutely describes the paradox that we must continually relearn: "Each individual has had to learn again and again that the symbolic body, as much as the 'real' material body, is always collapsing, always promising to slide into oblivion."[18] The *Final Cut* tugs at something fundamental about the body in relation to its image: the ongoing desire for the image to render the body and by extension the "self" in its truth. In a world that seems increasingly accessible to information and visual stimulation, the human impulse to establish and impose order is less about necessity than with something more emotionally and culturally complex. *The Final Cut* reveals the power of memory, even if it is fictitious.

NOTES

1. Will Leitch, "Saint Robin: How Social Media Turns Every Celebrity Death Into a Public Grieving Competition," *Matter: The Magazine Made by Matter Studios*. Aug 17, 2014. https://medium.com/matter/st-robin-76e0e72c3e06#.i2sw38y4m

2. This dark comedy explores the nature of posthumous desire to mythologize the dead. Williams's character Lance Clayton is a failed writer, high school English teacher and father of a teenage boy, who is revealed to be a rude, friendless, jerk. When his son dies in a freak accident, Lance/Williams restages the scene as a suicide and finds growing fame as the voice of his son as he pens his suicide note and diary.

3. Ruth Richardson, *Death, Dissection and the Destitute* (London: Phoenix Press: 2001 [1988]), 9.

4. Peter Brooks, *Body Work: Objects of Desire in Modern Narrative* (Cambridge: Harvard University Press, 1993), 257.

5. Robert G. Mayer and Daniel E. Buchanan, *Embalming History, Theory, and Practice* (New York: McGraw-Hill, 2000), 4.

6. Mary Douglas, *Natural Symbols: Explorations in Cosmology* (London: Cresset Press, 1970), 65.

7. Mary Douglas, *Purity and Danger* (London: Routledge, 1966), 35.

8. *Ibid.* p. 173

9. John O'Neill, *Five Bodies: The Human Shape of Modern Society* (Ithaca: Cornell University Press, 1985), 26.

10. *Ibid.*, p. 93.

11. Timothy Druckrey, "Revenge of the Nerds: An Interview with Jaron Lanier," *Afterimage* (May 1991): 9.

12. Roland Barthes, *Camera Lucinda* (New York: Hill and Wang, 1981), 19.

13. Susan Sontag, *Regarding the Pain of Others* (New York: Picador, 2003), 22.

14. Margrit Shildrick, *Embodying the Monster: Encounters with the Vulnerable Self* (London: Sage, 2002), 50.

15. Sigmund Freud, "Mourning and Melancholia" (Trauer und Melancholie, 1917), *S.E.* vol. XIV, 245.

16. Eve Kosofsky Sedgwick, "White Glasses" in *Tendencies* (Durham: Duke University Press, 1993), 257.

17. Cathy Caruth, *Unclaimed Experience: Trauma, Narrative, and History* (Baltimore: Johns Hopkins University Press, 1996), 7; emphasis in original.

18. Sander L. Gilman, *Making the Body Beautiful* (Princeton: Princeton University Press, 1999), 332.

BIBLIOGRAPHY

Barthes, Roland. *Camera Lucinda: Reflections on Photography*. Translated by R. Howard. New York: Hill and Wang, 1981.
Brooks, Peter. *Body Work: Objects of Desire in Modern Narrative*. Cambridge: Harvard University Press, 1993.
Caruth, Cathy. *Unclaimed Experience: Trauma, Narrative, and History*. Baltimore: Johns Hopkins University Press, 1996.
Douglas, Mary. *Natural Symbols: Explorations in Cosmology*. London: Cresset Press, 1970.
Douglas, Mary. *Purity and Danger: An Analysis of Concepts of Pollution and Taboo*. London: Routledge, 1966.
Druckrey, Timothy. "Revenge of the Nerds: An Interview with Jaron Lanier." *Afterimage,* May 1991: 9.
Freud, Sigmund. "Mourning and Melancholia" (Trauer und Melancholie). *S. E.* vol. XIV, 1917. *The Standard Edition of Complete Psychological Works [S.E.]*. Translated by James Strachey. London: Hogarth Press and Institute of Psycho-Analysis, 1953–1974, 24 vols.

Gilman, Sander L. *Making the Body Beautiful*. Princeton: Princeton University Press, 1999.
Kern, Stephan. *Anatomy and Destiny: A Cultural History of the Human Body*. Indianapolis: Bobbs-Merrill, 1975.
Leitch, Will. "Saint Robin: How Social Media Turns Every Celebrity Death into a Public Grieving Competition." *Matter: The Magazine Made by Matter Studios*. August 17, 2014. https://medium.com/matter/st-robin-76e0e72c3e06#.i2sw38y4m
Mayer, Robert G. and Daniel E. Buchanan. *Embalming History, Theory, and Practice*. New York: McGraw-Hill, 2000.
O'Neill, John. *Five Bodies: The Human Shape of Modern Society*. Ithaca: Cornell University Press, 1985.
Richardson, Ruth. *Death, Dissection and the Destitute*. London: Phoenix Press: 2001 [1988].
Ruby, Jay. *Secure the Shadow: Death and Photography in America*. Cambridge: MIT Press, 1995.
Sedgwick, Eve Kosofsky. "White Glasses" in *Tendencies*. Durham: Duke University Press,1993.
Shildrick, Margrit. *Embodying the Monster: Encounters with the Vulnerable Self*. London: Sage, 2002.
Sontag, Susan. *Regarding the Pain of Others*. NY: Picador, 2003.
Urwin, Rosamund. "Let's not reduce human tragedy to a retweet." *The Standard*. Thursday 14, August 2014. http://www.standard.co.uk/comment/rosamund-urwin-let-s-not-reduce-human-tragedy-to-a-retweet-9668169.html.

"Caught in a freeze-frame"

The Afterlife of Robin Williams

LISA K. PERDIGAO *and* ALAN M. ROSIENE

After Robin Williams's death on August 11, 2014, news outlets immediately began compiling lists of the actor's most memorable films. The postmortem assessments of Williams's work raise complex questions about the legacy left behind on film. Laura Mulvey writes, "To see the star on the screen in the retrospectives that follow his or her death is also to see the cinema's uncertain relation to life and death."[1] Williams's film career began in 1980 with *Popeye*, released three years after his first appearance on television. Following critically acclaimed and commercially successful films in the late 1980s and early 1990s such as *Good Morning, Vietnam* (1987), *Dead Poets Society* (1989), *Awakenings* (1990), *The Fisher King* (1991), *Aladdin* (1992), and *Mrs. Doubtfire* (1993), Williams's career evidences a transition that is reflective of the medium during this period. In the late 1990s, digital technologies revolutionized the industry, ranging from the introduction of DVDs in 1996 to the digital projection of *Star Wars: Episode I—The Phantom Menace* (1999). Where celluloid is ephemeral, prone to degradation over time, digital technologies offer and perhaps promise an enduring projection, the sustainment of a legacy onscreen.

Bill Forsyth's *Being Human* (1994) represents an important moment within the actor's career, not for its critical acclaim and box office success (the film had neither) but rather for its self-conscious meditation on what it means to present and preserve a life story onscreen. According to Forsyth's third draft of the screenplay dated January 1992, the film's structure, involving six interlocking characters and stories in its initial design, was a "novelty," "never before ... used in cinema."[2] In the director's vision, the film demonstrates the "endless, glorious playing and replaying of the simple drama of being alive."[3] However, the film's theatrical release presents a different story: an omniscient narrator was added to make the connections that Forsyth claimed for the viewers. At its center, the film, what the narrator describes as "the story of a story," replays the story of *nostos*: man's attempts to complete his journey and return home. In more expansive terms, the film is suggestive of the work of cinema writ large: translating individual moments in characters' lives into stories.

Two of Williams's films from the early 2000s, Mark Romanek's *One Hour Photo* (2002) and Omar Naïm's *The Final Cut* (2004), continue the self-conscious examination of film that *Being Human* presents, but to a different effect and end. They are self-reflexive works on the medium of film that offer insights into the categorization of film as relatively transient or permanent. In the two films, Williams's protagonists Seymour (Sy) Parrish and Alan Hakman embody the processes of assembling, editing, and projecting the still image onscreen. Sy and Alan are both outsider characters, looking in on strangers' lives, who find purpose in their work of documenting lives.[4] However, these snapshots can be deceptive, not fully representative of the whole story, as Sy notes, "No one ever takes a photograph of something they want to forget."[5] Alan's work as a "Cutter" involves assembling and editing the video footage recorded by Zoe implants for posthumous "Rememory" celebrations. He says, "My job is to help people remember … what they want to remember."[6] Like *Being Human*, the two films do not appear on many—if any—lists of Williams's "greatest" films; however, they have particular significance, especially after the actor's death. Williams's career evidences an endless "playing and replaying" of a singular quest to find wholeness and completion in and through film.[7]

The films' meditations on capturing and preserving a life story on film are reflective of those of an industry celebrating its one-hundredth anniversary and moving to digital technologies. Mulvey identifies that in 1995, cinema's centenary, "Suddenly, the cinema seemed to age."[8] Celluloid bears witness to and signs of its own decomposition. As Mulvey notes, it is an "essentially short-lived material, with chemical decay an inherent part of its physical makeup."[9] The sense of an "end of an era" signaled by the advent of digital technologies in the mid–1990s recalls the origins of the film industry.[10] Siegfried Kracauer writes, "Originally, film was expected to bring the evolution of photography to an end—satisfying at last the age-old desire to picture things moving."[11] The transition from the still image of photography to motion picture can be traced to Eadweard Muybridge's motion studies, which began in the 1870s and were published as *Animal Locomotion* in 1887, and introduction of the zoopraxiscope. On March 22, 1895, the public exhibition of the Lumière Brothers' *Workers Leaving the Lumière Factory* gave birth to the industry, introducing films as *actualités*, recordings of social and historical realities that animate snapshots of everyday life.[12] As Mary Ann Doane notes, "The actuality dominated the first decade of film production and produced continual evidence of the drive to fix and make repeatable the ephemeral."[13]

Reflecting the development of cinema, *One Hour Photo, The Final Cut,* and *Being Human* introduce complex questions about the relationship between still and moving images and offer self-reflexive examinations of film's re-presentation of time. Mulvey writes, "The cinema (like photography) has a privileged relationship to time, preserving the moment at which the image is registered, inscribing an unprecedented reality into its representation of the past."[14] Within and between the three films is the story of the development of the still photograph and the compilation and editing of video footage into story. Particularly and especially after Williams's passing, this trilogy of films offers insight into how an actor's legacy is constructed and remembered over time.

André Bazin's distinction between the photograph and cinematic image highlights the tensions depicted within *One Hour Photo.* He writes,

> Before the arrival of photography and later of cinema, the plastic arts (especially portraiture) were the only intermediaries between actual physical presence and absence.... But photography is something else again. In no sense is it the image of an object or person, more correctly it is its tracing. Its automatic genesis distinguishes it radically from the other techniques of reproduction.... But photography is a feeble technique in the sense that its instantaneity compels it to capture time only piecemeal. The cinema does something strangely paradoxical. It makes a molding of the object as it exists in time and, furthermore, makes an imprint of the duration of the object.[15]

Bazin's conception of the photographic image as an imperfect recording and measurement of time is a central focus and concern in *One Hour Photo.*[16] Sy's meditations on his work developing photos at the local SavMart store and the medium of photography itself present a compelling argument about the ways that photography has traditionally been regarded and reimagined in the early twenty-first century with digital technologies. Like its protagonist, Romanek's film is self-reflective about the construction and interpretation of the photographic image. The director utilizes the cinematic freeze-frame to depict the protagonist's condition: Sy is a static character whose childhood traumas prevent him from fully moving on and realizing the life that he envisions for himself within a collection of family photos.

The snapshot presents a metaphor for the hysterical paralysis brought on by Sy's childhood psychological trauma. This concept is visually realized in Romanek's film when the character is seen motionless standing in his spotless kitchen, sitting in the SavMart lunchroom, watching the Yorkin house from his car, sitting on a bed in the SavMart after he has been fired, standing in the Edgerton hotel elevator, and lying on the bed in his Edgerton hotel room. The climactic moment of stasis occurs when the police order Sy to "freeze" and, after a brief attempt to flee, he finally does as he is told. As the film reaches its end, Sy is again seen motionless, contemplating his photos through the one-way mirror of the interrogation room, a bordered window that evokes a 4 × 6 print. Romanek's juxtaposition—or, rather, frame within the frame—of photography captured in the cinematic image highlights how film more perfectly registers the object "as it exists in time."[17] Sy's existence, like the photograph, is an imperfect one, retrospective and stilled.

In contrast, Sy is visually surrounded by evidence of active family lives, individuals who grow and change over time.[18] Although Sy does not play a role in his customers' lives, through his work developing their photos, bringing them to life, he imagines himself moving from voyeur to participant. Sy's paralysis appears to coincide with his retreat into a fantasy life which substitutes for action in the real world. In effect, his imaginings allow him to bring the stilled frame to life, much like the cinema allows. Romanek depicts this concept as Sy, amidst the stasis of the SavMart lunchroom, stares at a Christmas photo that comes to life. When the camera pans from the Yorkin family within the picture's border to what lies beyond the margin, we see Sy beaming at the camera. Sy's staring at the Yorkin house introduces a lengthy fantasy of his entering the house—also by way of a left to right pan that fantastically crosses a border—and making himself at home.[19]

Although Sy tries to reenvision his life through the Yorkin family photos, the attempts are imperfect, casting him out of the frame as reality reasserts itself. Sy's manager, Bill Owens (Gary Cole), continually breaks into the fantasies and when he fires Sy, he denies him access to his photos. However, Sy has taken his work home with him, which, ironically, has led to his termination: he has duplicated the family's photos and created a wall of photos that shows their progress over time. As Sy stands before the wall, an iconic shot used in the film's advertisements, he initially appears in stark contrast. He is a voyeur to their life experiences. However, the image also highlights the idea that both the photographs and Sy are stalled out in time, incapable of change. It is the sequencing of the photos, which the movie camera pans over, that tells the story.

One Hour Photo is centrally concerned with and focuses on changing technologies. Sy appears out of touch with reality by insisting upon what some regard as a passé medium, even in 2002. While his manager fails to recognize the significance of Sy's job and work, Sy insists on his central role in the store and people's lives. Even though the AGFA repairman "seems to think that a plus point 3 shift to cyan is insignificant," Sy insists that "It's massive."[20] When Sy learns that Nina Yorkin's (Connie Nielsen) husband Will (Michael Vartan) wants her to "go digital," Sy responds, "Oh no, don't do that…. I'd be out of a job."[21] While Sy's protest can be read as symptomatic of a fear that he would also be out of the family's life, he is also objecting to the new technology. Doane notes that an 1895 story in *Scribner's Magazine* titled "The Kinetoscope of Time" "conveys something of the uncanniness of the new technology's apparent ability to transcend time as corruption by paradoxically fixing life and movement, providing their impossible record," condensing "many of the fears, desires, anxieties, and pleasures attached to the idea of the mechanical representability of time."[22] *One Hour Photo* projects this drama onscreen.

One Hour Photo frames its narrative of a fragmented character attempting to achieve wholeness through the development, preservation, and animation of photography. Its protagonist is an identifiable type: the hysteric and obsessional neurotic that Sigmund Freud and Slavoj Žižek describe. Žižek writes that the hysterical neurotic "'overtakes himself' and misses the object of desire precisely because of this impatience—because he wants to get at it too quickly—whereas the obsessional neurotic builds up a whole system enabling him to postpone the encounter of the object *ad infinitum*: the moment is never right."[23] Romanek perfectly conceives Sy's neuroses in relation to his ideas and concerns about photography, what he is able and unable to do with it.

Romanek's study of Sy's increasing fragmentation is played out in a conventional way on film, in keeping with both psychoanalytic and narrative theories. In a Charlie Rose interview, Romanek suggests that *One Hour Photo* is a standard three-act drama. If so, the second act likely begins when Sy encounters Jake's (Dylan Smith) father, Will, at the SavMart "in the flesh."[24] This meeting starts the process of dissolving the fantasy father figure Sy has constructed on the basis of the Yorkin family photos and his interactions with Nina and Jake over the years. Sy, the hysteric, tries to make himself the object of Will, the other's desire, but Will is short with Sy.[25] Seymour Parrish begins to "see more" about Yorkin, or "your kin." The marker of the fantasy father becoming real is the *Neon Genesis* toy that Sy will purchase for Jake in defiance of Will's prohibition.[26] Sy attempts to make himself the object of Jake's desire. Sy's encouragement of Jake's performance at soccer practice is contrasted by Jake's coach who tells the boy, "Jake, that's not good enough."[27] Although Sy ostensibly tries to replace the father by offering Jake the *Neon Genesis Evangelion* action figure that the boy had desired and Will refused to buy, Sy ultimately tries to offer conditional support of the absent father figure when he says, "He'd be here if he could" (*One Hour Photo*). Sy cannot become the father or husband, but he can be "Uncle Sy"; at least he "almost feel[s] like" him.[28]

After Sy discovers evidence of Will's adultery captured in another customer's film, he struggles to restore the family photo, recasting his imagined role. Initially, he attempts to avenge the wronged characters, embodying the

Evangelion character that Jake admires. However, Sy also remains the boy, with the action figure displayed in his room, watching over him as he sleeps. A contrast to Sy's earlier fantasy sequences, a nightmare depicts Sy with eyes bleeding—the Oedipal complex captured on film as Sy's eyes bleed developing fluid. After he awakens, Sy systematically erases Will from the family pictures, which he can do literally, but fails to do figuratively. When Sy places himself in the role of father, he *becomes* his own tyrannical father, or at least a reflection of him. Sy uses photography as a weapon against Will and his lover Maya (Erin Daniels), forcing them to engage in sexual acts that he can document on camera, providing more compelling evidence for Nina. However, Sy's actions go beyond capturing the affair on film; they reproduce his own childhood trauma at the hands of his father. He treats the actions as play—they are to "look like [they're] having fun ... like a game."[29] Where Sy had dreamed that he was part of the developing machine, excreting its fluid, he transitions into the photographer controlling the scene.

Sy is never able to realize his vision as part of the family; his own attempts at manipulating photography lead to his downfall. Although the film is self-conscious about the roles that film (shot, developed, and interpreted) play in individual lives and twenty-first century society, Sy is not. The hysteric revolts against a childhood psychological trauma and completely forgets the event. At work, Sy, describing the types of photos he processes on Mondays, can note that "we have to report kiddie porn and animal cruelty" without passion even though the remark bears a strong similarity to the words he later uses to confess his childhood trauma to Detective James Van Der Zee (Eriq La Salle) at the end of the film.[30] Sy's ability to refer dispassionately to the sexual abuse of children in the first part of the film shows the depth of his repressed traumatic memories. In the end, Sy is not redeemed by his past, but his present motivation is understood: when Sy says Will is "not a good father," Detective Van Der Zee replies, "I think I understand now, Sy."[31]

At the end of the film, Sy has regressed to playing the role of the child. It is fitting that Detective Van Der Zee oversee the case. The character bears the name of the famed Harlem Renaissance photographer who captured African American society and culture in the early twentieth-century; in particular, Van Der Zee's work *The Harlem Book of the Dead* (1978), a collection of his funereal photography, highlights the concept of a subject both still and preserved in time. As the film documents "many of the fears, desires, anxieties, and pleasure attached to the idea of the mechanical representability of time," its *mise-en-scène* depicts a static character frozen in and by his own medium.[32] Color is absent from Sy's kitchen, his aisle dream, and his final photos of the hotel room. The black and white (and orderly) world is a symptom of Sy's neurosis, his fixation at the anal stage of sexual development due to his father's abusive control. At Sy's request, Van Der Zee returns one roll of Sy's photos to him, a set of twenty prints that recalls Jake's innocent photographs of the Six Flags amusement park.[33] Sy's photos document his hotel room after the violence, a recollected state of innocence. The final scene uses a dissolve to juxtapose two versions of Sy: one alone and melancholic in the interrogation room and the other smiling in the Yorkin family photo. As the photograph comes into focus, fantasy replaces reality. Sy is "caught in a freeze-frame ... never changing," the perfect photographic subject.[34]

In *The Final Cut*, Alan, like Sy, possesses certain obsessive qualities that can be read as an extension of his medium, digital video. However, where Sy attempts to insert himself into his customers' lives—and photos—Alan immerses himself in his work, removing all traces of himself. Fletcher (Jim Caviezel), a former friend and Cutter, indicates that Alan suffers from delusion, obsession, and guilt.[35] The film begins with the source of Alan's guilt, a memory of his complicity in the death of a young friend, Louis. He is the obsessional neurotic replaying his childhood trauma over and over again, as if it were a film. Alan says, "One memory ... one single incident has made me who I am. It won't leave me. The guilt tears me apart...."[36] Initially unable to edit his own memories, Alan's work as a Cutter allows him to "help people remember ... what they want to remember."[37] However, unlike Sy, Alan is ultimately able to utilize advanced digital technologies to revisit and correct the past, allowing him to find completion and wholeness through film.

Throughout *The Final Cut*, digital video footage is depicted as superior to fallible memories as well as celluloid. In one of the DVD's special features, the EYE Tech sales pitch for the Zoe implant emphasizes the importance of capturing and preserving memories that will "slip away over time."[38] The EYE Tech representative says, "Memory fades. .... Colors change, participants are erased, added, and erased again. Even your most vivid memories are not quite how things actually happened. And when you pass away, those memories will disappear altogether."[39] While the film and sales pitch focus on the inferior quality of memories, they also highlight the perceived problems with celluloid: a degradation of the image over time. Film is marked with and by its own decay and losses.[40] Many of the stars of the Golden Age have passed, and, conceptually, film preserves their legacies onscreen indefinitely; however, the physical limitations of the medium—particularly celluloid—present an insurmountable challenge.

While the Zoe implant and Rememory celebrations are products of the film's science fiction future, they appear analogous to modern film. After its initial flashback sequence, *The Final Cut* introduces a pre-screening of scenes from Daniel Monroe's (George Gordon) Rememory, blurring the lines between Naïm's film, Alan's film within the film, and Daniel's Zoe implant footage. Alan says to Daniel's brother Jason (Chris Britton), "That's some of the opening sequence. The rest needs some fixes and tweaks" and "[R]ight now he's clocking in at one hour and forty minutes."[41] The standard formula for the Rememory echoes the normalized running time for narrative films that was established during the era of Classical Cinema.[42] *The Final Cut* also meets the industry standard, clocking in at one hour and thirty-five minutes. After the screening of Monroe's Rememory, the gathered audience gives the film a standing ovation. A headline introduces a name for the location of the screenings: the "Rememory Theater." When Alan goes to meet other Cutters, the group is assembled in the lobby of what appears to be an early twentieth-century movie theater; entering the building, Alan passes by a box office. *The Final Cut* exhibits the evolution of the production, distribution, and reception of film in the twentieth and twenty-first centuries.

Alan's role as a Cutter is to construct narratives from video footage recorded over subjects' entire lifetimes—for example, in the case of one of his subjects, Charles Bannister (Michael St. John Smith), 544,628 life hours. Human experience is divided and subdivided into seemingly infinite categories. When Alan reviews Bannister's footage, he sorts through categories such as childhood, sleep, puberty, eating, awkward phase, romantic life, temptation, personal hygiene, religion, tragedy, wedding, masturbation, fears, athletics, growth spurt, university, violence, school, courtship, and career. The list goes on indefinitely. As Alan watches Bannister's life unfold on multiple screens, Naïm introduces split screens: two become four, six, then twelve. Alan is positioned against a wall of moving images, bearing an uncanny resemblance to Sy before his wall of photographs in *One Hour Photo*. In *The Final Cut*, sixty-four screens represent Bannister's life, quickly flickering, fleeting. The immensity of the project of editing 544,628 hours into a one hour and forty minute film is visually realized in these sequences.

The potentially violent project of editing, involving suture, is central to Alan's work in the film and the project of *The Final Cut* more generally. Alan's keyboard contains CUT, DELETE, PIC, SWIPE, INSERT, END, SPLICE, SPLIT, and FOLD keys. When Alan discovers the secret that Bannister's widow, Jennifer (Stephanie Romanov), is trying to conceal about her husband and Fletcher is trying to release to the public, he simply presses DELETE and a new story emerges. Instead of revealing Bannister's incestuous relationship with his daughter Isabel (Genevieve Buechner), the daughter's proclamation of her love for her father following her recital is the last act of the evening. The name of the computer program, the Guillotine, highlights the violent acts of editing, of deleting, splicing, and splitting images.

Alan's love interest Delila's (Mira Sorvino) statement that he is like "a mortician … or a priest … or a taxidermist. All of them" highlights the funereal quality of his work, which is complemented by the computer's appearance onscreen.[43] The computer's wood frame gives a doubly suggestive appearance: the three computer screens resemble framed photographs and, from the other side of the monitors, the entire device looks like a coffin. Alan treats the footage as the embodiment of the life of the subject, even telling Monroe's brother "That's him" as he gestures to the Rememory CD.[44] Mulvey's description of cinema resembling the "central panel of a triptych that has blurred at the edges … reach[ing] both forwards and backwards" is realized in the triptych of monitors that represent the subject's life in seemingly infinite images and categories.[45] As Mulvey notes, "Throughout the history of cinema, the stilled image has been contained within the creative preserve of the filmmaker, always accessible on the editing table and always transferable into a freeze-frame on the screen."[46] Alan is both mortician and surgeon, suturing the footage and attempting to put it back together, a sometimes successful and other times doomed enterprise.[47]

Alan, like Sy, attempts to order his world of images, generating narratives that tell the life stories that he thinks his customers, the subjects' loved ones, want to exhibit. Although people's lives seem "so massive and so random" to Delila, the footage appears as "a miniature. Concise, symmetrical" to Alan.[48] Her question "What about all the bits in between?" is central to *The Final Cut* and film more generally.[49] Delila is identifying the point of suture. She questions the edits that are made and wonders what is sacrificed on the editing table in the attempt to create a film. The Cutters struggle with this problem within their own community. When Alan goes to visit Thelma (Mimi Kuzyk), another Cutter, she is engaged in a debate with her assistant Michael (Brendan Fletcher) about editing. Michael says, "You've taken this woman's entire life … and drawn a straight line from this particular moment. How can you make a decision like that? Whittling a life down to one …," and Thelma replies, "Michael, we have to make story decisions."[50] Her lines recall Alan's sense of the "One memory … one single incident" that has made him who he is.[51] However, by editing the Zoe footage, the Cutter is able to rewrite the story, the sequencing of events and their causality.

With Rememories, as with narrative film, individual lives are rendered as fictional creations rather than documentaries.[52] The Cutters appear as storytellers. Fletcher tells Alan, "These implants distort personal history and therefore all history… the past is rewritten for the sake of pleasant Rememories."[53] In the special feature "The Making of *Final Cut*," director Naïm notes his transition from editing a documentary to making a feature film. He says, "I really learned how … manipulative the medium can be… how much you can transform truth and reality."[54] Naïm's description of the editing process is indicative of Alan's work. Similar criticisms are expressed in Fletcher's attack—"You take people's lives and make lies out of them"—and those of the protestors of EYE Tech who bear picket signs reading "Remember for yourself" and "Live for today."[55]

While Alan is consumed by his work editing others' lives, he, like Sy, is unable to form lasting attachments with others. Alan's insistence that he does not work with an assistant emphasizes his loneliness; it is exacerbated by his strained relationship with Delila. Rather than being cast as a romantic lead, Delila is the spectator and viewer of Alan's life. She also plays the role of an amateur psychologist, diagnosing his symptoms and presenting a potential cure.[56] From her initial appearance in the film, Delila can be seen as a foil to Alan's technology-centered world. The contrast between the two characters' takes on the Zoe implant is rendered visually as Naïm juxtaposes scenes depicting the two characters observing each other in their respective work environments: Delila is at the bookstore that she runs and Alan is in front of his computer screens at home. When Delila tells a colleague, "Put it in archives very gently," she emphasizes the fragility of the page in contrast to the digital image.[57]

After discovering her ex-boyfriend's Zoe footage in Alan's "collection," borrowed memories that Delila believes Alan used to construct his relationship with her, she tells him that the footage is not Alan's to keep.[58] When Delila shoots at Alan's computer toward the end of the film, she severs Alan's connection to it and destroys the Bannister footage in the process. The images onscreen appear to disintegrate—a visual representation of the degradation of the celluloid image. The final image is a freeze-frame of an adult Louis discovered in the Bannister footage. While Alan had "drawn a straight line" from a particular moment in his childhood, this singular image, retrieved from 544,628 hours of footage, offers a different "story decision" through which Alan can remap his life. Although the freeze-frame, suggestive of the photograph, is lost to Alan, overwritten by code once the machine is destroyed, its significance and meaning persist. Alan assures the image—and himself— "You're still here" as he stares at the screen.[59]

Where Sy's efforts at controlling the photographic image ultimately lead to self-destruction, Alan's digital technologies allow him to revisit and correct his past through film. When Alan breaks into EYE Tech, looking for evidence that the boy survived the fall, he does not find Louis's file but instead discovers his own. Although the EYE Tech salesman tells expecting parents that they can reveal the information to their children once they reach maturation, Alan had lost his parents at a young age. Despite his belief in and (mostly) strict adherence to the Cutter's Code—i. A Cutter cannot sell or give away Zoe footage; ii. A Cutter cannot have a Zoe implant; iii. A Cutter cannot mix Zoe footage from different lives for a Rememory—Alan finds himself in violation of it.[60] He initially tries to hide proof of his implant, even going so far as to get an electrosynth tattoo to block its recordings; however, he soon realizes that the implant and its footage are the keys to unlocking his past and future. After Delila's destruction of the guillotine and implant brings an end to the freeze-frame search for Louis, Alan is only able to verify Louis's existence by accessing his own memories stored within the implant. Alan's journey into the Zoe archives is both enlightening and dangerous: if Alan remains in the image-world too long, his brain will suffer irreversible damage. Although Thelma warns, "You can only watch," Alan becomes more than a spectator of his own life; he is able to actively rewrite his story.[61]

This concept is rendered visually as Alan appears on multiple screens, not the split screens of the Bannister footage but screens within screens, the *mise en abyme*. Viewing his own footage, Alan learns that he did not encourage Louis to venture across an unsteady beam in an abandoned building; he encouraged him to retreat. He also learns that his friend survived the fall; the spilled blood that he remembers was only paint. After he reawakens, Alan tells Thelma and Hasan (Thom Bishops), "I'm all right. Now I remember."[62] As Mulvey says, "Return and repetition necessarily involve interrupting the flow of film, delaying its progress, and, in the process, discovering the cinema's complex relationship to time."[63] Repetition in *The Final Cut* directly relates to obsessional neurosis, indicated by Alan's statement "One memory … it won't leave me."[64] Alan's return to and correction of his childhood memory removes his compulsion to repeat it. After absolving himself of his guilt, Alan finds peace with the past and appears ready to start a new life. However, he does not get very far. Alan's video footage is important to Fletcher and Simon (Vincent Gale) who want to use it to expose Bannister's secrets. After Simon shoots Alan, Alan dies with a smile on his face. His audio goes out, followed by his video.

In the last act, *The Final Cut* depicts the persistence of digital technologies as Fletcher sits at a control panel, accessing and editing Alan's life. Fletcher appears like Alan, consumed by his work and his guilt. Fletcher's complicity in Alan's life and death is highlighted when Fletcher views footage of his own birthday celebration with Alan and Thelma. Alan's death emphasizes the connectedness of individual lives. The footage is from a first-person perspective, but other characters make appearances within it. The footage presents an immersive experience, the ability to see one's life story through multiple and seemingly infinite perspectives. The last image of Isabel watching Alan leave the Bannister home highlights this idea. At the bottom of the screen, I. Bannister: 10 years : 181 days : 8 hours appears. Fletcher believes that killing Alan is the only way to access the secret; however, Isabel—and her implant—cannot and will not forget.

Although *The Final Cut* emphasizes that the new Zoe technology is vulnerable and imperfect, like photography and celluloid before it, it suggests that digital technologies are resilient and persistent. In the film's final sequence, Fletcher stops at a scene depicting Alan brushing his teeth in front of a mirror, recalling the Rememory of W. Davis performing the same act over time, aging in reverse: 82 years, 72 years, 55 years, 44 years, 35 years, 21 years, 13 years, and 9 years before the screen fades to black. After Fletcher, wearing Louis's necklace, promises Alan that "It's for the greater good," ostensibly referring to the release of the Bannister footage, he says, "Your life will mean something. I promise."[65]

Arguably, *The Final Cut* ends with Alan's Rememory. In the film within the film, Alan leaves the room, walking out of the film's frame. It is an impossible shot, a glitch in the technology. Earlier in the film, Alan shows Delila a compilation of seemingly impossible images, daydreams and hallucinations—a girl taking flight from a swing, a man and woman in a car underwater, sheep walking into a building. He explains that "Some implants have a defect. They can't differentiate between what the eye sees ... and what the mind sees."[66] The film's final shot might be the product of such a glitch in Alan's implant or a symbolic representation of his escape from the endless "playing and replaying" of the guilt that almost destroyed him, something that Fletcher has now inherited as Cutter.[67] But also the last image embodies the tension inherent within the medium, of creating, preserving, and sustaining an individual life in and through film. Alan's appearance onscreen is both fleeting and enduring, capable (at least according to Fletcher) of inspiring meaning in the face of loss.

Where *One Hour Photo* and *The Final Cut* depict the attempts to animate a life in and out of still photographs and video footage, *Being Human*, released a decade prior to the two films, completes the picture by offering a study of the frustrated attempts of a director to assemble the footage and narrative into a "bigger picture." The representation of multiple versions of the character Hector (all played by Williams) across time suggests what we argue is at work in the actor's expansive body of work: an endless "playing and replaying" of a singular quest to find wholeness and completion in and through film.[68] Forsyth stated that "[Y]ou're going to live and die and you're going to cease, you're going to be an absolute nothingness. Instead of that being a problem, celebrate it and celebrate that you are connected to every other living being by the sheer fact that you've shared these experiences and that never stops."[69] *Being Human is* an Everyman narrative: Hector is the Everyman (everywhere everywhen) protagonist, a stark contrast to Sy, a hysteric, and Alan, an obsessional neurotic.[70] *One Hour Photo* creates dynamic narratives from static snapshots: e.g., the Christmas photo becomes video and pans to Sy outside the frame (fantasy), or the flipbook of Sy's photos animates the boss's daughter (reality), or the camera pans across Sy's wall of Yorkin photos (a real fantasy?). In *The Final Cut*, no materially new moments are created; the Cutter removes video footage from its original life context and deletes it or replaces it to form a narrative amenable to the customer's desires. In *Being Human*, the viewer is tasked with constructing a meta-narrative that connects the four discrete historical narratives the film provides. Unlike *One Hour Photo* and *The Final Cut* where Sy and Alan are spectators to the human experience, *Being Human* demonstrates a multitude of connections, most visibly through the multiplicity of Hectors who share a central quest to return home.

While Forsyth conceived his film as being a unique and even revolutionary experiment in modern filmmaking, it recalls what Doane notes of early cinema where "What was registered on film was life itself in all its multiplicity, diversity, and contingency."[71] She adds, "While photography could fix a moment, the cinema made archivable duration itself."[72] Here then is a reverse teleology from *One Hour Photo* to *Being Human*: the earlier film depicts Hector in his various incarnations (not reincarnations) as multiple, diverse, contingent, and enduring over time. Forsyth is adamant that time travel and reincarnation *not* be used to explain the transitions from time to time in *Being Human* (see beginning of screenplay), although Jonathan Murray admits the viewer might be tempted to adopt such explanations early in the film.[73] Instead, Hector embodies an essential quality of time—of cinematic time.

However, like *One Hour Photo* and *The Final Cut*, *Being Human* presents an essential drama repeated over time in Williams's career: "isolation—physical and psychological, intended and imposed—as the essential human state."[74] All three films involve family relations, but *Being Human* has the most hopeful outcome. It begins with the loss of prehistoric Hector's family, but the film is framed with the expectation that modern Hector will recover his relationship with his children and commit to remarry. *One Hour Photo* and *The Final Cut* show only dysfunctional families; both the protagonists and the seemingly normal characters they encounter are traumatized by child abuse, adultery, and sudden death. *One Hour Photo* is about recollecting a repressed memory by restaging a childhood trauma. Sy, who suffers from traumatic amnesia, has no memory of his child abuse until after he has taken the position of his abusive father to torment Will Yorkin. Detective Van Der Zee witnesses Sy's tentative allusions to his abuse; the detective understands Sy's past is relevant to his present case. *The Final Cut* is about correcting a false memory by recollecting a true memory (deconstructing a life of sin-eating penance based upon mistaken guilt). Alan's recollection of his innocence, the real story, dissolves the baseless guilt that drives him to create bowdlerized video memorials by cutting and decontextualizing dirty realities. In *Being Human*, memory/forgetting is mentioned in all four segments, usually in relation to absent family members, but no memory of these memories connects the isolated narratives of the film. *One Hour Photo* and *The Final Cut* concern the secret memories of Sy and Alan, but *Being Human* presents Hector's memories as only one of many repeated objects and ideas the viewer of the film must remember to consider.

For Forsyth, the protagonists in *Being Human* represent "the ultimate extension of all the characters [he's] written," and one could argue it is a representative type echoed throughout Williams's career in film, in works such as *Dead Poets Society* (1989), *The Fisher King* (1991), *Hook* (1991), *Mrs. Doubtfire* (1993), *Jack* (1996), *Good Will Hunting* (1997), *What Dreams May Come* (1998), and *Patch Adams* (1998).[75] *Being Human* can be broadly interpreted as a composite sketch of the actor's roles across time, and, more specifically, representative of a central interest in and concern with how film tells the story of a life.[76]

And yet that is not the whole story; in fact, that story has never been released. As Murray notes, the film is "little seen but widely known," its paradoxical status resulting from the film's "notable industrial, commercial and critical misfortunes."[77] It, perhaps even more than the self-reflexive films *One Hour Photo* and *The Final Cut*, highlights the frustrated attempts at producing, editing, and distributing films. *Being Human* did not test well and the studio made demands for changes to the original product, cutting down the original one hundred and sixty minutes into eighty-five before the director returned to the project and added an omniscient narrator, resulting in a final one hundred and seventeen minute theatrical release.[78] Delila's questions and ideas about the Zoe footage—"What are people's lives like? Do they make any sense? It all seems so massive and so random"—are addressed in *Being Human*, filling in the "bits in between" the other two films.[79] In contrast to the Rememory's "miniatures," *Being Human* appears epic, taking the character and actor from the prehistoric age to the modern world. However, the story behind the film is one of Cutting—by studio executives and eventually the director himself.

Murray argues that *Being Human*'s "deliberately unconventional narrative structure, premise, and use of *mise-en-scène*" reflect the film's "contemporary human urge to recycle" and its depiction of various Hectors is "marked by reiteration rather than (or as well as) progression," suggesting ways of reading the film in relation to the two later ones and, more expansively, Williams's entire body of work.[80] As *One Hour Photo*, *The Final Cut*, and *Being Human* represent a trajectory of the evolution from photography to the feature-length film, they are also sites of return and repetition, depicting "the cinema's complex relationship to time."[81] With the actor's passing, the films' experiments with and explorations of their medium are particularly insightful. Centrally concerned with and documenting the "aspiration to preserve the fleeting instability of reality and the passing of time in a fixed image," the films challenge a static representation of the actor's life and work, another kind of freeze-frame, encouraging endless returns and reassessments.[82]

NOTES

1. Laura Mulvey, *Death 24x a Second: Stillness and the Moving Image* (London: Reaktion Books, 2006), 17.
2. Bill Forsyth, *Being Human: Script* (Burbank: Warner Bros., 1992).
3. *Ibid.*

4. In *One Hour Photo*, Sy says, "And if these pictures have anything important to say to future generations, it's this: I was here. I existed. I was young, I was happy, and someone cared enough about me in this world to take my picture." *One Hour Photo*, writ. and dir. by Mark Romanek (Fox Searchlight, 2002), DVD.

5. *Ibid.*

6. The *Final Cut*, writ. and dir. by Omar Naïm (Lionsgate, 2004), DVD.

7. Forsyth, *Being Human*.

8. Mulvey, *Death 24x a Second*, 17.

9. *Ibid.*, 18.

10. *Ibid.*

11. Siegfried Kracauer, From *Theory of Film*, in *Film Theory and Criticism: Introductory Readings*, 5th ed., ed. by Leo Braudy and Marshall Cohen (New York: Oxford University Press, 1999), 171–182.

12. Bernard Dick, *Anatomy of Film*, 6th ed. (Boston: Bedford/St. Martin's, 2009), 2.

13. Mary Ann Doane, *The Emergence of Cinematic Time: Modernity, Contingency, the Archive* (Cambridge: Harvard University Press, 2002), 22.

14. Mulvey, *Death 24x a Second*, 9.

15. André Bazin, From *What is Cinema?*, in *Film Theory and Criticism: Introductory Readings*. 5th ed., ed. by Leo Braudy and Marshall Cohen (New York: Oxford University Press), 409.

16. In the film, Sy describes snapshots as "little stands against the flow of time," or "stopped time." *One Hour Photo*.

17. Bazin, *What is Cinema?*, 409.

18. As Sy comments, his world is comprised of "Family photos depict[ing] smiling faces … births, weddings, holidays, children's birthday parties," photo albums that evidence "a joyous, leisurely existence free of tragedy." *One Hour Photo*.

19. Although we do not have access to Sy's consciousness in his other static moments, we might suppose he is fantasizing at these moments of dissociation too, moments his Sav-Mart manager describes as "spacing out on the job." *Ibid.*

20. *Ibid.*

21. *Ibid.*

22. Doane, *The Emergence of Cinematic Time*, 1.

23. Slavoj Žižek, *Looking Awry: An Introduction to Jacques Lacan through Popular Culture* (Cambridge: MIT Press, 1991), 192.

24. *One Hour Photo*.

25. Will bluntly says, "no more toys" to Jake, and he reminds his son "not to talk to strangers," referring to Sy. *Ibid.*

26. Jake tells Sy, "He's a good guy. He can fly and he has a silver sword that can kill bad guys." *Ibid.*

27. *Ibid.*

28. *Ibid.*

29. *Ibid.*

30. Sy tells Detective Van Der Zee, "[Y]ou would never take disgusting, sick … degraded pictures of your children…. You would never treat your children like animals." *Ibid.*

31. *Ibid.*

32. Doane, *The Emergence of Cinematic Time*, 1.

33. The pictures also recall Sy's earlier thoughts: "Most people don't take snapshots of the little things … but these are the things that make up the true picture of our lives." *One Hour Photo*.

34. *A.I. Artificial Intelligence*, writ. and dir. By Steven Spielberg (Dreamworks, 2001), DVD. In the 2001 film, in which Williams voices the hologram Dr. Know, Professor Hobby's (William Hurt) description of the AI David highlights a recurring theme in Williams's oeuvre—the imaginary defeat of death through the perfected image.

35. The *Final Cut*.

36. *Ibid.*

37. *Ibid.*

38. *Ibid.*

39. *Ibid.*

40. As Mulvey notes, "Just as the cinema animates its still frames, so it brings back to life, in perfect fossil form, anyone it has ever recorded, from great star to fleeting extra," and yet "Aged 100, the cinema had also been inevitably affected by the natural mortality of the human figures whose existences it unnaturally preserved." Mulvey, *Death 24x a Second*, 17.

41. *The Final Cut.*

42. Timothy Corrigan and Patricia White, *The Film Experience: An Introduction*, 4th ed. (Boston: Bedford/St. Martin's, 2015), 357.

43. *The Final Cut.*

44. *Ibid.*

45. Mulvey, *Death 24x a Second*, 22.

46. *Ibid.*

47. As Paolo Cherchi Usai suggests, "Moving image preservation will be redefined as the science of gradual loss and the art of coping with consequences, very much like a physician who has accepted the inevitability of death even while he fights for the patient's life." *Ibid.*, 17.

48. *The Final Cut.*

49. *Ibid.*

50. *Ibid.*

51. *Ibid.*

52. When Alan is inquiring about the image of Louis in his subject's Zoe footage, he says that the man is "not a main character in Bannister's life." *Ibid.*

53. *Ibid.*

54. *Ibid.*

55. *Ibid.*

56. She tells him that "There's no place for me with you.... You haven't even made room for yourself," complaining that he is "always working." *Ibid.*

57. *Ibid.*

58. She says, "These moments ... they belong to me, Alan. The good and the bad. They're mine and his. Who are you to take them away from me?" *Ibid.*

59. *Ibid.*

60. *Ibid.*

61. *The Final Cut.*

62. *Ibid.*

63. Mulvey, *Death 24x a Second*, 8.

64. *Ibid.*

65. *Ibid.*

66. *Ibid.*

67. Forsyth, *Being Human.*

68. *Ibid.*

69. Jonathan Murray, *Discomfort and Joy: The Cinema of Bill Forsyth* (New York: Peter Lang, 2011), 186.

70. *Ibid.*, 187.

71. Doane, *The Emergence of Cinematic Time*, 22.

72. *Ibid.*

73. Murray, *Discomfort and Joy*, 202.

74. *Ibid.*, 186.

75. *Ibid.*

76. According to Forsyth's early notes, the film's experiments with the narrative and cinematography—"transitions across space and time"—will "let the audience grasp the simple truth behind our story ... the game of making the connections, feeling the bonds, even inventing or discovering associations of their own ... in this biggest of stories, smallest of stories." *Ibid.*

77. *Ibid.*, 189.

78. *Ibid.*

79. *The Final Cut.*
80. Murray, *Discomfort and Joy*, 193.
81. Mulvey, *Death 24x a Second*, 8.
82. *Ibid.*, 18.

BIBLIOGRAPHY

Bazin, André. From *What is Cinema?* In *Film Theory and Criticism: Introductory Readings,* 5th edition, edited by Leo Braudy and Marshall Cohen, 408–418. New York: Oxford University Press, 1999.
Corrigan, Timothy, and Patricia White. *The Film Experience: An Introduction.* 4th ed. Boston: Bedford/St. Martin's, 2015.
Dick, Bernard. *Anatomy of Film.* 6th ed. Boston: Bedford/St. Martin's, 2009.
Doane, Mary Ann. *The Emergence of Cinematic Time: Modernity, Contingency, the Archive.* Cambridge: Harvard University Press, 2002.
Forsyth, Bill. *Being Human: Script.* Burbank: Warner Bros., 1992. http://www.dailyscript.com/scripts/Being_Human.PDF.
Kracauer, Siegfried. From *Theory of Film.* In *Film Theory and Criticism: Introductory Readings,* 5th edition, edited by Leo Braudy and Marshall Cohen, 171–182. New York: Oxford University Press, 1999.
Mulvey, Laura. *Death 24x a Second: Stillness and the Moving Image.* London: Reaktion Books, 2006.
Murray, Jonathan. *Discomfort and Joy: The Cinema of Bill Forsyth.* New York: Peter Lang, 2011.
Žižek, Slavoj. *Looking Awry: An Introduction to Jacques Lacan through Popular Culture.* Cambridge: MIT Press, 1991.

Coda

Robin Williams—The Millennials' Mentor

KATHY MERLOCK JACKSON

> It might seem ridiculous for a generation to claim a universally loved celebrity as their own, but if there was ever a Millennial hero, it was Robin Williams.
>
> —Megan Gibson, *Time Magazine*

The entire world mourned when actor and comedian Robin Williams ended his life on August 11, 2014, at his home in Tiburon, California. However, no audience seemed more affected than the millennial generation, whose youths were shaped by Williams's work. An outpouring of emotion followed, as millennials shocked by the news took to social media with reminiscences and heartfelt tributes. One writer noted that when she awoke the morning after Williams's death, "[E]very single Facebook status in my News Feed and every single trending topic on Twitter—two clear indicators of Millennial mindset—were related to Williams."[1] In the days and weeks that followed, writers attempted to assess Williams's impact on a generation with a plethora of articles with such titles as "Why Robin Williams Was a Millennial Hero" by Megan Gibson in *Time*,[2] "Robin Williams' Death Hits Millennials Unusually Hard" by Ilia Blinderman in the *Toronto Star*,[3] and "For Millennials, Robin Williams Was Our Childhood" by Daniel D'Addario in *Salon*.[4] Kristin Iversen in *Brooklyn Magazine* expressed sentiments held by many when she wrote that Williams's death

> didn't feel like the loss of an icon; this felt like the loss of a family member ... intimate in a way specific to who the actor was for so many millions of his fans. For those who came of age in the [']90s, Robin Williams was a force larger than life; his performances were manic and magical, his jokes all the funnier for not even always making sense..., his earnestness at times embarrassing, and his compassion and humanity palpable.[5]

In an *Elle* article, "Why Losing Robin Williams Seems So Personal," Justine Harman characterized the actor as "a tremendously gifted performer who happened to have the unfortunate reality of being an entire generation's fantasy."[6] Daniel D'Addario, however, perhaps expressed it best when he simply stated, "Williams will be remembered for his edgy comedy and for dramatic turns, but for people my age, Williams was my childhood."[7] Each age, of course, has its heroes, personalities whose sensibilities resonate with the cultural moment. During the late 1980s and 1990s, an era characterized by the dominance of the VCR allowing young viewers to play favorite films over and over again, Williams held this distinction, but his importance goes deeper. His chosen roles and stunning performances dovetailed with cultural and family issues of the time and provided touchstone experiences for the generation that was growing up.

The millennial generation, according to demographers and social trend analysts Neil Howe and William Strauss who are generally credited with coining the term, was born between 1982 and 2004.[8] Other sources give different ranges: Pew between 1981 and 1997; the *New York Times*, in a 2015 article on Generation Z, between 1980 and 1995; the U.S. Department of Commerce between 1980 and 1999; and Eric Greenberg, in *Generation We*, between 1978 and 2000.[9] Despite these discrepancies, the millennial generation is defined by its shared life experiences and values. Also called Generation Y, the millennials are the largest generation alive, numbering 77.9 million.[10] They grew up with in-home televisions, VCRs, videogames, and DVD players. They are digital natives, shaped by the availability of computers, the Internet, cellphones, and social media. Their world was marred by the September 11 terrorist attacks and the Columbine High School massacre, causing their parents and caretakers to assume a greater vigilance than had been customary and contributing to the phenomenon of the overinvolved "helicopter parent."[11] Technology allowed for more monitoring, feedback, and immediate recognition but in some cases less human interaction. More than previous generations, millennials value fun and movement; they enjoy games and gaming and were early adopters of "multi-tasking," thus doing several things at once rather than in succession. Diagnoses of attention-deficit disorders increased in their lifetimes as attention spans shrank, and as Jean M. Twenge reports in *Generation Me*, they experienced depression at younger and younger ages, with the number of children on mood-altering drugs tripling between 1987 and 1996.[12] Fewer millennials lived in traditional nuclear families as the rate of divorce and single-parenthood increased, along with the number of blended families, interracial adoptions, and gay parents. As young adults, millennials have been more likely to perpetuate childhood, delay responsibilities, and move back home with family in a phenomenon Jeffrey Jensen Arnett coins "emerging adulthood."[13] Childhood and adolescence are not easy for any generation, and as the millennials faced the challenges of growing up, Robin Williams gained popularity as an entertainment personality, gearing many of his performances to the young.

Perhaps the reason that Williams was so able to tap into the emotions of youth was that his own childhood bore signs of sadness and isolation. He was born in Chicago on July 21, 1951, to wealthy, preoccupied parents who later moved to a thirty-room mansion on twenty acres of land near Detroit, Michigan. "I was living on this huge estate," said Williams "It was *miles* to the next kid."[14] Williams attended elite private schools, where the short, overweight child was often bullied by classmates calling him names such as "dwarf" and "leprechaun."[15] He spent a lot of time alone and entertained himself by talking in different voices, which contributed to the impersonation style that later became his trademark. Dr. Jonice Webb, a clinical psychologist and author of the book *Running on Empty: Overcome Your Childhood Emotional Neglect*, points to several factors that suggest that Williams was a victim of Childhood Emotional Neglect (CEN), a condition that affected the way he navigated the world as an adult. She enumerates these as follows:

1. Robin's father was a high-level GM executive and his mother a fashion model. He grew up surrounded by wealth and privilege, but not by attention. His parents were seldom home, and he was raised mostly by the maid, who was also his primary companion.

2. Robin's description of himself as a child: "short, shy, chubby and lonely." He described spending much of his childhood in the family's huge house, playing with toy soldiers, alone.

3. In 2009, Robin told *People Magazine* that in his childhood home, "the ideal child was seen, not heard." This mantra is a hallmark of the CEN family.

4. During a 2001 episode of *Inside the Actor's* [sic] *Studio*, Robin gave credit to his mother for helping to develop his humor because as a child, he worked to be funny as a way to get her attention.

All who knew Robin agreed that he kept his pain hidden, deep underground. Only those who spent considerable time with him or knew him well got glimpses of his true sadness and hurt. Carefully guarded pain: it's the stamp of CEN.[16]

No one will ever know the veracity of this diagnosis or whether CEN contributed to Williams's suicide. Williams's biographer, Andy Dougan, for example, claims that although Williams was isolated and lonely, "he still felt loved" and did not grow up "feeling neglected by a cold and aloof paterfamilias."[17] By the time he entered high school, he had shed his baby fat, taken up sports, and become a popular, outgoing class clown. One attribute is certain, however: Williams was sensitive to the emotional needs of youths, selecting roles and crystalizing performances that offered therapy. He shunned violence as a solution, offering laughter and inclusion.

This new dimension to his career began in the mid 1980s. According to Williams's *New York Times* obituary, his early stand-up comedy was marked by profanity and irreverence: "Onstage, he was known for ricochet riffs on politics, social issues and cultural matters both high and low; tales of drug and alcohol abuse; lewd commentaries on relations between the sexes; and lightning-like improvisations on anything an audience member might toss at him."[18] Typically, his best-regarded early movies such as *The World According to Garp* (1982), *Moscow on the Hudson* (1984), and *Good Morning, Vietnam* (1987) tackled social problems for an adult audience; even the comic-and-cartoon-inspired *Popeye* (1980), directed by Robert Altman, portrayed a dark, brutal world and did not really represent an exception. However, when Williams and his then-wife Valerie Valardi had their first child, Zachary Pym ("Zak"), in 1983, he thought about making movies that his son could watch that would make him proud of his father. Two more children followed, Zelda Rae, born in 1989, and Cody Alan, born in 1991, both with second wife Marsha Garces, who had previously been Zak's nanny. Williams enjoyed fatherhood, saying, "My children give me a great sense of wonder. Just to see them develop into these extraordinary human beings."[19] Williams's own millennial children inspired him to plead for kindness and a better world and to reach out to a youth audience.[20] As Williams once said of his child-oriented roles, "I do them because of my own children and for other people's children."[21] In particular, he was sensitive to children's struggles, such as his son Zak's difficulties navigating his parents' divorce. Williams's movies became safe spaces for children, places in which those struggling could find relatable circumstances, laughter, and comfort.

One way Williams first captured the youngest of millennial viewers was through his many guest appearances on *Sesame Street*, beginning in 1990, long after his debut television sitcom, *Mork & Mindy*, which aired from 1978 to 1982, ended. In one segment, he uses improvisation to teach Elmo the many acts one can do with a stick. In another, he talks about his knees and the wonders of his feet. In a lesson on similarity and difference, Williams tells a robin that he is a Robin too, and the two agree that, although they are different, they are the same as well. On one episode, Williams educates his young viewers on conflict through interaction with the Two-Headed Monster, but they end up laughing. Finally, in one of Williams's most memorable spots, he uses his shoe to explain what makes something alive. To be alive, he says, one must eat, breathe, and grow. Using word play, he jokes that his shoe has a sole (soul) and then proceeds to water it, check its breathing, and feed it a banana and nuts in order to prove that his shoe is not alive. Wearing a baseball cap or bright plaid shirt, Williams engages his young audience, using puns, pantomime, and humor to instruct the littlest children on creativity, science, and values. He even appeared twice on the cover of *Muppet Magazine*, including its inaugural issue.

Millennials most remember Williams as a warm paternal figure or caregiver, often a playful man-child with traces of arrested development. Whether in the role of a teacher, a father, or a counselor, he comes across as flawed, unaware of himself or what is expected of him, perhaps because of a personal tragedy from which he survived intact but not unscathed. However, he emotes love and caring, infusing his acting with childlike qualities of wonder, enthusiasm, and optimism. As Kristin Iversen recalls, "For those of us who grew up as part of the Millennial generation, Williams was more than just an actor, he was the quintessential father figure, the ultimate movie dad."[22] In an increasingly technological society that was moving quickly and marked by change, Williams struck a chord. Bruce Weber writes that he's "primarily known for his physically energetic and vocally subtle stand-up routines that … absurdly link the disparate elements of our shared contemporary culture and ricochet from shtick to shtick at dizzying speed."[23] Herein lies Williams's appeal: he exudes quiet caring and frenetic mania all at once, catering to an audience looking for authenticity, meaning and attention but still wanting to move quickly, do multiple things simultaneously, and be entertained at a dizzying clip. He captures space between leisurely childhood discovery and purposeful multi-tasking mania.

Perhaps Williams's first film to suggest this was *Dead Poets Society* (1989), in which he played John Keating, a brilliant, inspiring, but decidedly unconventional teacher at an elite 1950s boarding school called Welton Academy. Directed by Peter Weir, this film enabled Williams to draw on his own adolescent experience at a private all-boys school near Detroit. As he recalled in an interview, "Blazer. Latin motto. I was getting pushed around a lot. Not only was there like physical bullying, but there was intellectual bullying going on. It made me toughen up, but it also made me pull back a lot. I had a certain reticence about dealing with people. Through comedy, I found a way to bridge the gap."[24] In key scenes in *Dead Poets Society*, John Keating shocks his young charges by encouraging them to rip pages out of their textbook's boring, pompous introduction and jump atop their desks to see things from a different perspective. "Carpe, carpe. Carpe diem," the former Rhodes Scholar and lover of poetry shouts to his students in Latin, urging them to live in the moment and follow their dreams. "Seize the day, boys. Make your lives extraordinary." Recalling his mantra, Williams says, "I like the point of the movie, … of trying to find the passionate thing in your life, finding some sort of passion."[25] His mercurial performance reflects idealism, non-conformity, the importance of ideas and freedom of expression, and the essence of what makes one human. As millennial writer Megan Gibson reflects on *Dead Poets*

Society, "To this day, I still can't resist Williams' line, 'But poetry, beauty, romance, love, these are what we stay alive for.'"[26] Through John Keating, Williams spoke to a youth audience seeking mentors who care and who give license to following personal passions. *Dead Poets Society* became one of the highest-grossing films of the year and a home VHS and high-school English class staple for subsequent years.

Although *Dead Poets Society* spoke to youth, for Williams it was a prestige project, and he was nominated for an Academy Award for Best Actor. However, as Daniel D'Addario observes, "something shifted" with his next film, *Hook* (1991): "[T]he movie about Peter Pan rediscovering the joy of Neverland had the same effect, perhaps on Williams, who'd always been wacky and loose on-screen but was suddenly acting like he'd never grown up."[27] Child fare became part of Williams's DNA and the man-child his chosen role. In *Hook*, Williams teamed up with director Steven Spielberg, whose understanding of childhood experience secured his place as one of America's best-known cinematic story tellers for young people. Williams also spent a lot of time with the many children on the set, acting as their mentor and making them laugh. In the film, Williams plays Peter Banning, a workaholic lawyer out of touch with his wife Moira, his children Jack and Maggie, and his own inner child. When on a trip to London to visit his mother Wendy for a charity event for orphans, Peter discovers that his children have been kidnapped by Captain Hook and learns that he is the real Peter Pan but that his memories were erased when he was adopted. He returns to Neverland as Peter Pan, regains his youthful spirit, and after a period of soul-searching and a confrontation with Captain Hook, reclaims his children and returns to his mother's home. When Wendy suggests that Peter's adventures are over, Peter expresses his transformation and newfound appreciation for family: "To live would be an awfully big adventure." Although *Hook* was panned by the critics, it led to a lifelong friendship between kindred spirits Spielberg and Williams, who later did the voice of Dr. Know in the director's lost-child science-fiction epic, *A.I. Artificial Intelligence* (2001). *Hook* did well at the box office and found an audience that clung to its message. As Megan Gibson reported after Williams's death, "To this day my husband—also Millennial, although a British one—still raves about how much he loves *Hook*. (Not *loved*. Loves.)"[28]

Williams's next cinematic foray into children's fare led him to animation. He played the voice of Batty Koda in *FernGully: The Last Rainforest* (1991), directed by Bill Kroyer. In the early 1990s animation studios discovered the marketing value of casting major stars in voice roles, and Disney was intent on landing Williams for a major role as the Genie in *Aladdin*. According to Williams, he initially returned the script when he learned it was a Disney project, rejecting the role because of his objection to Disney's commercialization and marketing directly to children. However, Disney persevered, and

Williams finally relented, saying, "The one thing I said was I will do the voice. ... I'm doing it basically because I want to be part of this animation tradition. I want something for my children. One deal is, I just don't want to sell any-thing—as in Burger King, as in toys, as in stuff."[29] Williams did the part for union scale, about $75,000, but Disney reneged on its promise not to use the Genie to sell products, fostering a sometimes-uneasy relationship between the actor and the giant media conglomerate.

Directed by Ron Clements and John Musker, *Aladdin* appeared in 1992 and proved to be the perfect vehicle for Williams's irrepressible, manic form of comedy. According to Dave Itzkoff, "His gigs were always rife with frenetic, spot-on impersonations that included Hollywood stars, presidents, princes, prime ministers, popes, and anonymous citizens of the world."[30] Although the Genie is not the main character in the film, he stole the show, and Williams's ad-libbed vocal performances, reflective of his stand-up style and impersonations, made an imprint on an impressionable audience. Kristin Iversen recalls her childhood delight with Williams's magical Genie when she saw him for the first time: "I vividly remember laughing so hard at his opening scene in *Aladdin* that I was in tears, almost unable to breathe."[31] Williams also did the voice of the Peddler in the film, which became the biggest box-office blockbuster of 1992 and one of Disney's best-selling videos of all time. As children played it over and over again, the Genie's song "Friend Like Me" and signature phrases—such as "Yo, Rugman! Haven't seen you in a few millennia. Give me some tassel!" or "I'm history. No, I'm mythology. Nah, I don't care what I am. I am free hee!"—became as popular as the film's magic-carpet-ride theme song "A Whole New World." Williams once again created a character with a good heart and a frenetic style. He reprised his voice role as the Genie in *Aladdin and the King of Thieves*, directed by Tad Stones, a direct-to-video release. According to Williams, making the film was a good experience, reflecting his childlike streak: "I went into a room and started improvising and these guys kept throwing things at me. ... It just got wild. They let me play. That's why I loved it—it was like *carte blanche* to go nuts."[32] Just like an enthusiastic child, Williams's Genie could not be con-tained.

Williams's stint as the Genie prepared him for another unconventional caretaker's role in *Mrs. Doubtfire* (1993). In this Disney family comedy directed by Chris Columbus, he plays a divorced father, Daniel Hillard, who cross-dresses to assume the identity of British housekeeper Euphegenia Doubtfire in order to be close to his children. Although studio executives wanted a happy ending with Daniel and Miranda Hilliard getting back together, Williams fought for a more realistic ending, saying, "To have shown it otherwise would have been a negative fantasy. What I wanted to do was just put across something that my therapist was saying to me after my divorce.

Just focus on your child. Try to make things better for him."[33] Williams's flamboyant performance spoke to children of divorce, assuring them that, although their parents might not still love one another, they did love their children. As Megan Gibson writes,

> Beyond the laughs, for kids with divorced parents locked in an ongoing custody battle—kids like me, that is—*Mrs. Doubtfire* was a real comfort, without being afterschool-special cheesey. … It feels almost corny to say this now but at the time I needed reassurance that no matter how ugly the divorce was, my parents had nothing but love for me. Williams, who never panders to his onscreen kids or the kids in the audience, seemed to *get it*, and that was a rare thing.[34]

In Williams's films, things do not always end happily. For a generation intent on finding "authenticity," this is important. Good teachers are accused of making students self-indulgent and reckless and get fired, all wishes do not come true, and parents do not get back together. However, Williams's performances raise questions, address the complexities of life, and show that while there are no easy answers, the goodness of the human spirit prevails. Perhaps because of this, *Mrs. Doubtfire* became the second biggest moneymaker of 1993, behind only Steven Spielberg's *Jurassic Park*, and the most successful cross-dressing film to date.

By the mid 1990s, Williams continued using his comedic talents to connect with a young audience by merging child and adult roles. In *Jumanji* (1995), directed by Joe Johnston, he plays twelve-year-old Alan Parrish, who following a disagreement with his father was trapped in a jungle-themed board game for twenty-six years and is finally released when siblings Judy and Peter Shepherd find the long-forgotten game in the attic in their new home in New Hampshire and begin playing. The rules are as follows: "A game for those who seek to find a way to leave their world behind. You roll the dice to move your token; doubles get another turn. The first player to reach the end wins."[35] Williams recalls what attracted him to the part: "I think maybe I was just possibly working out something from my own childhood. … Maybe I'm drawn to it because I sympathize with it. The character in *Jumanji* is an only child who gets picked on. I was that child who was picked on not only physically but intellectually too and it's like a whole other thing when you get both."[36] He too wanted to leave the world behind.

Based on the children's literary classic *Jumanji* by Chris Van Allsburg, the film recalls Williams's role as the Genie in *Aladdin* who erupts from his magic lamp after being held captive for ten thousand years. With Judy and Peter, the newly-freed and now-adult Alan seeks out his best friend, Sarah Whittle, with whom he was playing the game back in 1969, and upon finding her, the four seek to replay the game to counteract the damage that has occurred following Alan's being sucked into the game decades before when he drew a card that read "in the jungle you must wait, 'till the dice reads four or eight." What they discover is horrific: rolls of the dice release predatory jungle vines, stampeding animals, a big-game hunter, and general chaos throughout the city. Alan eventually makes a winning roll, reversing all havoc that the game created and allowing for a happy ending, but the story may not be over: far away two girls walking on the beach in France edge closer to Jumanji buried in the sand. *Jumanji* appealed to a generation who loved games, and Williams's zany performance and the images of jungle calamity fueled its box-office performance. Despite mixed reviews the movie did well. It also spawned a popular board game, adding to millennials' childhood experiences.

Williams followed up *Jumanji* with *Jack* (1996), another film that combines childhood and adulthood. This film, directed by Francis Ford Coppola, features Williams as Jack Powell, a boy whose rare disease makes him age four times faster than normal. Williams recalled what drew him to the role: "I think what made me want to play Jack was that innocent time before all that, riding bikes, friends in treehouses, all those things that loom on the boundaries of child and boy."[37] He was also taken with his character's vulnerability, saying, "At ten or eleven you are still a boy, and that time right before puberty, which hits as 12—or 11 if you live somewhere where the milk is different—is so incredible. A boy is so vulnerable then. Boys that age don't have a lot of chops in terms of hiding feelings. What they feel is right there on their faces."[38] This unconventional portrayal of a fifth grader who looks forty provides a vehicle for Williams to explore embarrassment, rejection by peers, and a boy's first crush on a favorite teacher. Eventually, Jack finds acceptance and, as an old man, makes the valedictory speech at this high school, imploring his classmates to "make your life spectacular." Although the message of *Jack* recalls *Dead Poets Society*, the film neither pleased critics nor attracted a wide audience. Even Williams himself said of his adult-child portrayal, "This is the last one. This is the ultimate one. This is the metaphor gone beyond hyperbole into simile. I can't do it after this. I'm 45. This is way beyond the Peter Pan syndrome."[39] Nevertheless, the day after Williams's death, Megan Gibson paid tribute to it, saying, "Yet it was one of the movies that struck a chord with my best friend, who sobbed so hard while watching the VHS tape that her mother had to turn it off. But it stayed with her. Last night, nearly 20 years after she first saw the movie, my best friend sent me a text in the middle of the night that simply said, 'Thinking of the movie *Jack*.'"[40] In his list of "7 Robin Williams Movies that Made Your Childhood," Rande Iaboni chose to include it too.[41] For some millennials, the combination of manic energy and heartfelt emotion still worked.

Yet for others, it did not. Times were changing. By the late 1990s, Williams began to lose his luster with the child audience who had grown up with him. The sentimentality that had always been part of Williams's appeal was becoming too much. If audiences stayed away from *Jack* because it did not ring true, *Patch Adams* (1998) proved even more disappointing. In this film, directed by Tom Shadyac, Williams plays clownish doctor Hunter "Patch" Adams, based on a real person who shakes up the hospital and lives of his young patients with his optimism, humor, and unconventional methods. It is a story that Williams, with his zany mannerisms and red bulb nose, had played effectively before, but this time it came up lacking. Kristin Iversen called it "lame and embarrassing" and "missing the mark" and observed that "so many people in my generation had stopped paying attention to Williams's career, despite the fact that any of us could rattle off quote after quote of his half-a-dozen movies that made our childhoods brighter and full of laughter."[42] Another child-oriented feature, *Flubber* (1997), did only slightly better. The comedy, a remake of Disney's 1961 *The Absent-Minded* Professor starring Fred MacMurray, highlighted Williams's uncontrollable energy in a nonsensical plot. Williams decided to take the role because his five-year-old son Cody loved the original. Directed by Les Mayfield, *Flubber* stars Williams as Professor Philip Brainard, a chemist so preoccupied in the process of developing a new energy source of gooey green flying rubber dubbed "Flubber" that he misses his own wedding twice. As the substance grows and bounces, it creates mayhem. The film, which portrays Williams as a childlike figure immune to real-world responsibility, had a good opening weekend but floundered, not doing nearly as well as the Disney original.

Only *Good Will Hunting* (1997), written by Matt Damon and Ben Affleck and directed by Gus Van Sant, rivaled the earlier Williams sagas directed at youth. Like *Dead Poets Society*, it was a prestige project, the two films acting as bookends for the millennial audience's Robin Williams youth oeuvre. Williams plays the role of therapist Sean Maguire, who treats twenty-year old blue-collar laborer Will Hunting (Matt Damon), an unrecognized mathematical genius, and helps him to re-evaluate his life. In this film, Williams plays his familiar role of a paternal caretaker but without the uncontrollable-child traits that characterized so many of his earlier performances. Both Sean Maguire and Will Hunting suffered abuse as children and misfortune in later in life but through disclosure and trust in one another find ways to move forward. Following a poignant scene in which Maguire repeats nine times to Hunting that the abuse was not his fault and the men weep, the script describes a quintessential image: "Two lonely souls being father and son together."[43] Showcasing Williams's dramatic talents, *Good Will Hunting* proved to be a critical and popular success and earned Williams his first and only Academy Award, despite three previous nominations, for best supporting actor. Once again, Williams created a character of compassion, demonstrating to his millennial audience how to think about life in an unbridled, creative way.

Williams emerged as one of America's most prolific actors and comedians, and his projects involving childhood and youth comprise only part—albeit an important one—of his total cinematic legacy. Other less notable films, such as *Toys* (1992), directed by Barry Levinson, in which he plays Leslie Zevo, the son of a toymaker passed over to inherit his father's business because he is too childlike, and *In Search of Dr. Seuss* (1994), directed by Vincent Paterson, in which he plays the Father in a five-minute humorous, frenetic reading of *The Cat and the Hat* to two little girls, attest to Williams's interest in childhood and its artifacts. A study of Williams's life reveals his fascination with toys, such as his cherished collection of thousands of toy soldiers, children's books, and, especially, video games. As his friend and personal photographer Arthur Grace once recalled, "As long as I knew him, Robin was in love with video games and took them seriously.... When Robin was engrossed in any action video game, you quickly learned that the area around him was a 'no-fly' zone."[44] Williams espoused play and fun to a generation that valued those qualities and, many feel, have resisted growing up and accepting adult responsibility. His movies gave millennials safe spaces where what they did and what they cared about were valued. In the chaotic worlds of Williams movies and millennials, it is acceptable to maintain childlike qualities as a way of coping.

What millennials recall about Williams, and the reason why they mourned him so deeply, is that he exemplified for them the caring protector that they sought as well as the children that they were, all at once. He could be fatherly and irresponsible, yet loving and distracted. His skill at mimicry revealed his insight into people's feelings and motivations. Perhaps most important, though, was his mania: his improvisational, free-associational style that captures the fragmented, lightning-quick quality of digital technology. Williams's fast-moving humor entertained millennial viewers, striking a chord in the fast-moving Internet age, while his heartfelt concern, which eventually became too mawkish, soothed them when families fractured and bad things threatened, making them feel safe and special. Kristin Iversen suggests this when she writes, "Growing up as an adolescent in the late [']90s, it was easy to have a pure and simple love for this man whose goal was to entertain us, to make us happy and protect us from the Jafars and Captain Hooks of the world."[45] Played over and over again on VHS and DVD recorders, Williams's touchstone films with their key scenes and signature lines became part of millennials' cultural memory. In role after role, he encouraged his youthful observers to express themselves freely and follow their dreams, lessons that every generation needs to hear, but this generation's spokesperson for them was Williams. Because of his own painful youthful experiences, he understood the challenges of growing up and drew upon his sunny presence, humor, and insight to help. As Williams's acting school teacher John Houseman once told him, "Mr. Williams, you are damaged but interesting."[46] Perhaps no generation has been more maligned than the millennials, characterized as childlike in their reluctance to give up games and play and accept responsibility, socially fragile and in need of recognition and safe places, frenetic and distracted with their overuse of technology, and slow to launch. They identified with this damaged, interesting actor, who gave them the gift of mirroring the frailties and possibilities within themselves.

NOTES

1. Megan Gibson, "Why Robin Williams Was a Millennial Hero" in *Time*, August 12, 2014, http://time.com/3103255/robin-williams-dead-millennial-hero/

2. *Ibid.*

3. Ilia Blinderman, "Robin Williams' Death Hits Millennials Unusually Hard" in *Toronto Star*, August 13, 2014, https://www.thestar.com/opinion/commentary/2014/08/13/robin_williams_death_hits_millennials_unusually_hard.html.

4. Daniel D'Addario, "For Millennials, Robin Williams Was Our Childhood" in *Salon*, August 11, 2014, http://www.salon.com/2014/08/12/for_the_kids_of_the_90s_robin_williams_was_the_ultimate_movie_star/

5. Kristen Iversen, "Remembering Robin Williams: The Ultimate Film Dad Has Died" in *Brooklyn Magazine*, August 12, 2014, http://www.bkmag.com/2014/08/12/remembering-robin-williams-the-ultimate-film-dad-has-died/

6. Justine Harman, "Why Losing Robin Williams Feels So Personal" in *Elle*, Aug. 12, 2014, http://www.elle.com/culture/movies-tv/news/a25166/losing-robin-williams-feels-personal/

7. D'Addario, "For Millennials, Robin Williams Was Our Childhood."

8. Brown, Sarah, "Who Are Millennials, Anyway?" *The Chronicle of Higher Education*, Section B, The Academic Workplace. (25 July 2016): B5.

9. *Ibid.*; Greenberg, Eric with Karl Weber, *Generation We: How Millennial Youth Are Taking Over America and Changing Our World Forever* (Emeryville, CA: Pachatusan, 2008), 4.

10. Thom S. Rainer, and Jess W. Rainer, *The Millennials: Connecting to America's Largest Generation* (Nashville: B&H Publishing Group, 2011), 8.

11. Paul Taylor, *The Next America: Boomers, Millennials, and the Looming Generational Showdown* (New York: PublicAffairs, 2014), 27.

12. Jean Twenge, *Generation Me: Why Today's Young Americans Are More Confident, Assertive, Entitled—and Miserable—Than Ever Before* (New York: Atria, 2014), 106.

13. Jeffrey Jensen Arnett, *Emerging Adulthood: The Winding Road From the Late Teen Through the Twenties* (New York: Oxford Univ. Press, 2004), 4.

14. Qtd. in David, Jay. *The Life and Humor of Robin Williams* (New York: William Morrow, 1999), 3.

15. David, *The Life and Humor of Robin Williams*, 3.

16. Jonice Webb, "Robin Williams and Childhood Emotional Neglect" in *Psych Central*, September 4, 2014, https://blogs.psychcentral.com/childhood-neglect/2014/09/robin-williams-and-childhood-emotional-neglect/.

17. Andy Dougan, *Robin Williams* (New York: Thunder's Mouth Press, 1998), 8–9.

18. Dave Itzkoff, "Robin Williams, Oscar-Winning Comedian, Dies at 63" in *New York Times*, Aug. 11, 2014, https://www.nytimes.com/2014/08/12/movies/robin-williams-oscar-winning-comedian-dies-at-63.html

19. "Robin Williams: It's Time for a Convoluted Stream of Consciousness. Ask Me Anything" in Reddit.com, September 25, 2013, https://www.reddit.com/r/IAmA/comments/1n41xl/robin_williams_its_time_for_a_convoluted_stream/

20. Bruce Weber, "Robin Williams, the Comic, Confronts Robin Williams, the Actor" in *The New York Times*, May 28, 1989, http://www.nytimes.com/1989/05/28/movies/robin-williams-the-comic-confronts-robin-williams-the-actor.html

21. Qtd. in Dougan, *Robin Williams*, 207.

22. Iversen, "Remembering Robin Williams: The Ultimate Film Dad Has Died."
23. Weber, "Robin Williams, the Comic, Confronts Robin Williams, the Actor."
24. Qtd. in Strauss, Valerie, "How High School Changed Robin Williams' Life" in *The Washington Post,* August 11, 2014, https://www.washingtonpost.com/news/answer-sheet/wp/2014/08/11/how-robin-williams-joked-about-school/
25. Qtd. in Weber, "Robin Williams, the Comic, Confronts Robin Williams, the Actor."
26. Gibson, "Why Robin Williams Was a Millennial Hero."
27. D'Addario, "For Millennials, Robin Williams Was Our Childhood."
28. Gibson, "Why Robin Williams Was a Millennial Hero."
29. Qtd. in McDonald, Soraya Nadia, "Robin Williams Almost Didn't Make 'Aladdin,' and a Generation of Children is Grateful That He Did" in *The Washington Post,* August 15, 2014, https://www.washingtonpost.com/news/morning-mix/wp/2014/08/15/robin-williams-almost-didnt-make-aladdin-and-a-generation-of-children-are-grateful-that-he-did/
30. Itzkoff, "Robin Williams, Oscar-Winning Comedian, Dies at 63."
31. Iversen, "Remembering Robin Williams: The Ultimate Film Dad Has Died."
32. Qtd. in Dougan, *Robin Williams,* 223.
33. Qtd. in David, *The Life and Humor of Robin Williams,* 44.
34. Gibson, "Why Robin Williams Was a Millennial Hero."
35. Qtd. in Spignesi, Stephen J., *The Robin Williams Scrapbook* (Secaucus, NJ: Citadel, 1997), 155.
36. Qtd. in Dougan, *Robin Williams,* 207.
37. Qtd. in Strauss, "How High School Changed Robin Williams' Life."
38. *Ibid.*
39. Qtd. in Spignesi, *The Robin Williams Scrapbook,* 155.
40. Gibson, "Why Robin Williams Was a Millennial Hero."
41. Rande Iaboni, "7 Robin Williams Movies That Made Your Childhood" in CNN.com, August 13, 2014, http://www.cnn.com/2014/08/12/showbiz/movies/robin-williams-best-roles/index.html
42. Iversen, "Remembering Robin Williams: The Ultimate Film Dad Has Died."
43. Dougan, *Robin Williams,* 231.
44. Arthur Grace, *Robin Williams: A Singular Portrait, 1986–2002* (Berkeley: Counterpoint, 2016), 10.
45. Iversen, "Remembering Robin Williams: The Ultimate Film Dad Has Died."
46. Qtd. in Dougan, *Robin Williams,* 230.

BIBLIOGRAPHY

Arnett, Jeffrey Jensen. *Emerging Adulthood: The Winding Road From the Late Teen Through the Twenties.* New York: Oxford University Press, 2004.
Blinderman, Ilia. "Robin Williams' Death Hits Millennials Unusually Hard." *Toronto Star,* August 13, 2014. Accessed July 22, 2016. https://www.thestar.com/opinion/commentary/2014/08/13/robin_williams_death_hits_millennials_unusually_hard.html
Brown, Sarah. "Who Are Millennials, Anyway?" *The Chronicle of Higher Education,* Section B, The Academic Workplace, July 25, 2016: B5.
D'Addario, Daniel. "For Millennials, Robin Williams Was Our Childhood." *Salon,* August 11, 2014. Accessed July 22, 2016. http://www.salon.com/2014/08/12/for_the_kids_of_the_90s_robin_williams_was_the_ultimate_movie_star/
David, Jay. *The Life and Humor of Robin Williams.* New York: William Morrow, 1999.
Dougan, Andy. *Robin Williams.* New York: Thunder's Mouth Press, 1998.
Gibson, Megan. "Why Robin Williams Was a Millennial Hero." *Time,* August 12, 2014. Accessed July 22, 2016. http://time.com/3103255/robin-williams-dead-millennial-hero/.
Grace, Arthur. *Robin Williams: A Singular Portrait, 1986–2002.* Berkeley: Counterpoint, 2016.
Greenberg, Eric, with Karl Weber. *Generation We: How Millennial Youth Are Taking Over America and Changing Our World Forever.* Emeryville, CA: Pachatusan, 2008.
Harman, Justine. "Why Losing Robin Williams Feels So Personal." *Elle,* August 12, 2014. Accessed July 22, 2016. http://www.elle.com/culture/movies-tv/news/a25166/losing-robin-williams-feels-personal/

Iaboni, Rande. "7 Robin Williams Movies That Made Your Childhood." CNN.com, August 13, 2014. Accessed July 22, 2016. http://www.cnn.com/2014/08/12/showbiz/movies/robin-williams-best-roles/index.html

Itzkoff, Dave. "Robin Williams, Oscar-Winning Comedian, Dies at 63." *New York Times,* August 11, 2014. Accessed July 5, 2016. https://www.nytimes.com/2014/08/12/movies/robin-williams-oscar-winning-comedian-dies-at-63.html

Iversen, Kristin. "Remembering Robin Williams: The Ultimate Film Dad Has Died." *Brooklyn Magazine,* August 12, 2014. Accessed July 22, 2016. http://www.bkmag.com/2014/08/12/remembering-robin-williams-the-ultimate-film-dad-has-died/

McDonald, Soraya Nadia. "Robin Williams Almost Didn't Make 'Aladdin,' and a Generation of Children is Grateful That He Did." *The Washington Post,* August 15, 2014. Accessed July 22, 2016. https://www.washingtonpost.com/news/morning-mix/wp/2014/08/15/robin-williams-almost-didnt-make-aladdin-and-a-generation-of-children-are-grateful-that-he-did

Rainer, Thom S. and Jess W. Rainer. *The Millennials: Connecting to America's Largest Generation.* Nashville: B&H Publishing Group, 2011.

"Robin Williams: It's Time for a Convoluted Stream of Consciousness. Ask Me Anything." Reddit.com, Sept. 25, 2013. Accessed July 24, 2016. https://www.reddit.com/r/IAmA/comments/1n41xl/robin_williams_its_time_for_a_convoluted_stream/

Spignesi, Stephen J. *The Robin Williams Scrapbook.* Secaucus, NJ: Citadel, 1997.

Strauss, Valerie. "How High School Changed Robin Williams' Life." *Washington Post,* August 11, 2014. Accessed July 24, 2016. https://www.washingtonpost.com/news/answer-sheet/wp/2014/08/11/how-robin-williams-joked-about-school/

Taylor, Paul. *The Next America: Boomers, Millennials, and the Looming Generational Showdown.* New York: PublicAffairs, 2014.

Twenge, Jean. *Generation Me: Why Today's Young Americans Are More Confident, Assertive, Entitled—and Miserable—Than Ever Before.* New York: Atria, 2014.

Webb, Jonice. "Robin Williams and Childhood Emotional Neglect." *Psych Central,* September 4, 2014. Accessed July 23, 2017. https://blogs.psychcentral.com/childhood-neglect/2014/09/robin-williams-and-childhood-emotional-neglect/

Weber, Bruce. "Robin Williams, the Comic, Confronts Robin Williams, the Actor." *The New York Times,* May 28, 1989. Accessed July 24, 2016. http://www.nytimes.com/1989/05/28/movies/robin-williams-the-comic-confronts-robin-williams-the-actor.html

Films Referenced

A.I. Artificial Intelligence. Director, Steven Spielberg 2001; Universal City, CA: Dreamworks, 2002 DVD.

Aladdin. Director, John Musker and Ron Clements 1992; Burbank, CA: Walt Disney Co., 2004 DVD.

Alive. Director, Frank Marshall 1993; Burbank, CA: Buena Visa Home Video, 2002 DVD.

American Beauty. Director, Sam Mendes, 1999. Universal City, CA: DreamWorks, 2017.

Anaconda. Director, Luis Llosa 1997; Golden Valley, MN: Mill Creek Entertainment, 2014 DVD.

Anacondas: The Hunt for the Blood Orchid. Director, Dwight H. Little 2004; Culver City, CA: Sony Pictures Home Entertainment, 2004 DVD.

Apocalypse Now. Director, Francis Ford Coppola, 1979; Santa Monica, CA: Lions Gate, 2010 DVD.

Avalon. Director, Barry Levinson, 1990; Culver City, CA: Columbia TriStar Pictures, 2001 DVD.

Awakenings. Director, Penny Marshall, 1990; Culver City, CA: Columbia Pictures, 2010 DVD.

Being Human. Director, Bill Forsyth 1994; Burbank, CA: Warner Bros., 2010 DVD.

The Birdcage. Directed by Mike Nichols. 1996. Santa Monica, CA: MGM Home Entertainment, 2005 DVD.

Boulevard. Director, Ditto Montiel 2014; Beverly Hills, CA: Starz Anchor Bay 2015 DVD.

Bugsy. Director, Barry Levinson, 1991; Culver City, CA: Columbia TriStar Pictures, 2006 DVD.

Butch Cassidy and the Sundance Kid. Director, George Roy Hill 1969; Los Angeles, CA: 20th-Century Fox, 2000 DVD.

Cannibal Ferox. Director, Umberto Lenzi 1981; Los Angeles, CA: Grindhouse Releasing, n.d. DVD.

Carnival of Blood. Director, Leonard Kirtman 1970; Lynwood, Washington: Something Weird Video, 2002 DVD.

Carnival of Souls. Director, Herk Harvey 1962; Criterion Collection, 2016 DVD.

Dead End. Director, William Wyler, 1937; Beverly Hills, CA: Goldwyn Pictures/MGM, 2005 DVD.*Dead Poets Society.* Director, Peter Weir 1988; Touchstone Pictures: Touchstone Home Entertainment, 1998 DVD.

Death to Smoochy. Director, Danny DeVito. 2002. Jersey Films: Warner Home Video, 2016 DVD.

Death Wish. Director, Michael Winner, 1974; Hollywood, CA: Paramount Pictures, 2017 DVD.

The Deer Hunter. Director, Michael Cimino, 1978. Universal City, CA: Universal Studios Home Entertainment, 2012 DVD.

The Devil's Carnival. Director, Darren Lynn Bousman 2012; Los Angeles, CA: Cleopatra Entertainment, 2014 DVD.

Disclosure. Director, Barry Levinson. 1994; Burbank, CA: Warner Bros, 2012.

Dr. Strangelove, Or: How I Learned to Stop Worrying and Love the Bomb. Director, Stanley Kubrick, 1964; Culver City, CA: Sony Pictures Home Entertainment, 2001 DVD.

Eaten Alive!. Director, Umberto Lenzi 1980; Hertfordshire, U.K.: Arrow Video, 2015 DVD.

Escape from New York. Director, John Carpenter 1981; Los Angeles, CA Embassy Pictures/ MGM, 2000 DVD.

Father's Day. Director, Ivan Reitman 1997; Burbank, CA: Warner Bros., 1997 DVD.

FernGully: The Last Rainforest. Director, Bill Kroyer 1992; Beverly Hills, CA: Fox Video, 2001 DVD.

The Final Cut. Director, Omar Naïm, 2004; Santa Monica, CA: Lions Gate, 2008 DVD.

Final Destination 3. Director, James Wong 2006; Burbank, CA: Warner Brothers, 2007 DVD.

The Fisher King. Director, Terry Gilliam, 1991. Burbank, CA: Warner Home Video 2010 DVD.

Flubber. Director, Les Mayfield 1997; Burbank, CA: Buena Vista Home Entertainment, 2003 DVD.

Freaks. Director, Tod Browning 1932; Burbank, CA: Warner Bros., 2005 DVD.

French Connection, The. Director, William Friedkin 1971; Los Angeles, CA: 20th-Century Fox, 2006 DVD.

Full Metal Jacket. Director, Stanley Kubrick, 1987. Burbank, CA: Warner Bros., 2007 DVD.

The Funhouse. Director, Tobe Hooper 1981; Los Angeles, CA: Shout! Factory, 2012 DVD.

The Ghost and the Darkness. Director, Stephen Hopkins 1996; Burbank, CA: Warner Bros., 1998 DVD.

Good Morning, Vietnam. Director, Barry Levinson, 1987. Burbank, CA: Buena Vista Home Entertainment, 2006 DVD.

Good Will Hunting. Director, Gus Van Sant.; 1997. Los Angeles, CA: Be Gentlemen Limited Partnership, 2011 DVD.

The Green Inferno. Director, Eli Roth 2013; Universal City, CA: Universal Home Studios Entertainment, 2016 DVD.

Hamburger Hill. Director, John Irvin, 1987; Santa Monica, CA: Lionsgate, 2008 DVD.

Hook. Director, Steven Spielberg, 1991; Universal City, CA: Amblin Entertainment/Sony Pictures Home Entertainment, 2015 DVD.

Insomnia. Director, Christopher Nolan, 2002; Alcon Entertainment: Warner Brothers, 2010 DVD.

Insomnia. Director, Erik Skjoldbærg, 1997; New York, NY: The Criterion Collection, 2014 DVD.

Jack. Director, Francis Ford Coppola 1996; Burbank, CA : Buena Vista Home Entertainment, 2004 DVD.

Jumanji. Director, Joe Johnston 1995; Culver City, CA: Sony Pictures Home Entertainment, 2000 DVD.

Jumanji: Welcome to the Jungle. Director, Jake Kasdan, Sony Pictures Entertainment, 2017.

Jungle Holocaust. Director, Ruggero Deodato 1977; New York City, NY: Shriek Show, 2002 DVD.

Junior. Director, Ivan Reitman 1994; Universal City, CA: Universal, 1998 DVD.

Jurassic Park. Director, Steven Spielberg 1993. Universal City, CA: Amblin/Universal, 2012 DVD.

Jurassic Park III. Director, Joe Johnston 2001; Universal City, CA: Universal Studios Home Entertainment, 2015 DVD.

Killer Clowns From Outer Space. Director, Stephen Chiodo 1988; Los Angeles, CA: MGM, 2012 DVD.

The Last Circus. Director, Álex de la Iglesia 2010; New York City, NY: Magnolia Home Entertainment, 2011 DVD.

Liberty Heights. Director, Barry Levinson, 1999; Los Angeles, CA: Warner Home Video, 2000 DVD.

Man of the Year. Director, Barry Levinson; 2006. Los Angeles, CA: Universal Pictures, 2007 DVD.

Mary Poppins. Director, Robert Stevenson, 1964; Burbank, CA: Walt Disney Studios, 2013 DVD.

Mean Streets. Director, Martin Scorsese, 1973; Burbank, CA: Warner Bros., 2004 DVD.

Midnight Cowboy. Director, John Schlesinger, 1969. Beverly Hills, CA: United Artists, 2012 DVD.

Missing in Action. Director, Joseph Zito, 1984; Beverly Hills, CA: MGM, 2012.

Moscow on the Hudson. Director, Paul Mazursky 1984; Culver City, CA: Columbia Pictures, 1984 DVD.

The Mountain of the Cannibal God. Director, Sergio Martino 1978; Culver City, CA: Sony Pictures Home Entertainment, 2007 DVD.

Mrs. Doubtfire. Director, Chris Columbus, 1993; Los Angeles, CA: 20th Century–Fox, 2007 DVD.

The Mummy. Director, Stephen Sommers 1999; Universal City, CA: Universal Home Studios Entertainment, 2005 DVD.

The Naked Jungle. Director, Byron Haskin 1954; Burbank, CA: Paramount Pmt / Warner Archive, 2013 DVD.

The Nanny. Director, Seth Holt, 1965. London: Hammer Film Productions, 2008 DVD.

Nanny McPhee. Director, Kirk Jones. 2005. Universal City, CA: Universal, 2012 DVD.

Night at the Museum. Director, Levy, Shawn, 2006; Los Angeles, CA: 20th-century Fox, 2006 DVD.

Night at the Museum 3: Secret of the Tomb. Director, Levy, Shawn 2014; Los Angeles, CA: 20th-century Fox, 2015 DVD.

On the Waterfront. Director, Elia Kazan 1954; Los Angeles, CA: Columbia Pictures, 2001 DVD.

One Hour Photo. Director, Mark Romanek. 2002. Catch 23 Entertainment: Fox Searchlight, 2003 DVD.

Patch Adams. Director, Tom Shadyac 1998; Universal City, CA: Universal Pictures, 2016 DVD.

Pirates of the Caribbean: The Curse of the Black Pearl. Director, Gore Verbinski 2003; Burbank, CA: Walt Disney Studios Home Entertainment, 2003 DVD.

Platoon. Director, Oliver Stone, 1986. Beverly Hills, CA: MGM, 2011 DVD.

Popeye. Director, Robert Altman 1980; Hollywood, CA: Paramount Home Video, 2010 DVD.

Predator. Director, John McTiernan 1987; Los Angeles, CA: 20th Century–Fox, 2010 DVD.

Rain Man. Director, Barry Levinson, 1988; Los Angeles, CA:: United Artists/MGM, 2014 DVD.

Rambo: First Blood Part II. Director, George P. Cosmatos, 1985. Santa Monica, CA: Lionsgate, 2004 DVD.

Red Tails. Director, Anthony Hemingway 2012; Los Angeles, CA: 20th Century–Fox, 2012.

RV. Director, Barry Sonnenfeld, 2006; Los Angeles, CA: Sony Pictures, 2006 DVD.

Sleepers. Director, Barry Levinson, 1996; Los Angeles, CA: Astoria Films, 1997 DVD.

Something Wicked This Way Comes. Director, Jack Clayton 1983; Burbank, CA: Walt Disney Studios Home Entertainment, 2004 DVD.

Sphere. Director, Barry Levinson, 1998; Los Angeles, CA: Warner Bros., 1998.

Taxi Driver. Director, Martin Scorsese. 1976. Columbia Pictures: Sony Pictures Home Entertainment, 2007 DVD.

Thief of Baghdad. Director by Raoul Walsh 1924 (Silent, b&w); Beverly Hills, CA: United Artists, 2015 DVD.

Thief of Baghdad. Directors, Ludwig Berger, Michael Powell, and Tim Whelan 1940 (Color); Beverly Hills, CA: MGM 2002.

31. Director, Rob Zombie 2016; Santa Monica, CA: Lionsgate, 2016 DVD.

Tootsie. Director, Sidney Pollack, 1982; Hollywood, CA: Columbia Pictures, 2008 DVD.

Toys. Director, Barry Levinson 1992; Century City, CA: Twentieth Century–Fox, 1992 DVD.

The Tuskegee Airmen. Director, Robert Markowitz, 1995; New York: HBO pictures, 2010 DVD.

Unfaithful. Director, Adrian Lyne. 2002. Los Angeles, CA: 20th Century–Fox, 2011 DVD.

Vampire Circus. Director, Robert Young 1972; Romulus, MI: Synapse Films, 2010 DVD.

Wag the Dog. Director, Barry Levinson, 1997; Los Angeles, CA: New Line, 2005 DVD.

Waxwork. Director, Anthony Hickox 1988; Santa Monica, CA: Lionsgate, 2016 DVD.

West Side Story. Directors, Robert Wise and Jerome Robbins 1961; Beverly Hills, CA: United Artists/MGM 2012 DVD.

What Dreams May Come. Director, Vincent Ward. 1998. Universal Studios Home Entertainment, 2003 DVD.

The Wizard of Oz. Director, Victor Fleming 1939; Burbank, CA: Warner Bros., 2014 DVD.

The World According to Garp. Director, George Roy Hill 1982; Burbank, CA: Warner Bros. Entertainment, 2014 DVD.

World's Greatest Dad. Director, Bobcat Goldthwait 2009; Dallas, TX: Magnolia Pictures, 2009 DVD.

About the Contributors

Johnson **Cheu** is an assistant professor in the Department of Writing, Rhetoric, and American Cultures at Michigan State University. He is also the editor of two previous essay collections on film topics, *Diversity in Disney Films,* and *Tim Burton,* both from McFarland. He has received three Pushcart Prize nominations for his poetry.

Michelle Catherine **Iden** is an assistant professor at the County College of Morris in Randolph, New Jersey. She has taught at the University of Maryland, University College, Europe. Her research focuses on memory and American cultural history. She has written on the cultural impact of the Vietnam Veterans' Memorial in Washington, D.C., and the Irish Famine memorials in New York City and Philadelphia.

Kathy Merlock **Jackson** is a professor of communication at Virginia Wesleyan University, where she specializes in media studies, animation, and children's culture. She has published over a hundred articles, reviews, and chapters and eight books. She is vice president/president-elect of the Popular Culture Association/American Culture Association and edits *The Journal of American Culture.*

Sue **Matheson** is an associate professor of English at the University College of the North where she teaches American film and popular culture, Canadian literature, and children's literature. She is the editor of *Love in Western Film and Television* and *A Fistful of Icons and* is also the author of *The Westerns and War Films of John Ford.*

Cynthia J. **Miller** is a cultural anthropologist, specializing in popular culture and visual media. She is the editor or coeditor of numerous scholarly volumes, including *Divine Horror.* She is the series editor for Rowman & Littlefield's Film and History book series and an editorial board member for the *Journal of Popular Television* and Bloomsbury's "Guide to Contemporary Directors" series.

Prajna **Parasher** is a professor of art, film and cultural studies, chair of the Arts, Design and Communication Department, and program director of the film and digital technology program and interdisciplinary design program at Chatham University. Her films are part of the canon in ethnic, diaspora, cultural and women's studies.

Stacy C. **Parenteau** is an assistant professor of psychology at Auburn University at Montgomery. She received her Ph.D. in clinical psychology, with a specialization in health psychology, from the University of Kansas in 2008. Her main line of research examines the association between religiosity/spirituality and health outcomes.

Lori L. **Parks** is a visiting assistant professor in the Department of Humanities and Creative Arts at Miami University. Her research interests include art and visual culture with a particular focus on an interdisciplinary and cultural approach to the body and its representation.

Lisa K. **Perdigao** is the humanities program chair and a professor of English at Florida Institute of Technology. Her research and teaching interests are in the areas of American literature, film, television, comics, and YA literature. She is the author of *From Modernist Entombment to Postmodernist Exhumation* and coeditor, with Mark Pizzato, of *Death in American Texts and Performances*.

Tom **Prasch** is a professor and the chair of history at Washburn University. His publications include chapters on Robert Eggers's *The Witch*, Michael Palin's travel documentaries, Alfred Russel Wallace's spiritualism and evolutionary thought and Richard Lester's *Bed Sitting Room*.

Alan M. **Rosiene** is the associate head of the School of Arts and Communication, English and languages program chair, and an assistant professor of English at Florida Institute of Technology. He has presented papers on the short stories of J. G. Ballard, Joss Whedon's *Firefly*, and China Mieville's young adult novel *Un Lun Dun*.

Elizabeth Leigh **Scherman** is a senior faculty member at Bates College, also teaching with the graduate school of education at UC Berkeley. She researches representations of divergent bodies in media as well as the rhetoric that accompanies such portrayals, whether in scientific literature, cinema, television, or other forms of popular culture.

Philip L. **Simpson** serves as provost of the Titusville Campus and eLearning of Eastern Florida State College. He is president of the Popular Culture Association/ American Culture Association and is also the author of *Psycho Paths* and *Making Murder*. He coedited *Stephen King's Contemporary Classics* and The Walking Dead Live!

Andrew **Slade** is an associate professor and the chair in the Department of English at the University of Dayton. His research focuses on the philosophy of art and literature, with special attention to postmodernism and the aesthetic of the sublime. He has published scholarly articles on the theory of tragedy and the aesthetics of representations of traumatic histories.

Ludovic A. **Sourdot** is an associate professor of curriculum and instruction in the Department of Teacher Education at Texas Woman's University. His research focuses on the pedagogical possibilities television programming offer for teacher education; he is the coeditor with Edward Janak, of *Educating Through Popular Culture*.

Eric J. **Sterling** earned his Ph.D. in English from Indiana University. For the past 24 years he has taught English at Auburn University–Montgomery, where he won the Distinguished Teaching Professor Award, the Distinguished Research Professor

Award, and the Ida Belle Young Professorship. He has published four books and seventy-five refereed essays.

Gael **Sweeney** teaches writing, creative nonfiction, and cultural studies in the Department of Writing Studies, Rhetoric, and Composition at Syracuse University, and has published articles about White Trash Culture, Elvis, Hugh Grant, Johnny Depp, and The Beatles, as well as *The Lion King's* Timon and Pumbaa.

Rebecca A. **Umland** is a professor of English at the University of Nebraska at Kearney. With Samuel J. Umland, she has coauthored two books: *The Use of Arthurian Legend in Hollywood Film* and *Donald Cammell*. She has published book chapters on Arthurian legend, British literature, and world cinema and a book, *Outlaw Heroes as Liminal Figures of Film and Television*.

Samuel J. **Umland** is a professor and the chair of the English Department at the University of Nebraska at Kearney. With Rebecca A. Umland, he has coauthored a book on Arthurian film and on film director Donald Cammell. He also published *The Tim Burton Encyclopedia*.

A. Bowdoin **Van Riper** is a historian whose research focuses on images of science and technology in popular culture. After teaching for 21 years at the university level, he is a research librarian at the Martha's Vineyard Museum. He is the author, editor, or coeditor of fourteen books, including *Teaching History with Science Fiction* and *What's Eating You*, coedited with Cynthia J. Miller.

Kenya **Wolff** is an assistant professor of early childhood education within the School of Education at the University of Mississippi. Her research utilizes critical qualitative methodologies and focuses on various social contexts of childhood. She serves on the editorial board for the Southern Early Childhood Association Journal, *Dimensions,* and as an assistant editor for *International Critical Childhood Studies.*

Index